The Fabric of Cultures

Fashion, identity, and globalization

Edited by Eugenia Paulicelli
and Hazel Clark

Routledge
Taylor & Francis Group

LONDON AND NEW YORK

7838

Cover image: *Eleanor Hewitt*, Yinka Shonibare MBE, 2005. Mannequin, Dutch wax, printed cotton textile, steel stand and stilts. Commissioned by the Cooper-Hewitt National Design Museum, New York, 2005. Courtesy of the artist, Stephen Friedman Gallery (London), and James Cohan Gallery (New York).

First published 2009
by Routledge
2 Park Square, Milton Park, Abingdon, Oxon OX14 4RN

Simultaneously published by Routledge USA and Canada
270 Madison Ave, New York, NY 10016

Routledge is an imprint of the Taylor & Francis Group, an informa business

Typeset in Sabon by The Running Head Limited, Cambridge,
www.therunninghead.com
Printed and bound in Great Britain by
CPI Antony Rowe, Chippenham, Wiltshire

British Library Cataloguing in Publication Data
A catalogue record for this book is available from the British Library

Library of Congress Cataloging in Publication Data
The fabric of cultures: fashion, identity and globalization / edited by Eugenia Paulicelli and Hazel Clark.
    p.   cm.
Includes bibliographical references and index.
1. Clothing and dress—Social aspects—Cross-cultural studies.   2. Fashion—Social aspects—Cross-cultural studies.   3. Globalization—Social aspects.   I. Paulicelli, Eugenia, 1958–   II. Clark, Hazel.
GT525.F33 2009
391—dc22
                                                        2008019120

ISBN10: 0–415–77542–6 (hbk)
ISBN10: 0–415–77543–4 (pbk)

ISBN13: 978–0–415–77542–7 (hbk)
ISBN13: 978–0–415–77543–4 (pbk)

To our children, Anna Ward and Jacob Clark Dilnot

Contents

List of figures   ix
Notes on contributors   xi
Acknowledgements   xv

Introduction   1
EUGENIA PAULICELLI AND HAZEL CLARK

1 From potlatch to Wal-Mart: courtly and capitalist hierarchies
  through dress   13
  JANE SCHNEIDER

2 Dressing the nation: Indian cinema costume and the making of a
  national fashion, 1947–1957   28
  RACHEL TU

3 Made in America: Paris, New York, and postwar fashion
  photography   41
  HELENA C. RIBEIRO

4 Framing the Self, staging identity: clothing and Italian style in
  the films of Michelangelo Antonioni (1950–1964)   53
  EUGENIA PAULICELLI

5 The art of dressing: body, gender, and discourse on fashion in
  Soviet Russia in the 1950s and 1960s   73
  OLGA GUROVA

6 Fashioning appropriate youth in 1990s Vietnam   92
  ANN MARIE LESHKOWICH

7 Youth, gender, and secondhand clothing in Lusaka, Zambia: local and global styles   112
   KAREN TRANBERG HANSEN

8 Fashion design and technologies in a global context   128
   MICHIEL SCHEFFER

9 Fabricating Greekness: from fustanella to the glossy page   145
   MICHAEL SKAFIDAS

10 Fashion Brazil: South American style, culture, and industry   164
   VALÉRIA BRANDINI

11 Fashioning "China style" in the twenty-first century   177
   HAZEL CLARK

12 From factories to fashion: an intern's experience of New York as a global fashion capital   194
   CHRISTINA H. MOON

   Index   211

Figures

2.1	Poster from the film *Andaz* (1949)	29
2.2	Still from the film *Andaz* (1949)	31
2.3	Advertisement for Cinthol soap (1957)	33
2.4	Still from the film *Pyaasa* (1957)	37
3.1	Suzy Parker with Robin Tattersall and Gardner McKay, evening dress by Lanvin-Castillo, Café des Beaux-Arts, August 1956	44
3.2	Suzy Parker with Robin Tattersall, dress by Dior, Place de la Concorde, Paris, August 1956	48
4.1	Sketch by Adriana Berselli: Anna's costume (Lea Massari), left, and Giulia's (Dominique Blanchard), right	55
4.2	Lucia Bosè and Massimo Girotti in *Cronaca di un amore* by Michelangelo Antonioni (1950)	58
4.3	Maria Gambarelli, Eleonora Rossi Drago, and Yvonne Fourneaux in *Le amiche* by Michelangelo Antonioni (1955)	60
4.4	Michelangelo Antonioni during a pause while filming *Le amiche*	61
4.5	Monica Vitti and Richard Harris in *Il deserto rosso* by Michelangelo Antonioni (1964)	67
4.6	Monica Vitti and Richard Harris in *Il deserto rosso* by Michelangelo Antonioni (1964)	67
4.7	Monica Vitti in *L'avventura*, by Michelangelo Antonioni (1960)	69
5.1	Official fashion—1953—in *Rabotnitsa* magazine	75
5.2	Lolita Torres on board the motor ship *Rionges* in *Rabotnitsa* (1957)	80
5.3	"If you've got plumper" in *Rabotnitsa* (1966)	83
5.4	"Dress for work" in *Rabotnitsa* (1954)	85
5.5	"On a dance floor" in *Rabotnitsa* (1966)	87
6.1	Contestants model clothing for school or work	93
6.2	An evening gown selection	94
6.3a	Attire for vocational students in *Tuoi Tre* (Youth) (1978)	104

6.3b	Attire for Youth Union office workers and administrators in *Tuoi Tre* (Youth) (1978)	105
7.1	Sign painting on small-scale fashion shop, 2003	113
7.2	Display of shirts and other garments in a *salaula* market, 1993	117
7.3	Young man wearing his first ready-made suit, 1993	121
7.4	Women dressed up for a party occasion, three in *chitenge* suits, and one in a tailor-made office outfit, 1997	124
8.1	Back-pocket selection	134
8.2	The jeans wall	140
9.1	Young Greek fighter with long fustanella	149
9.2	The short version of the fustanella—or *fustanellitsa*—as worn by the Presidential Guard	151
9.3	Reinterpreting the fustanella on the glossy page. Concept and styling: Tassos Sofroniou. Photograph: Konstantinos Rigos. *Free* magazine, October 2007	152
9.4	Reinterpreting the fustanella on the glossy page. Concept and styling: Tassos Sofroniou. Photograph: Konstantinos Rigos. *Free* magazine, October 2007	153
9.5	The cover of the first issue of Greek *Vogue*: "At Last Greek!" ("Επιτέλους Ελληνίδα!"), March 2000	159
9.6	"Fashion Onwards": the cover of the Greek *Marie Claire*, November 2007	161
10.1	Rosa Chá bikinis	168
10.2	André Lima fashion show	169
10.3	Design by Ronaldo Fraga	171
10.4	Design by Alexandre Herchcovitch	173
11.1	Shanghai Tang short cheongsam, shown at a benefit in Hawaii, 2006	181
11.2	Shanghai Tang black embroidered cheongsam, 2007	184
11.3	Blanc de Chine, denim cheongsam, pants, and shirt from the Bleu de Chine line, launched in 2008	185
11.4	Interior of the Blanc de Chine New York store, 2006	188
11.5	Tan Yuan Yuan, principal dancer with the San Francisco Ballet, practicing tai chi in a silk tunic and pants by Blanc de Chine, 2006	189

Contributors

Valéria Brandini is a Cultural Anthropologist, PhD in Communication Science, and Master in Marketing and Advertisement, who works on research about fashion, culture, and business. Her books include *Dressing the Streets, Fashion, Culture, and Metropolis*, and *For an Ethnography of Luxury: A Fashion Brand Study*. She works as a brand consultant for many companies in South America, and teaches on many postgraduate courses in Brazil, in universities including UEL, UAM, and SENAC; she is also the Research Coordinator of the Business and Consumption Cultures Group at the Department of Anthropology in UNICAMP, Brazil.

Hazel Clark is Dean of the School of Art and Design History and Theory at Parsons the New School for Design, New York. She is a design historian and theorist, with a specialist interest in fashion, and design and cultural identity. Her recent publications include *The Cheongsam* (Oxford University Press 2000); she has edited *Design Issues* on design in Hong Kong (MIT Press, Spring 2003); and co-edited, with Alexandra Palmer, *Old Clothes, New Looks: Second Hand Fashion* (Berg 2005), and, with David Brody, *Design Studies: A Reader* (Berg 2009).

Olga Gurova holds a PhD in Cultural Studies from the European University at St. Petersburg, Russia. She teaches sociology of consumption in the State University Higher School of Economics in St. Petersburg, Russia. She is the author of articles on the history of the body and underwear in Russia and author of the book *Soviet Underwear: Between Ideology and Everyday Life* (Moscow: Novoe Literaturnoe Obozrenie 2008).

Karen Tranberg Hansen is Professor at Northwestern University, USA, and is an urban and economic anthropologist. Her books include *Distant Companions: Servants and Employers in Zambia 1900–1985* (Cornell University Press 1989); *Keeping House in Lusaka* (Columbia University Press 1997); *Salaula: The World of Secondhand Clothing in Zambia* (University of Chicago Press 2000); she edited *African Encounters with Domesticity* (Rutgers University Press 1992) and co-edited, with Mariken

Vaa, *Reconsidering Informality: Perspectives from Urban Africa* (Nordic Africa Institute 2004).

Ann Marie Leshkowich is Associate Professor of Anthropology at College of the Holy Cross, Worcester, MA, USA. Her research focuses on gender, entrepreneurship, globalization, fashion, and kinship in Vietnam. Her publications include "Wandering Ghosts of Late Socialism: Conflict, Metaphor, and Memory in a Southern Vietnamese Marketplace," *Journal of Asian Studies*, 2008; Sandra Niessen, Ann Marie Leshkowich, and Carla Jones (eds.), *Re-Orienting Fashion* (Berg 2003); and Ann Marie Leshkowich and Carla Jones, "What Happens When Asian Chic Becomes Chic in Asia?" *Fashion Theory*, 2003.

Christina H. Moon is a Doctoral Student in Anthropology at Yale University currently engaged in fieldwork in New York City. Her dissertation research explores the cultural and social relationships between design work and creative labor in the New York City fashion industry and its relation to global garment production. Her project interests include global subjectivity and its relation to cultural products and globalization, as well as cities and the politics of urban space.

Eugenia Paulicelli is Professor of Italian, Comparative Literature, and Women's Studies at Queens College and the Graduate Center of the City University of New York. Here she co-directs the interdisciplinary concentration in Fashion Studies. She is the originator and co-curator of the exhibit "The Fabric of Cultures: Fashion, Identity, Globalization" (Godwin-Ternbach Museum at Queens College, Spring 2006). She is the author of *Fashion under Fascism: Beyond the Black Shirt* (Berg 2004); editor of *Moda e moderno dal Medioevo al Rinascimento* (Meltemi 2006). She has written several essays on fashion that have appeared in volumes and journals such as *Fashion Theory*, *Annalecta Husserliana*, *Annali d'Italianistica*, *Athanor*, and *Gender & History*.

Helena C. Ribeiro is a Doctoral Student in English at the Graduate Center of the City University of New York. She is working on a dissertation project that explores democracy and the aesthetics of contrariness in Ezra Pound and Edgar Allan Poe.

Michiel Scheffer is Professor in Fashion and Textile Management at Saxion University Enschede (NL). He is trained as a geographer (Utrecht, LSE). His PhD was on the globalization of clothing production (Utrecht University, 1992). He worked for ten years with the Dutch Fashion Industry Association before working as an industry consultant and professor.

Jane Schneider is Professor Emeritus of Anthropology at the Graduate Center of the City University of New York. Her anthropological field research has been in Sicily. Her publications include: co-authored with Peter Schneider,

Culture and Political Economy in Western Sicily (1976); co-edited with Annette B. Weiner, *Cloth and Human Experience* (1987); and the recent edited collection, with Ida Susser, *Wounded Cities: Destruction and Reconstruction in a Globalized World.*

Michael Skafidas is a Doctoral Student in Comparative Literature at the Graduate Center of the City University of New York, a Teaching Fellow at Queens and City Colleges, a contributing editor of *Global Viewpoint* for the Los Angeles Times Syndicate, and editor-at-large at *Vogue Hellas, Marie Claire International,* and *Status* magazine. He is also the editor of the Greek edition of *NPQ* and co-author with N. Gardels of *Bright Minds at the Turn of the Century* (Terzo Books 2000)

Rachel Tu is currently Research Assistant for the Mellon Costume Documentation Project at the Brooklyn Museum. She earned her Master of Arts in Visual Culture: Costume Studies at New York University and her Bachelor of Arts in Cultural Anthropology at the University of California, Santa Barbara. She is previously published under the name Rachel Morris.

Acknowledgments

This book would not have been possible without the enthusiasm for the project that came from our editor Natalie Foster at Routledge and the encouraging comments that came from the three anonymous readers who read our initial proposal. Thanks are also due to Charlotte Wood at Routledge who has been always prompt and patient in answering all our questions as the manuscript was being prepared. We would like to thank all our contributors. They have been responsive and wonderful to work with in the course of a long process of sharing, comparative scholarly research, expertise, and friendship. Thanks also to John Mackay (Slavic Languages and Literatures and Film Studies at Yale University) for his expertise on Soviet Russia.

The volume is the fruit of a multidisciplinary dialogue within the scholarly community of The City University of New York and particularly the Graduate Center and Queens College. It was here that the project "The Fabric of Cultures. Fashion, Identity, Globalization" was born in the spring of 2006. Eugenia Paulicelli, in particular, would like to express her deepest gratitude to a number of colleagues who have made the whole project of approaching fashion in a scholarly manner through PhD graduate seminars: Stephen Brier (Vice President for Information Technology and External Programs); Joseph Glick (Executive Officer in the Department of Psychology), who embraced with enthusiasm the chance to design and co-teach two PhD seminars on fashion; Acting Provost Julia Wrigley, who kindly participated in the "The Fabric of Cultures" conference and supported the creation of a new Fashion Studies Concentration at the CUNY Graduate Center. Thanks also to Jane Schneider (included in the volume), David Harvey, Sharon Zukin, Stuart Ewen, and Janet Cox-Rearick, who either took part in the conference or gave lectures around the issues of global fashion, time–space relations, consumption, shopping, and art. Their wonderful lectures stimulated and nourished in many ways the development of the research project as a whole.

Eugenia Paulicelli would also like to thank Amy Winter and her staff at the Godwin-Ternbach Museum at Queens College for the enthusiam and hard work they displayed in mounting and co-curating a wonderful exhibition on "The Fabric of Cultures," where dresses and textiles from around the world were admired. The exhibition enjoyed the expertise of two other co-curators, Elizabeth Lowe and Julia Sharp. She offers thanks too to all the students who have animated and participated in the project in a variety of ways. In particular, to Helena Ribeiro, a PhD candidate in English (CUNY), whose paper is included in the collection; Michael Skafidas, PhD candidate in Comparative Literature, who is also included in the volume and whose support, expertise as a journalist, and his enthusiasm to research global culture were very much appreciated; Leonardo Rivera, who offered technological expertise, invaluable help at the conferences at Queens and the Graduate Center, and support in the reproduction of stills for Eugenia Paulicelli's essay; Monica Hanna, PhD candidate in Comparative Literature, and Anne Brownstein, PhD candidate in Urban Studies, who both moderated panels at "The Fabric of Cultures" conference. Without the support of these wonderful students, their intellectual curiosity, and their generosity and friendship this project would have not taken the shape it now has.

Grazie as always to my husband David Ward, for his continuous support, with critical and honest feedback at all the stages of the project, and to our daughter Anna for her jokes and witticisms (E.P.). Also, my thanks to Clive and Jacob for their unwavering support (H.C.).

Introduction

Eugenia Paulicelli and Hazel Clark

This volume is the latest of the fruits of a multidisciplinary project that was originated at Queens College and the Graduate Center of the City University of New York. The project, which bears the same title as the present volume, included an exhibition held at the Godwin-Ternbach Museum at Queens College (February 14–June 1, 2006), a PhD seminar at the Graduate Center co-taught by Eugenia Paulicelli and Joseph Glick, a series of lectures, and an international symposium in spring 2006 that took place at the Graduate Center, co-sponsored by the Women's Studies Certificate Program, the Renaissance Studies Certificate Program, the Center for Culture, Politics, and Place, the Office of Interdisciplinary Studies, and the Office of the Provost, all at the CUNY Graduate Center; and by the Department of Art and Design Studies, Parsons the New School for Design, Casa Italiana Zerilli-Merimò, New York University, and the Italian Cultural Institute, New York. Most of the papers contained in the volume were initially delivered at the CUNY conference. This and all the other events organized around the project saw a wonderful synergy of scholars, undergraduates, and doctoral students from a variety of disciplines and cultures interacting with each other, engaging in conversation and sharing their findings and expertise. As in a multicolored tapestry, scholars and students explored a series of topics: the relationship of fashion to identity; the global and the local; the interrelations of cultures, to name but a few. The aims of the Fabric of Cultures project were threefold: to show the complexity in the production and consumption of fashion; to investigate the mechanisms of cultural production; and to examine the interaction between personal, national, and transnational identities.[1] At the core of both the project and this volume is the claim that fashion is a privileged lens through which to gain a new understanding of cultures, and individual lives, as well as of the mechanisms regulating cultural and economic production in the past and in the present. Breward and Evans have written that "fashion is a process in two senses: it is a market-driven cycle of consumer desire and demand; and it is a modern mechanism for the fabrication of the self. It is in this respect that fashion operates as a fulcrum for negotiating the meeting of internal and external worlds" (Breward and

Evans 2005: 3). Fashion, however, is also a cultural system of meanings and an ongoing process of communication. The meanings of clothes are acquired through a process of cultural mediation that takes place in a variety of ways, such as film, photography, the internet, publicity, and magazines, as well as individual taste and choices.

Fashion as a manufacturing industry would not exist without the textile industry that in turn was at the core of the social, political, and economic transformations that marked the early modernization of Europe in the eighteenth-century industrial revolution; at the heart of colonialism; and central to the consequent struggle for independence from colonial empires, as in the case of India. Fashion is also key to gaining an understanding of the current shifts in the global economy and markets, as well as to the projection of identity and aesthetics. Think, for instance, how in the world of cultural production and the media fashion has always been and still is linked to a desirable model of modernity, style, and chic (e.g. Paris in the nineteenth century and the first half of the twentieth; Milan, and Italy generally, from the late 1970s onwards; Antwerp and Belgium for avant-garde design in the 1990s; Japanese designers in the 1980s; New York sportswear and ready-to-wear from the inter-war period onwards, etc.). These are just some examples of what seems to constitute the power fashion has to portray and invent national and global identities, branding particular countries, lifestyles, and cities on a global scale as the chapters in this volume show.

It has been our aim to examine fashion vis-à-vis issues of identity and globalization in a relational mode linked by time–space relationships. Tied to a "national fabric," but also aiming to widen its remit, fashion is always traveling and ultimately aims at a global market. This is why the production of fashion goes hand in hand with the process of branding and rebranding of the products that become icons and symbols of a desirable lifestyle and look. Indeed, this process of branding and rebranding includes not only objects but places, cities, and countries. Fashion again has a lot to say about, and contributes greatly to, the shaping of the perception of a country or culture. Several chapters in the volume address and focus on this aspect of fashion, by way of a variety of methodologies.

This book examines the impact fashion has, and has had, as a manufacturing industry and as a culture industry that shapes the identities of nations and cities, in a cross-cultural perspective within a global framework. At the same time our aim is to look into local histories and industries and to offer, for the first time, a wide spectrum of case studies that draw on primary sources and focus on a diversity of geographical spaces and places. The uniqueness of the study lies in the fact that it offers essays from all over the world, including the renowned global capitals of fashion like New York, but also from and about countries less known or identifiable as centers of fashion, such as contemporary Greece and Soviet Russia. One of the aims of the volume is to show how similar mechanisms can be observed in different countries or continents in fashion production and consumption practices. Another is to call attention to the local realities in the four continents of Asia, Europe, Africa, and America (North and South America/ Latin America) to see if there are ways of resisting the leveling mode of globalization, the Orientalizing of the Other, and how and where these attempts have failed. In addition, the book offers chapters that examine fashion culture and production in countries that are now emerging with their own fashion and design in the global market or are undergoing a process of reinventing and reusing their own tradition and "national fabric" in order to produce their own vision in fashion and design. This process also entails a reexamination and rereading of one's own nation's history. Fashion is an open window through which to observe such phenomena. As several scholars have stressed, clothing is part of material culture and has a double face. It is at one and the same time public and private, material and symbolic, always caught within the lived experience and providing an incredible tool with which to study culture and history. Emerging from all the papers and from the project as a whole is a growing perception that we need to see "globalization" in problematic terms and not just as an umbrella that encompasses modes of production and consumption or is identifiable with a Western model.

This does not mean that we accept uncritically the homogenizing mechanisms of the fashion system. Rather, an awareness of these subtle and not so subtle mechanisms and operations comes to the fore when we consider the fact that cloth and clothing are an integral part of the human experience at both the material and symbolic levels. But how does the national fabric of a given country and society interact and relate to processes of economic and cultural globalization? Can we rightly talk about a postnational condition and fashion? Or does fashion go beyond "nation"? How can we explain, for instance, that although we live in a globalized world, we still see ways in which fashion defines its own boundaries in terms of style, luxury, and chic, working at the same time with different geographies of the cultural imaginary? How do we address issues of "homogenizing heterogeneity" that co-opt the Other in the discourse and political economy of the still predominant West? How do we define and/or pinpoint the local and the global, as well as tradition and modernity, craft and technology? In what ways do these aspects recur in defining fashion, its industry, and its culture worldwide?

Some of these issues are at the core of the chapters of the volume and are developed in depth in the collection's opening chapter by Jane Schneider, "From Potlatch to Wal-Mart: Courtly and Capitalist Hierarchies through Dress." She argues that cloth and clothing constitute the widest imaginable category of material culture, covering a spatial domain that extends from the miles of textiles annually produced by hand or in the factory to the most intimate apparel of the human body, and a temporal domain whose earliest moments, lost to archaeology, predate the Neolithic. Encompassed within the category are the familiar dualities of Western social thought: production versus consumption, utility versus beauty, the gift versus the commodity, symbolism versus materiality. Many accounts of the capitalist industrialization of cloth and clothing center around the duality most integral to the triumphalist narrative of European civilization: the West versus "the rest."

One of the great merits of this chapter is its attempt to transcend these oppositions. Rather than label the political-economic and cultural systems of sartorial production and consumption that existed prior to the emergence of capitalism as "pre-" or "noncapitalist," it defines them as "courtly," a word that highlights their relation to hierarchy and acknowledges their persistence. Regarding the capitalist system of production and consumption, the analysis points in two directions: on the one hand, to technological innovation, the mobilization of wage labor, and the "capture" of raw materials through colonial and imperial projects; on the other hand, to the special genius of capitalism, and its ongoing (and antihierarchical) democratization of the possibility for self-enhancement through consumption. Because this democratization presupposes low-cost goods, the two aspects—heavy-handed interventions in production and the cultivation of desire—are shown to be integrally related.

Jane Schneider's chapter structures the approach and questions that are raised and developed, although using different methodologies, by the other chapters. The essays in the first part (Gurova, Tu, Ribeiro, Paulicelli) focus their attention on the period following World War II, a crucial time in the transformation and reconstruction of the national fabric, and the succeeding case studies are presented and analyzed in the light of the great transformations that have affected countries around the globe after the collapse of the Berlin Wall in 1989 (as shown in Leshkowich, Skafidas, Hansen, et al.). Although historically different from one another, these two phases show striking similarities both in the mechanisms at work that produce fashion and project a style more attuned to concepts of modernity, and in the complex interaction between local and global in the symbolic significance of fashion and its culture industries and media apparatus.

While the chapters by Gurova, Tu, Ribeiro, and Paulicelli focus on countries that range from the totalitarian Soviet Union to independent India and Marshall Plan-reconstructed Italy and France, it is interesting to see how fashion, the search for a distinct local style responding to visions of modernity to be projected globally, plays a major role in refashioning these nations' narratives. Indeed, in these contexts fashion becomes a powerful mechanism of inscription of these economic and cultural transformations and the transition between what is seen as "traditional" and what is seen as "modern" (by which is meant that which is sexy and appealing). These chapters show how fashion as a manufacturing industry and a culture industry, in league with the power of the popular press, fashion magazines and images, photography and film, constructs and invents a "new" national narrative that inevitably and constantly relates to global issues of identity, production, and consumption.

Olga Gurova, in her chapter "The Art of Dressing: Body, Gender, and Discourse on Fashion in Soviet Russia in the 1950s and 1960s," focuses her attention on the reconstruction of the fashion discourse in socialist Russia in the 1950–60s. Here the female body and how it is dressed and decorated is produced by means of discourse in women's popular press. In particular, women's magazines in Soviet culture had two specific features: they were limited in number, and all of them were under the control of state institutions. The fashion discourse, then, was the medium through which state ideology was written as a text and its norms enforced on the surface of the female body. Indeed, in the 1950s and 1960s, fashion discourse took on an idea of "Soviet style" (*sovetskii stil'*), placing the Soviet look in the context of oppositions between Soviet and Western, socialist and capitalist, domestic and imported. The Soviet style was, of course, identified by simplicity, modesty, and a sense of measure. These categories were opposed to the sexiness and casual look that were associated with Western culture and, at the same time, with bad taste. Gurova presents fashion as a set of practices considered historically as a way of disciplining and normalizing the female body according to the Soviet look. This also undermines the idea that fashion and its discourse are the sole product of a capitalist economy. Rather, they have a great deal to say about issues of national identity, nationalism, and globalization.

In fact, Rachel Tu's "Dressing the Nation: Indian Cinema Costume and the Making of a National Fashion, 1947–1957" examines how popular cinema is crucial in conveying messages similar to those carried by the popular press or fashion magazines. As she points out, in the decade following Indian independence, from 1947 to 1957, cinema played an integral role in the public sector. Not only did it provide an escape from the harsh realities of political transition, but it was also a guide to the integration of national sentiments into daily life. Associating with film characters, cinema viewers, residing primarily in metropolitan areas across the subcontinent, assumed new modes of public dress that they had never worn before. On an individual level, this adoption created a tactile relationship between the film characters and viewers. On the larger social level, with many individuals across the subcontinent wearing and admiring similar elements of dress, a national fashion was born. Operating under the premise that Indian cinema reflects the negotiation of national ideology and imagery, this chapter identifies the semiotic role of costume in cinema, its glamorized image in high fashion, and finally its adaptation into daily dress in the decade following Indian independence. Focusing on three Hindi popular films—*Andaz, Taxi Driver,* and *Pyaasa*—the chapter identifies several key costume types and reveals shifting attitudes about acceptable attire. It also examines related film advertisements and editorials in the periodicals *Filmfare, Illustrated Weekly,* and *Blitz* that project film actors simultaneously as fashion icons and model citizens. As awareness of diverse fashions spread, dress—one of the most malleable mediums of self-expression—allowed individuals to redefine their relationships with each other in a new social and political environment.

The chapter by Helena Ribeiro, "Made in America: Paris, New York, and Postwar Fashion Photography," focuses on the fashion photography of Richard Avedon, who after World War II, along with other New York-based fashion photographers, was sent by *Harper's Bazaar* to photograph French fashion on French streets in line with the aim of the Marshall Plan to encourage Europe to rediscover and reconstruct itself. What Avedon and others did was to rebrand and refashion the allure and chic of Paris through cultural mediation, almost as a constant reminder to France of who had been responsible for liberating the nation from the Nazi occupation. Ribeiro stresses the idea that Avedon reconstructed, in an American magazine, an alternate Paris, and an alternate Paris mythology, via an alternate cityscape peopled with American models draped in French couture, and that this helped to rebuild Paris from the ashes and the havoc left by the war. Avedon's work does not sell only Dior and Cardin, it sells Paris itself.

The ability to create a sense of a "national" style that is projected onto a global scene can be a powerful mechanism in the relationship between costume and the movies. Eugenia Paulicelli's chapter on "Framing the Self, Staging Identity: Clothing and Italian Style in the Films of Michelangelo Antonioni (1950–1960)" shows how in Antonioni's films clothing has a dual function. On the one hand, it is integral to his ability as a filmmaker to create a new language that shares an intimate space with visual poetry; clothing participates, with its texture, cut, and design, in the creation of an atmosphere and a landscape that affect feelings. On the other hand, clothing is used by Antonioni, as by any performing artist, to comment on and illustrate his characters' roles and status as a macro-structure of signification. Many of Antonioni's characters are linked directly to the world of fashion, such as the protagonist in *Le amiche* (1955) or the photographer in *Blow-Up* (1966), or are involved in professions that deal with appearances, media culture, and cinema. It is far from surprising, then, that Antonioni is one of the most quoted sources of inspiration for fashion photography in contemporary fashion magazines, such as American *Vogue.* Often they set their high-fashion shoots in the context of the Italian *dolce vita* where sexiness, sophistication, beauty, and warmth are blended with the kind of ideal lifestyle that has so lulled foreign travelers to the peninsula. Italian cinema of the boom years, and especially Antonioni and Fellini, have contributed to launching Italian style globally at the same time as American directors populated the Eternal City, produced their films at the Cinecittà studios, and frequented Roman fashion houses, clubs, and the Via Veneto epitomized in Fellini's film *La dolce vita* (1960). This theme of the creation, development, and projection of national style and image is developed further, in different cultural contexts, in the chapters that follow.

Ann Marie Leshkowich's chapter, "Fashioning Appropriate Youth in 1990s Vietnam," marks the second part of the book which focuses on the 1990s and after and on new cultural geographies of fashion (Leshkowich, Hansen, Skafidas, Brandini, Clark, and Moon), and on ways of rethinking "global fashion" (Scheffer). By the late 1990s, a decade of economic reform had dramatically improved standards of living in Vietnam. Ho Chi Minh City was in the throes of a "fashion craze," yet many worried that the allure of the new and foreign might lead Vietnamese youth to forget the sacrifices elder generations made in the name of independence and revolution. These concerns were vividly displayed in an event that forms the central focus for the chapter: a New Year's fashion contest for youth sponsored by the Ho Chi Minh Communist Youth League. The event concluded with a nationally known designer denouncing the female contestants for choosing clothes that were impractical and immodest. To explain why contestants' outfits proved controversial, Leshkowich traces the changing relationship between the Vietnamese Communist Party, state officials and media outlets, and youth. In contrast to accounts of late- or postsocialist states as retreating from involvement in citizens' daily lives, or claims that party politics are irrelevant to cosmopolitan and materialistic urban youth, Leshkowich's chapter illuminates the dynamics of nationalism, socioeconomic change, and globalization that have made youth fashion an important object of governmentality and have prompted state officials to attempt to position themselves as expert—and entrepreneurial—arbiters of style.

In the next chapter, "Youth, Gender, and Secondhand Clothing in Lusaka, Zambia: Local and Global Styles," anthropologist Karen Tranberg Hansen employs empirical research based on the local use of secondhand clothing by young people in Zambia to develop further our understanding of "global" dress practices. Hansen argues that cities like Lusaka are in the primary stages of translating globalization into local terms. She uncovers the role of the local geography of consumption with its spaces, agents, and performances in the global framework in which dressed bodies become the point of contact between local knowledge and the broader global context. Today in Lusaka, influences "from outside" of Zambia are more present, and more visibly evident, than they have ever been. Increasing interaction across space and the consciousness of such processes are due to globalization understood broadly. Yet the "newness" of fashion does not mean a slavish following of Western models, nor does it depend on new clothes. In tracing the secondhand clothing commodity chain to Lusaka, Hansen uncovers African consumer demand and more specifically indicates how the desire to be well dressed is a driver for the clothing industry. This preoccupation constitutes an aesthetic sensibility that draws its discernment from a variety of sources to create an overall look that gives the wearer pride, pleasure, and the experience of feeling good. Hansen reminds us how clothing is part of the aesthetic of everyday life, and what we are calling in this book "the fabric of culture." Mediating between self and society, the dressed body also construes desires, including global imaginaries. Hansen illustrates how, as a cultural and material resource, secondhand clothing does all of these things.

Like Hansen, Michiel Scheffer in his chapter "Fashion Design and Technologies in a Global Context" deals with another example of what may be viewed as materially mundane and globally ubiquitous clothing, in this case blue jeans. Using David Harvey's seminal work *The Condition of Postmodernity* (1989) as his critical framework, Scheffer considers the effects of the transition from Fordism to post-Fordism, and from modernism to postmodernism, on the global production and appearance of blue jeans. He describes jeans in fashion terms, and relative to deeper trends, such as speeding up the turnover time of capital and the shift of production to developing countries. Scheffer reveals how jeans were transformed from a classic item of workwear to a fashion item with subtle design features that serve to identity styles and distinguish brands. Detailed design differences facilitated a speeding up of fashion cycles, increased profit margins, and gave jeans a broader appeal, especially at the luxury end of the consumer market. Yet while the technical modification of jeans began in the 1980s, the effects were not felt fully commercially until the second half of the 1990s, when the global dominance of Levi's was finally challenged by newly emerging brands. Developed in specific regional clusters, particularly in the Veneto in Italy, and in southern France, western Japan, and California, these brands created differentiation through new methods of washing in combination with traditional spinning and weaving techniques. These innovations recuperated a post-Fordist logic in their accumulation of capital, high labor-intensiveness, vertical systems, and use of information technology to feed sales data back to the design and manufacturing units.

Scheffer argues that the geography of design innovation in jeans in developed countries is fed by strong clusters in manufacturing, with predominantly regional characteristics, and a market structure which comprises dominant global brands and a small number of global production alliances. Thus, he concludes, postmodern jeans production reflects very intricate arrangements in terms of global capital and production.

Taking a different approach from Scheffer, part of Michael Skafidas's chapter, "Fabricating Greekness: From Fustanella to the Glossy Page," focuses on the fustanella vis-à-vis its revival especially on the occasion of the Olympics. Skafidas focuses on some paradoxes surrounding national dress and how the history of the fustanella is questioned and linked to its mixed origins (including Albanian ones), something that does not emerge in the contemporary narratives of "Greekness." Skafidas goes on to investigate the nature of authenticity in national dress and the constructed nature of national identity. Focusing on how, during the Olympics, the fustanella was glamorized in an exhibition held at the Benaki Museum in Athens, he explains how in countries like modern Greece fashioning the self means reinventing one's historical self and challenging the imported aesthetics of Western fashion.

The waning of the fustanella coincided with the advent of the Western two-piece suit. Yet Skafidas explains that the fustanella is a product of theft, snatched by the Greek state from the national dress of the Arvanites and then established as a military uniform that copied the English. Today, for younger-generation Greeks, the fustanella represents a bygone era of tradition that most do not identify with. Fashion magazines cashed in on the post-Cold War euphoria in Greece as they addressed effectively the needs of previously unexplored markets at a crucial moment of change and transition which followed a century of pessimism. The launching of the local edition of such an internationally acclaimed fashion magazine as *Vogue* offered its audience, among other things, accessibility to a system of signs previously largely unavailable. Here we see the postmodern fashion industry's grand ambition to turn "fashionization" into a global phenomenon. But, Skafidas argues, the aesthetic gentrification that derives from the fashionization of modern lifestyle leads to a bifurcation on a local level, as in the case of Greece. It creates the *fashionable* and the *unfashionable* citizen, and from a global perspective it divides the new world map in the light of a softer post-Cold War prejudice: the *fashionable* and the *unfashionable* world.

The sense of what constitutes the fashionable in newly developing fashion geographies formerly marginal to the global systems of haute couture and ready-to-wear is further explored by Valéria Brandini in "Fashion Brazil: South American Style, Culture, and Industry." She takes as her point of reference "Latin style" fashion, with her focus centered in particular on Brazil. Brandini charts the differences between the establishment of the Brazilian clothing industry by Jewish immigrants from Central and Eastern Europe at the end of the nineteenth century, and the development of a fashion industry at the end of the twentieth century. Contemporary Brazilian fashion does not depend on the cultural stereotypes epitomized by the Carmen Miranda style of the 1950s. The new generation of Brazilian fashion designers who have gained a global reputation, notably Alexandre Herchcovitch, are referencing the exotic, but also the urban and the marginal, as sources of design innovation. The fact that their work might not "look Brazilian" to a global audience is not of great significance. Their reference to the darker side of Brazilian culture, to the streets, prostitution, poverty, the *favelas*, and gang behavior, as well as to Brazilian beach life, are providing a needed stimulus to a once dwindling clothing industry. As Brazilian fashion professionals begin to gain global recognition, Brazil's ethnic and creative identity is becoming a new focus of attention in European and North American fashion circuits. Operating under a fashion system that expresses the cultural differences between the Old World (Europe) and the New World (America), Brazilian fashion highlights the differences between the values of tradition and modernity.

Consideration of these same values also underpins the next chapter, Hazel Clark's "Fashioning 'China Style' in the Twenty-First Century." Like Brandini, Clark considers the role of cultural identity in the conscious formation of design identities by fashion designers and fashion brands. Focusing her research on two Hong Kong-based fashion brands, Shanghai Tang and Blanc de Chine, both established just prior to the 1997 handover of Hong Kong sovereignty from Britain to the People's Republic of China, she examines their mutual aspirations to become luxury global fashion brands. Each brand has developed its own, subtly distinct interpretations of Chineseness or "China style," which is integrated into their design strategies on four key levels: visually, materially, spatially, and textually. Clark indicates how the brands have developed over the course of a decade away from stereotyped traditional tropes to more distinct and "modern" design identities. These changes are discussed in the context of the wider global distribution of the brands, and in particular with reference to their stores in New York City. The chapter asks whether "China style" is simply another fashion trend, a new version of chinoiserie and nostalgia, or rather something more: an indication of a substantial design shift in the Western-dominated global fashion system.

An interest in New York City as a global fashion capital is also the subject of the final chapter of the book, Christina Moon's "From Factories to Fashion: An Intern's Experience of New York as a Global Fashion Capital." In her chapter Moon employs her unique perspective as a student of anthropology undertaking fieldwork as an intern in a fashion design company on Seventh Avenue, working toward the fall/winter 2006 runway shows. As background Moon portrays the cultural and economic changes that occurred in the garment district during the 1990s. This provides the context for the shifting scales of perspective of the everyday spaces that she experiences as an intern. In the course of the neoliberalization of global trade that took place in the 1990s, two powerful forces in the New York garment district drastically transformed the social, economic, and cultural geography of the neighborhood. The first was the near complete destruction of the local garment production factories, which coincided with the second, the simultaneous expansion of design and culture industries in the New York fashion industry. Amidst the destruction, visions of an imagined fashion capital emerged alongside new forms of design, culture, and entrepreneurial labor. By the end of the decade the establishment of space for New York Fashion Week and its change in global fashion timing marked New York City as an emerging global fashion capital.

Moon concludes that in an era of globalization, where points in the apparel production process are described as economic, anonymous, and abstract, the experience of the global also needs to be articulated within the tangible and intimate spaces of everyday life and work. This can be achieved through new scholarly research that combines the theory and practices of both production and consumption. Moon aims to find spaces in which to understand more clearly the mechanisms that support the fashion system as a manufacturing industry, as a symbolic force that has rebranded a global city like NYC. At the same time she pays attention to producers, the very people and workforce that make the clothes. Hers is an attempt at finding both a meeting place and a vantage point from which to observe the local and the hidden (intimate) spaces within the homogenizing effects of global capitalism.[2]

In presenting a variety of case studies across space and time it has been our aim with this volume to both explore and question the standardizing effects of fashion and global capitalism. We have sought to explore the extent to which fashion, approached by scholars whose expertise, training, and approaches differ, might be better understood in a comparative perspective, from which the local and the global, and the power clothes have to affect feelings, emotions, and perceptions, can be seen to share a common terrain. It has been the two editors' main concern to frame the diversity of case studies presented in this volume in such a way that they embrace these two important sides of fashion, but without ever losing sight of the impact and power fashion has on individual lives and how it has transformed local and global economies, cultures, and identities.

Notes

1. See the catalog of the exhibition *The Fabric of Cultures* (Winter 2008), especially E. Paulicelli, "Where It All Began" (6–7) and "Fashion, Identity, Globalization" (8–15).
2. See *Women's Studies Quarterly*, issue on "The Global and the Intimate," 2006.

References

Breward, C. and Evans, C. (2005) *Fashion and Modernity*, Oxford and New York: Berg.

Pratt, G. and Rosner, V. (guest eds.) (2006) special issue "The Global and the Intimate," *Women's Studies Quarterly*, 34(1–2).

Winter, A. (ed.) (2008) *The Fabric of Cultures: Fashion, Identity, Globalization*, catalog of exhibition, The Godwin-Ternbach Museum, Queens College, City University of New York.

Chapter 1

From potlatch to Wal-Mart

Courtly and capitalist hierarchies through dress

Jane Schneider

Cloth and clothing constitute an illuminating lens through which to consider the history of inequality—that is, social relations of vastly unequal wealth, status, and power. This is especially so if we take into account both the production and the consumption of these fundamentally important exemplars of material culture. An emphasis on consumption alone risks reproducing the simplistic notion that what one wears merely indexes and communicates one's social position. Conversely, focusing only on production reproduces the triumphalist narrative of capitalist industrialization and marketing, a narrative in which the West dominates "the rest."

As is well known, productivist understandings of capitalism focus on the mobilization of proletarianized wage labor as the central characteristic. Capitalist accumulation is also closely associated with the "capture" of raw materials through colonial and imperial projects. At the same time, however, these sources of profit are utterly dependent on the special genius of capitalism, which is its ongoing democratization of the possibility of enhancing the self through consuming. Because this democratization presupposes low-cost goods and services, the two aspects—exploitative interventions in production and the cultivation of desire—are integrally related.

Self-enhancement is admittedly a vague idea. Loosely it stands for energizing ourselves and our close others through life-affirming, death-denying, initiatives. Examples involving clothes include transforming our bodies and surroundings in ways we believe are aesthetically or sexually attractive; displaying ourselves to accrue prestige or feel worthy and empowered; generously distributing clothing or accessories to consolidate friendships and followings; signaling through clothes an identification with particular ideas or affiliation with particular groups; and discarding old clothes, perhaps redefined as rags or clutter, in order to make room for more. Clothing consumption is always restless and multidimensional—a mix of these and other elements. The point is that, in modern capitalist societies, its enhancing qualities are, or can be, the purview of virtually everyone.

As a political-economic and cultural system, capitalism historically overlaid and displaced, but did not eliminate, arrangements that privileged elite consumption, in which the opportunities for enhancement were intensely hierarchically distributed. Rather than label these earlier arrangements "precapitalist" or "noncapitalist"—appellations that imply, in the first instance, their eventual disappearance and, in the second, an absence or lack—I will (experimentally) refer to them as "courtly," highlighting their relation to hierarchy. This choice of words challenges several well-worn assumptions: that capitalist and "other" consumption practices are related to each other as the commodity is to the gift; that the modern consumer was newly constituted as a rational individual, exercising choice in the marketplace; and that the debate over whether modern consumer choices are really "free" or manipulated by image and advertising is worth the ink it absorbs. As the explication of the term "enhancement" suggests, modern consumer practices are fully continuous with, and indeed illuminated by, the ethnography on which Marcel Mauss based his brilliant theory of the gift (Mauss 1954 [1923–1924]).

But whereas in the consumption sphere continuities between courtly and capitalist practice are considerable, a deep rupture splits the sphere of production. Unmarked by the proletarianizing and colonizing strategies alluded to above, the courtly production of cloth and clothing hinges on the ability of nobles and chiefs to acquire rare and precious materials through deputized trade and barter, and to frequent, patronize or attach to their courts, in some cases through a form of enslavement, beehives of artisan activity— skilled, knowledgeable, artistically inclined, selflessly dedicated as the case may be. Under such arrangements, manufacturers are in control of product design and decisions and, we surmise, of the organization and rhythm of work. In short, they enjoy a modicum of autonomy that is all but lost in industrialized textile and garment manufacturing.

This chapter examines the self-enhancing qualities of cloth and clothing in the context of courtly societies, identifying both the continuities and the discontinuities with capitalism. It further highlights the artisan production of these goods as contrasted with industrial capitalist manufacture. Two historical moments of exuberant clothing consumption are then compared: the distributions of Chilkat "blankets" at potlatching feasts in the late nineteenth century on the Northwest Coast, and the credit-intensified purchase of logo-branded clothes in late twentieth-century US Wal-Marts. The comparison, it is hoped, validates paying simultaneous attention to production and consumption when asking big questions of cloth and clothing history, specifically what this history reveals about the dynamics of social inequality under capitalism.[1]

Enhancement and the spirituality of cloth and clothing

The ethnography and archaeology of Africa, Asia, Melanesia, and Latin America, carried on throughout the twentieth century, is rich with details supporting the notion that cloth and clothing are integral to self and small-group enhancement. Two kinds of description stand out: one related to the spirituality of cloth, the other to its aesthetic properties. That objects can have a spiritual dimension was long ago established by Mauss, who theorized that gifts are a fundamentally political phenomenon, staving off sentiments of envy or resentment that might otherwise lead to the evil eye, and even to open warfare. Once given, they compel reciprocity because the spirit of the giver is embodied in them, adding moral weight (Mauss 1954 [1923–24]: 10). Objects often also encode the names, biographies, memories, and histories of past "owners," deepening the significance of their transmission. In the 1970s and 1980s, Annette B. Weiner applied these ideas specifically to cloth. One of her case studies was Western Samoa, where women traditionally soaked, dried, and plaited the narrow fibers of the pandanus to make large, linen-like mats. Lasting as long as 200 years, these mats absorbed value through association with ancestors and mythical events; reinforcing claims to the past, they were desired, and kept, as treasure. And yet they frayed at the edges—a poignant reminder of the fragility of the human condition (see Weiner 1989; 1992).

Whether the spiritual endowment of cloth and clothing is believed to derive from soaking up historical and mythical associations, from the intrinsic quality of impermanence, or from artisans' incantations as described below, it is an endowment that ensures their centrality in the multiple exchanges connecting humans with the world of spirits and divinities, and with one another. In episodes of spirit possession, a returning or restless essence is frequently believed to seek not only a human body in which to dwell, but human apparel, and to reveal its identity through demands for specific items of cloth and clothing (e.g. Verger 1954). A transforming medium, cloth also delineates and adorns sacred spaces; bedecks ceremonial dancers; drapes temples, shrines, icons, chiefs, and priests; and enriches umbrellas and palanquins. Mayan brocaded blouses called *huipiles* clothe images of patron saints and the Virgin Mary, while Andean herders propitiate earth and mountain spirits with a special textile bundle (Morris 1986; Zorn 1985).

Cloth intensifies sociality in rituals of birth, initiation, and curing. As James J. Fox summarized for Indonesia's outer islands, it "swaddles the newborn, wraps and heals the sick, embraces and unites the bride and groom, encloses the wedding bed, and in the end, enshrouds the dead" (1977: 97). In many societies, spouses provide each other's wedding attire and minimum future wardrobes, thereby tightening the knot (e.g. Kendall 1985). Textiles that a bride prepares herself—spinning, weaving, embroidering, adding appliqué or lace—constitute her personal gift, her trousseau, to her new household and its eventual descendants.

The capacity of cloth to enhance who we are and deepen our social relationships is especially evident in ethnographies of mortuary rituals, in which the living wrap their dead, whether for burial, reburial, or cremation, in textiles believed to ensure their continuance as social beings. So compelling is the idea that cloth constitutes a continuing tie that often the dead are understood to demand it on pain of sorcery or possession (Darish 1989; Feeley-Harnik 1989). In investiture ceremonies conferring entitlements, cloth also plays a central role. In India, writes Bernard S. Cohn (1989), the Mughal court stored as treasure piles of memory-saturated fabrics, considering them a medium for the transfer of essential substances and an emblem of "honor for posterity." How appropriate, then, to place such fabrics on the shoulders of a successor. When a new emperor is installed in Japan, textiles crafted by the rustic method of laboriously soaking, rotting, boiling, and beating coarse, uncultivated fibers convey a simultaneously material and spiritual blessing derived from the "most ancient core of Japanese culture" (Cort 1989: 379).

These brief descriptions of cloth and clothing as spiritually enhancing are drawn from the work of ethnographers, historians, and archaeologists of societies we have defined as courtly, who not only conducted their research a few decades ago, but who also considered themselves, at the time, to be documenting "traditional" practices. "Preindustrial" or "noncommercial" clothes and fabrics have a dominant presence in their accounts, as does what most social theory considers to be a "premodern" orientation toward religious phenomena, emphasizing their presence *in* the material world. It can be argued, however, that the spiritual and the material are inseparable in the minds of humans everywhere, including those who inhabit fully modern industrial–capitalist societies. Here, too, people keep and store items of cloth and clothing for reasons that include the memories encoded in them—for example, the memory of receiving them from a particular relation as a gift. Here, too, the clothes of deceased loved ones elicit intense affect, a feeling of connection. And, a point we return to below, here, too, the idea lives on, despite two centuries of modern scientific discourse, that cloth and clothes enhance the person in magical ways, promoting his or her success as a vital, loved, admired social being.

Enhancement and artisan production

The idea that cloth and clothing are spiritually imbued materials is reinforced by ethnographic descriptions of artisans performing rituals and observing particular taboos in the course of spinning, weaving, embroidering, brocading, dyeing, finishing, and thereby animating their product. Pueblo men spun, wove, and embroidered in their male ritual center, the *kiva*. Older Kodi women in Sumba, Indonesia, likely practitioners of midwifery and, more covertly, of witchcraft, specialized in the resist-dyeing of warp yarns with earth tones and indigo. Supplying these yarns to younger women for the production of warp-faced ikats on backstrap looms, they let it be known through song, lament, and ritual offerings that dyeing was analogous to childbirth. Imperfectly dyed cloth signified miscarriage, so much so that a pregnant woman should refrain from looking into the dye pots, lest the sight of the dark, churning, and foul-smelling liquid dissolve the contents of her womb (Hoskins 1989).

Beyond contributing spirituality, artisans contribute beauty—an equally critical ingredient in the capacity of cloth and clothing to infuse persons with vitality and widen their social worlds. Nor are these aspects separable; design motifs such as "god's eyes" and genealogical crests, and symbolically coded colors, are at once beautiful and the conduits of spiritual power. Essential elements in textile aesthetics are the interlacing of warp and weft, "post-loom" decoration (e.g. embroidery, appliqué, reverse appliqué), and the feel and color harmonies of the finished piece. Clothing hinges as well on shape, whether the soft contours of wrapped and folded lengths of fabric or the sculptural architecture that is achieved by tailoring—cutting, fitting, and sewing. Throughout the history of cloth and clothing production, male and female artisans have elaborated on one or more of these variables, inspired by other arts, by the availability of raw materials, by rivalries with other producers, by the support of patrons, and through interaction with one another.

No cloth or clothing tradition was ever static, although many traditions became known to very wide audiences for particular, excellent, or unusual qualities, and are today collected by aficionados and museums—Chilkat (Northwest Coast) dancing capes and leggings among them. Experts appreciate artisans having seized opportunities and overcome obstacles in order to produce a textile worthy of such prestige. The difficulties of obtaining fast colors—yellows, blues, and above all reds—in the centuries before the invention of aniline dyes included this challenge: although protein fibers bond with dyestuffs, cellulose fibers (e.g. linen and cotton) repel them unless treated with special mordants. No wonder that, historically, dyers occupied a particularly auspicious position among cloth makers. The reputations of many renowned textiles, some of them objects of royal monopolies, depended on dyers' ability and special knowledge (Schneider 1978, 1987: 427–431).

Although we can only guess at the everyday quality of productive relations for the distant past, pockets of oppression surely existed. The most telling instances were based on gender. In some courtly contexts, cloth was manufactured wholly or largely by men. The Lele of Central Africa, studied by Mary Douglas, assigned women to cultivate food, leaving men to weave fine raffia textiles (Douglas 1967). In the characteristic "men's cloths" of West Africa, men brocaded imported (and colorful) silk or woolen yarn into a cotton ground whose fibers were cultivated, processed, and spun by women. Especially in polygynous households, or where Muslim rules of female seclusion prevailed, this rendered their contribution subordinate. In certain circumstances, however, women developed their own cloth styles, rooted in the resist-dyeing of commercial cloth, and did not spin for men. Similarly, urban-centered Javanese batiking was a women's craft. Nevertheless, in most historical societies, when men's and women's styles coexisted, women more often than men produced their cloth in rural households and villages, men in the towns and cities; men more than women benefited from the opposite gender's dedication to tasks of minor aesthetic relevance, like processing fibers and spinning.

Forms of enslavement appear in some accounts of artisanal cloth production. As shifting trade patterns opened the door for the Bushong Kuba, neighbors of the Lele, to create their "velvet" elaboration of raffia in what is now southern Zaire, the royal authority imported slaves to tend the plantations of raffia palms and harvest the fiber. They also exercised their marital privileges to bring women to their court, tasking them with adding plush-pile designs to male-woven lengths of raffia (Vansina 1978). As with the Inka, the instruction of court-bound women in the textile arts—here the skill was embroidery, with the Inka it was tapestry weaving—must have been controlling. And yet, even under these circumstances, because the artisans in question possessed admired skills and specialized knowledge, they can be presumed to have had the leverage to connect ideas about design, motif, and color with the movements of their own hands. Nor did most cloth artisans work under conditions of near-enslavement. One should not, of course, romanticize their "mode of production"—work could be extremely tedious, foul-smelling and even dangerous; apprentices were demeaned as much as they were encouraged; materials could fail, or fail to be available. The point is that, compared with factory laborers, artisans are a fortunate lot. Garnering the respect of elites who value their talents, they also enjoy relative equality in the workplace, which is minimally dominated, if at all, by overseers and bosses. In short, they benefit in the production sphere from the treasured condition of autonomy—a "gift" that industrial capitalism took away.

Courtly consumption

In contrast, in courtly societies, the consumption sphere is all about hierarchy; the most beautiful "things," and the most spiritually powerful as well, circulate upward toward the chiefs and royals and aristocrats at the top. Louis Dumont's labels for Western and (in his terms) "non-Western" ideological systems—*Homo equalis* and *Homo hierarchicus*, respectively— aptly capture the courtly-capitalist contrast in this regard (Dumont 1970). Pursuant to the *Homo hierarchicus* ideology, elites, and particularly male elites, accumulated prestigious cloth and clothing in part to adorn and make splendid themselves and their surroundings, in part to store as treasure, and in part for dispersal in grand distributions aimed at embarrassing rivals and winning loyal followers. In a well-known analysis of cloth and its functions in the Inka state, John Murra, for example, showed that surpluses of peasant cloth, woven with "magical precautions" and mobilized through the Inka tribute system, were piled so high in the royal warehouses as to stagger the Spanish conquerors (Murra 1989 [1962]).

Inka rulers further appropriated cloth from weavers in the state's administrative centers and at court—source points for exquisitely fine tapestries. Constructed of strong cotton warps acquired through exchanges with the coast, and softer, brightly dyed alpaca wefts obtained from the highlands, these textiles were in great demand for purposes of diplomacy and foreign exchange. Kings offered them as gifts to attract the fealty of lords in newly incorporated peripheries and forbade their wear or display in the absence of royal approval. Especially valued for this overtly political purpose were cloths from the royal wardrobe, steeped with associations of past rulers and deeds. An "initial pump primer of dependence," suggests Murra (1989 [1962]: 293), cloth of this sort was hoarded by the lords of the provinces for four or more generations, symbolizing at once their obligations to Cuzco and Cuzco's bestowal of citizenship in return.

In courtly societies, hierarchy depended upon sumptuary paraphernalia to objectify and communicate rank, and to constitute material bonds between the past and the present, the rulers and the ruled. To quote Murra again, "no political, military, social, or religious event was complete without textiles being volunteered or bestowed, burned, exchanged, or sacrificed" (ibid.). As noted above for the Mughals, inaugural regalia, passed on from generation to generation, was itself the substance of rule. One sees these principles at work in the cloth and clothing distributions associated with late nineteenth- and early twentieth-century Native American potlatch ceremonies on the Northwest Coast.

Potlatching on the Northwest Coast

The groups involved, primarily salmon fishers and hunters, of which the Kwakiutl are the best known, experienced a dramatic transformation of their world following the installation, in the early nineteenth century, of forts and collecting stations in support of the fur trade.[2] With the founding of the Hudson Bay Company's main post at Alert Bay in the 1870s, the "White economy" took off, causing natives to further lose some of their hunting and fishing grounds, and to become more involved in waged employment and trade. Numerous men worked for the Whites' canneries, coal mines, logging and shipping companies; women serviced White settlers as prostitutes and domestics. Several groups ceased earlier practices of raiding and warfare while taking on the role of middlemen between Athabascan fur-trappers to the north and European fur exporters on the coast (see Wolf 1982: 182 ff.; 1999: 69 ff.). European-introduced diseases against which no immunities existed added the most dramatic source of insecurity. The Kwakiutl, for example, were reduced from an estimated pre-contact population of 19,000 to 7,600 by 1862 and around 1,000 in 1924 (Wolf 1999: 77).

It is in the context of this transformed political economy and demographic collapse that potlatches, held to celebrate critical junctures in the life cycle—birth, adolescence, marriage, house construction, death—and accession to rank or chiefly office, became marked by agonistic competition. The ritualized distributions of valuables on the part of the chiefly hosts, and the attempts to reciprocate on the part of followers and guests, took on an increasingly aggressive tone, the chiefs being challenged by entrepreneurial upstarts making claims to chiefship. In 1888 the Canadian government banned the ceremonies, defining them as "wasteful" and "barbaric" and authorizing the Royal Mounted Police, missionaries, and schoolteachers to repress them, although to limited effect until 1921 (ibid.).

Traditionally, the highest-ranking chiefs of the Northwest Coast region claimed ancestral rights to hunting and fishing grounds from which they were owed a portion of the take as tribute—a fifth of the salmon, for example, and a half of the mountain goats. Additional chiefly prerogatives included houses, masks, feast dishes, mythic songs bestowed by ancestors and spirits, and, most important, the right to distribute valuables at grand ceremonial events. The anthropological literature on potlatch ceremonies tracks the escalation, after the 1870s, in the quantity of the circulating valuables—most commonly copper shields, canoes, boxes, dishes, foods, and slaves. One item, "blankets," appears with special frequency and is often also presented as a measure of value. In the early part of the nineteenth century, distributions of "blankets" among the Kwakiutl averaged perhaps 300. After 1849, when Hudson Bay blankets entered the picture, the numbers climbed, with 9,000 circulating in one potlatch in 1869, 13,000 in another in 1895, and over 30,000 in the last Kwakiutl ceremony of 1921 (Wolf 1982: 192).

Obscured by this vast inflation of a commodity introduced by Whites were the far more significant cedar bark textiles of native artisans. Misnamed "blankets" by the Hudson Bay colonizers, these consisted of dramatic capes, dance skirts, kilts, and leggings, variously decorated in a patterned weave of, predominantly, blue and yellow and believed to transmit a kind of spiritual energy or vital force. The commanding figure in the rear of the Haida canoe in the Seventy-seventh Street entrance hall of the Museum of Natural History in New York City is wearing a cape and leggings in this genre.

Within the genre, Chilkat "blankets" were the most renowned and coveted, and the most generative of enthusiasm in the smashing "giveaways" of the late nineteenth century. The Chilkat part of the name refers to a Tlingit subgroup centered on Alaska's Chilkat River whose women put together new factors of production as their menfolk, competitors of the Kwakiutl, began collecting pelts from interior trappers and delivering them to the coastal depots (Wolf 1982: 182–192). Like the southern Salish, another native group, the Tlingit wove mountain goat hair. Indeed, as hunters of this animal, their access to its fibers outdistanced that of the Salish who, not being hunters, had to send women and children into the mountains in the goats' birthing season to collect tufts of hair from bushes and trees (Gustafson 1980: 217). Goat hair conferred a critical advantage to the textile for, as noted above, in the absence of the modern aniline dyes, cellulose fibers repel most colors whereas protein fibers absorb them. And yet the lovely softness of goat hair could not be maximized in a weft-faced textile until a strong warp fiber became available. The realignments associated with fur trading brought cedar bark, the basis of the coastal cloth traditions, into the configuration. In other words, goat hair carried the color while cedar bark gave the strength (Emmons 1907; Boas 1927; Drucker 1955; 1965; Holm 1982; Samuel 1982).

Adopting the unusual "half-loom" of the coast, which consisted of only one beam, Tlingit women wrapped goat hair, spun and dyed into two-ply yarn, around the dangling cedar warps, creating discrete designs as in a tapestry. The patterns derived from the genealogical crests that men painted on various wooden surfaces—zoomorphic figures whose symmetrically arranged oval-shaped eyes, multiple profiles, and distorted anatomical relationships filled every space (Holm 1982). To accomplish this craft, the weavers required yarns that replicated as many of the paint pigments as possible. Their group's location on the northern and interior trade routes gave them access to Alaskan copper from which they made a well-reputed yet fugitive blue. Additionally, they boiled indigo-dyed commercial cloth— those Hudson Bay blankets—for blue (ibid.; Samuel 1982). All told, the possibilities for blue, as well as for the cedarbark warping fibers, gave the Tlingit an edge in the textile rivalries that crisscrossed the region. An over-the-top potlatching gesture for chiefs of any group was to tear Chilkat capes and dance skirts into small pieces for distribution among lowly recipients, who might then reconstitute them as leggings and aprons (Emmons 1907: 344–346).

Although Mauss is often superficially associated with the idea that Northwest Coast gifting was about reciprocity, in fact he considered the gift's most crucial feature to be its capacity to create obligatory relations of unequal power, almost as a substitute for aggression. Whereas to give is to demonstrate superior rank, accepting without giving in return, or without giving more, is to become a client or servant (Clarke 2003: 39). This observation is particularly apt for gifts that convey vital forces, a realization that inspired Georges Bataille, in the mid-1980s, to add to Mauss's ideas the almost metaphysical principle of squandering which he called "expenditure." Excessive giving, the conspicuous destruction of worldly goods, the extravagant offer of considerable riches, was a way for a chief to humiliate, challenge, or obligate a rival, driving him to a higher pitch of aggressive generosity—to "pay back with interest." According to Bataille, the "need to lose or squander" (quoted in Clarke 2003: 40) implicit in these behaviors renders waste the "flip side" of accumulation. Living in a greatly destabilized world characterized by excess, chiefs were compelled to expend, "willingly or not, gloriously or catastrophically." This insight about courtly consumption resonates with today's consumerism, with the difference that today, ordinary, everyday people are as likely as elites to contribute to the exuberance—and to do so in part by gifting to themselves.

Wal-Martism

Like the Northwest Coast of a century ago, the United States has recently undergone a dramatic upheaval of its political economy. Among the shaping forces are the deregulation of financial markets following the oil shock of the mid-1970s, the rapid spread of new informational technology, the disinvestment in "Fordist" industrial manufacturing and concomitant weakening of the industrial labor unions, the redirection of public investment away from social services and transfer of service provisioning to the private sector, and the vast increase in low-wage, benefit-deprived service-sector jobs. Contemporaneously we find the consolidation of corporate power on a global scale, based on flexible strategies of production: for example, outsourcing, ease of relocation, dispersal to export-processing zones, recruitment of vulnerable immigrant labor. Taken together these processes point, on the one hand, to new entrepreneurial opportunities yielding a rash of new billionaires and, on the other hand, to the increased likelihood of dispossession and disemployment at one or more points in the life cycle (see Harvey 2003: 137–183). In the case of the United States, the top 1 percent of the population gained more than 115 percent in after-tax income during the final two decades of the twentieth century; the bottom fifth lost 9 percent while categories in between remained stagnant or gained only modestly. Whereas CEOs earned thirty-five times as much as the average worker in 1973, by the year 2000 they were earning more than 200 times as much (see Manning 2000).

Consumption of course intensified among the new rich, caricatured as gripped by a "luxury fever." Stunningly, however, ordinary people also succumbed to the fever, almost across the board. Consider Sharon Zukin's observation that "as American manufacturers reshaped or abandoned their traditional role, shopping took on greater weight in the economy," evidenced both by a "new feeling of entrepreneurial freedom" and by new entrepreneurs and government officials defining shopping as a national pastime if not a national duty (Zukin 2004: 204). By the turn of the twenty-first century, annual retail sales approached "more than $3 trillion a year [while] consumer spending is thought to account for (an unprecedented) two-thirds of economic growth." Correspondingly, the "Consumer Confidence index" became a barometer of the public mood while the number of shopping malls overtook the number of high schools (ibid.: 17). Over the past thirty years, suggests Zukin, each of us has gained, on average, four times more retail space and will enjoy even more as the biggest stores continue to expand. "You can't help but be struck by the pervasiveness of shopping," she writes (ibid.).

In other words, purchasing became to the late twentieth-century US what potlatching was to the late nineteenth-century Northwest Coast—an alignment between a shattered political-economic environment and an exuberant squandering of things. Yet, as noted above, any comparison between US consumerism and potlatching is severely limited by the elitism of the latter. Only chiefs had piles of Chilkat "blankets"; they alone commanded their distribution at feasts. Commoners went without, or received these items in humiliating shreds and patches. In the US system, money can buy you anything if you have enough of it; no sumptuary laws interdict trying to materially emulate elites, who now include a widely publicized array of entertainment and sports celebrities as well as the more traditional pacesetters. On the contrary, ever more accessible lines of credit have enticed us to do just this. Tellingly, the personal savings rate of Americans declined from 13.6 percent of income in the 1940s to 8.5 percent around the time of the 1981–1982 recession, to almost zero by 1998 (Manning 2000: 60–61). The year 2000 dramatized what Robert Manning calls a triangle of debt, in which US corporate debt stood at US$4.3 trillion, the public (federal) deficit at US$5.8 trillion, and household debt at no less than US$6.5 trillion (ibid.: 34).

Underlying these figures was the transcendence, during the 1980s, of what might be called the "Fordist" credit system based on installment loans for high-ticket items (home mortgages, cars, furnishings, and appliances)— loans that ballooned from US$45 billion in 1960 to US$104 billion only a decade later. In the same decade, new suburban malls and corporate chain stores wiped out many smaller outlets that had long been sources of personal credit, creating the need for an "all-purpose bank card." Fortuitously, banking deregulation, initiated in the late 1970s, made the provisioning of such cards attractive. The issuers could borrow at 4–5 percent but collect an interest rate of from 17 to 20 percent, earning billions. Thanks in part to a generous gifting campaign—2.7 billion preapproved solicitations went out in 1995 alone—noninstallment credit card debt rose from US$257 billion in 1992 to US$600 billion in 1999, threatening to suck up more than half of the disposable incomes of many, many families. "If you have five credit cards . . . it makes it very easy to look richer than you are," says Juliet Schor in *The Overspent American* (see Manning 2000; Schor 1998).

Reminiscent of Chilkat "blankets," late twentieth-century American-sold clothes are infused with an almost magical vitality. Distinguishing between standardized and fashionable items, the post-Fordist clothing industry has privileged the latter, investing in design innovations, branding, and image creation. Its heavily promoted logos and labels, especially when mixed with seductive evocations of the sexual being beneath (and barely beneath) the clothes, convey a kind of spiritual power—a resource for self-enhancement—not unlike the totally decorated "dancing" capes and aprons of the Northwest Coast. Consistent with the spirit of capitalism, however, no consumer need be marginalized from this flow of energy as commoners were at the potlatches; relatively similar products are fine-tuned for highly differentiated publics, from the very expensive to the very cheap (see Dicken 1998).

The products appear, moreover, in similar places. In the late twentieth century, a series of mega-stores, most notably Wal-Mart, improved on the merchandising strategy earlier pioneered by the Woolworth chain: offering fashion-conscious name-brand goods as well as generic items at bargain prices. In effect, they have combined state-of-the-art communications technology, design capability, and far-flung "parts producers" into a singular colossus capable of supplying an expanding number of fashion seasons with "just-in-time" new styles (Dicken 1998: 294–295). What is "truly revolutionary" about these merchandising giants, writes Zukin, is that they are "the same for everyone. The emphasis on low prices tends to minimize social class distinctions" (2004: 69) as bargain hunters are attracted from every group. "A realm of freedom from work and politics . . . a form of democracy open to all, [shopping is] an exercise of skill to get the cheapest and the best" (ibid.: 34; see also Miller 1998]. But the democratization of shopping, and with this of dressing up, is predicated upon vast and growing inequalities in the sphere of production.

In the time since the industrial revolution, cloth and clothing manufacture have been remarkably resistant to technological change. Synthetic fibers, made by forcing petroleum products through shower-head-like "spinnerets," render laborious spinning unnecessary, while their high tensile strength enables speed-ups in weaving. Machine innovations have also reduced wastage in cutting. Nevertheless, labor is, has always been, and will always be the largest cost factor in making cloth and clothing. Assembly and sewing in particular remain highly demanding of the human hand; most fabrics are simply too fluid to trust to machines alone. As of the late 1990s, 13 million people were formally employed in textile manufacture worldwide, 6 million in garment manufacture, and this is not counting the millions who work in the informal sector, at home or in clandestine workshops (Dicken 1998: 283–286).

Between 1970 and 1993, 420,000 jobs were lost in textiles in the United States, and 180,000 (mostly unionized) jobs in the garment sector, cutting and tailoring. In the same period, the "revolutionary retailers" launched a dual assault on labor, on the one hand paying substandard wages to clerks and stock boys in their own outlets, explicitly discouraged in the case of Wal-Mart from unionizing; and on the other hand contracting for product from export-processing zones, maquiladoras, and sweatshops around the world. In such locations, employees tend to be young and female, often pressed into spinning or sewing by rural families suffering from crises of agricultural dislocation. The fragmented nature of the contracting arrangements constitutes a formidable obstacle to regulating what are often appalling working conditions: seven-day weeks with twelve to fourteen hours a day at times of peak demand, poor ventilation, accidents related to speed-up, and vulnerability to disemployment as the contractors relocate to zones where wages are lower still.

In the words of geographer Peter Dicken (1998: 294–295), the concentrated purchasing power of the great chains like Wal-Mart gives them "enormous leverage over textile and clothing manufacturers"—this being the extraordinarily unequal counterpart to the democratization of fashion. Yet even when consumers are aware of the exploitative conditions under which their purchases are manufactured, most feel gratitude for capitalism's incredible gift: the possibility for sartorial self-enhancement under the almost affordable combination of credit and bargain sales. Tellingly, the young, exploited women who toil in the sweatshops desire, themselves, to partake of this gift.

Notes

1. For a more developed presentation of this approach to textile history, which also considers the emergence of "fashion" between the courtly and the capitalist, and the interactions of the Western fashion system with Asian, African, and Latin American cloth and clothing traditions, see Schneider (2006).
2. My account of this transformation relies on Eric R. Wolf's comprehensive synthesis of Northwest Coast history, archaeology, and ethnology, presented in Wolf (1982 and 1999).

References

Boas, Franz (1927) *Primitive Art*, Oslo: H. Aschehoug.

Clarke, David B. (2003) *The Consumer Society and the Postmodern City*, London and New York: Routledge.

Cohn, Bernard (1989) "Cloth, Clothes and Colonialism: India in the Nineteenth Century," in Annette B. Weiner and Jane Schneider (eds.), *Cloth and Human Experience*, Washington and London: Smithsonian Institution Press.

Cort, Louise (1989) "The Changing Fortunes of Three Archaic Japanese Textiles," in Annette B. Weiner and Jane Schneider (eds.), *Cloth and Human Experience*, Washington and London: Smithsonian Institution Press.

Darish, Patricia (1989) "Dressing for the Next Life: Raffia Textile Production and Use among the Kuba of Zaire," in Annette B. Weiner and Jane Schneider (eds.), *Cloth and Human Experience*, Washington and London: Smithsonian Institution Press.

Dicken, Peter (1998) *Global Shift: Transforming the World Economy* (3rd edition), New York and London: Guilford Press.

Douglas, Mary (1967) "Raffia Cloth Distribution in the Lele Economy," in G. Dalton (ed.), *Tribal and Peasant Economies: Readings in Economic Anthropology*, New York: American Museum of Natural History Press.

Drucker, Peter (1955) *Indians of the Northwest Coast*, New York: American Museum of Natural History Press.

—— (1965) *Cultures of the North Pacific Coast*, San Francisco: Chandler.

Dumont, Louis (1970) *Homo Hierarchicus: An Essay on the Caste System*, Chicago: University of Chicago Press.

Emmons, G. T. (1907) "The Chilkat Blanket," *Memoire, American Museum of Natural History*, 3(4): 329–409.

Feeley-Harnik, Gillian (1989) "Cloth and the Creation of Ancestors in Madagascar," in Annette B. Weiner and Jane Schneider (eds.), *Cloth and Human Experience*, Washington and London: Smithsonian Institution Press.

Fox, James J. (1977) "Roti, Ndao and Savu," in M. H. Kahlenberg (ed.), *Textile Traditions of Indonesia*, Los Angeles: County Museum.

Harvey, David (2003) *The New Imperialism*, Oxford: Oxford University Press.

Holm, Bill (1982) "A Wooling Mantle Neatly Wrought: the Early Historical Record of Northwest Coast Pattern-Twined Textiles," *American Indian Art*, 8: 34–48.

Hoskins, Janet (1989) "Why Do Ladies Sing the Blues? Indigo Dyeing, Cloth Production, and Gender Symbolism in Kodi," in Annette B. Weiner and Jane Schneider (eds.), *Cloth and Human Experience*, Washington and London: Smithsonian Institution Press.

Kendall, Laurel (1985) "Ritual Silks and Kowtow Money: the Bride as Daughter-in-Law in Korean Wedding Rituals," *Ethnology*, 24: 253–269.

Manning, Robert D. (2000) *Credit Card Nation: the Consequences of America's Addiction to Credit*, New York: Basic Books.

Mauss, Marcel (1954) [1923–24] *The Gift: Forms and Functions of Exchange in Archaic Societies*, Ian Cunnison (trans.), Glencoe: Free Press.

Miller, Daniel (1998) *A Theory of Shopping*, Ithaca: Cornell University Press.

Morris, W. F. (1986) "Maya Time Warps," *Archaeology*, 39: 52–59.

Murra, John (1989) [1962] "Cloth and Its Functions in the Inka State," in Annette B. Weiner and Jane Schneider (eds.), *Cloth and Human Experience*, Washington and London: Smithsonian Institution Press. (Reprinted from a paper originally published in *American Anthropologist*, 64: 710–728.)

Samuel, C. (1982) *The Chilkat Dancing Blanket*, Seattle: Pacific Search Press.

Schneider, Jane (1978) "Peacocks and Penguins; the Political Economy of European Cloth and Colors," *American Ethnologist*, 5: 413–447.

—— (1987) "The Anthropology of Cloth," *Annual Review of Anthropology*, 16: 409–448.

—— (2006) "Cloth and Clothing," in Chris Tilley et al. (eds.), *Handbook of Material Culture*, London: Sage Publications.

Schor, Juliet B. (1998) *The Overspent American: Upscaling, Downshifting, and the New Consumer*, New York: Basic Books.

Vansina, John (1978) *The Children of Woot: a History of the Kuba Peoples*, Dawson: University of Wisconsin Press.

Verger, P. (1954) *Dieux d'Afrique: Culte des Orishas et Vodouns à l'ancienne côte des esclaves en Afrique à Bahia, la baie de tous les saints au Brésil*, Paris: P. Hartman (160 photos by author).

Weiner, Annette B. (1989) "Why Cloth? Wealth, Gender, and Power in Oceania," in Annette B. Weiner and Jane Schneider (eds.), *Cloth and Human Experience*, Washington and London: Smithsonian Institution Press.

—— (1992) *Inalienable Possessions: The Paradox of Keeping while Giving*, Berkeley: University of California Press.

Wolf, Eric R. (1982) *Europe and the People Without History*, Berkeley and Los Angeles: University of California Press.

—— (1999) *Envisioning Power; Ideologies of Dominance and Crisis*, Berkeley and Los Angeles: University of California Press.

Zorn, Elaine (1985) "Textiles in Herders' Ritual Bundles of Macusani, Peru," paper presented at American Anthropological Association, 84th Annual Meeting, Washington, DC.

Zukin, Sharon (2004) *Point of Purchase: How Shopping Changed American Culture*, New York and London: Routledge.

Chapter 2

Dressing the nation

Indian cinema costume and the making of a national fashion, 1947–1957

Rachel Tu

In the decade following Indian independence, from 1947 to 1957, Hindi commercial cinema played an integral role in public life not only as a source of entertainment, but also as a vehicle for disseminating nationalistic ideals. On the screen, films expressed genuine concerns that were arising out of the transition between colonialism and independence through melodramatic themes, costume, music, and language. Beyond the screen, film advertisements and magazines infiltrated the urban landscape, further integrating the cinematic image into daily life. Magazines in particular, such as *Filmfare* and *The Illustrated Weekly of India*, bombarded readers with every aspect of cinema culture and were clearly targeted toward a female readership.[1]

Cinema had a particularly influential impact in metropolitan areas, where increasingly women were entering the public sector. Looking to film characters as models of the new order, urban women from all sectors of society assumed modes of dress that they had never worn before. As women across the continent engaged in the highly personal and tactile act of donning the new dress, they embodied the national ideology. "Thus, rather than . . . an observation of everyday Indian life . . . Hindi commercial cinema . . . bec[a]me part of everyday life, part of its 'habits of speech, dress, and manners, background and foreground'" (Dwyer and Patel 2002: 8). This chapter identifies the role of cinema costume and its subsequent internalization as national fashion, revealing the emergence of the modern Indian woman in the decade following independence. Three successful film melodramas of the period, *Andaz*, *Taxi Driver*, and *Pyaasa*, contextualize women within an exaggerated moral universe. With additional support from popular magazines, *The Illustrated Weekly of India* and *Blitz News Magazine*, the films are placed within the larger arena of public life and illustrate their successful infiltration into the national psyche.

Costume and gender relations

In a 1949 advertisement for Mehboob Khan's film *Andaz*,[2] a smiling young woman stands confidently between two equally dapper young men (Figure

Figure 2.1
Poster from the
film *Andaz* (1949).
Courtesy of copyright
owner Mehboob
Productions Private
Ltd, Mumbai, India.

2.1). She wears a bright floral sari, while the men are dressed in Western suits. The characters' fashionable clothing and self-assured stance suggest the elegant and worldly milieu of this film, which is further underscored by the title *Andaz*, meaning a manner of style, emblazed in English, Hindi, and Urdu across the bottom. To would-be moviegoers, the poster articulates the basis for the story's conflict, a classic love triangle in which a woman must choose between two men, and alludes to the glamorous setting in which it will unfold.[3] In fact, the film is a morality tale that warns against the ambiguity of platonic relationships between men and women, a relatively new social development that was associated with Western values.

Neena, the protagonist, is a young socialite who has adopted the fashionable Western activities and attire of the international set. She is betrothed to the rakish Rajan, who is abroad at university in London. In Rajan's absence, Neena befriends Dilip, the son of a wealthy expatriate, with whom she plays tennis and attends parties. Captivated by Neena's demonstrative charms,

Dilip misinterprets her friendship for love. Just as he is about to proclaim his romantic feelings for her, Neena's father dies and her betrothed returns from London. Forced to assume the adult responsibilities of running the family business, but thrilled to finally marry her beloved, Neena sheds her Western clothing for the Indian sari. O. P. Joshi describes Neena's shift in attire as a standard cultural phenomenon, in which "the unmarried girls who await marriage . . . have the freedom of being fashionable and adopting new dresses . . . aware that marriage will restrict their freedom of dress" (Joshi 1992: 228).

Eventually, Dilip's secret love is revealed to Neena and Rajan. Apparently totally surprised by Dilip's declaration, Neena confronts him, and in the heat of the moment accidentally kills him. Sentenced to life in prison, Neena, in the last frame of the film, is shown close-up with metal bars casting shadows on her face. She says, "I was at fault, but so was the society I was a part of . . . Keep our daughters away from that atmosphere . . . foreign land and culture can never be suitable for our children."

Joshi writes, "In India, 'fashion' both as a word and as a concept, denotes a deviation from the norms of dress, and in the feminine context, generally means the adoption of alien and . . . Western dress" (Joshi 1992: 220–221). Certainly Neena's Western attire reflects a keen interest in current fashion, but her subsequent adoption of the sari is not free of fashion's dictates (Figure 2.2). Rather, Neena's saris, which feature sheer chiffons and keyhole neckline bodices that alluringly conceal and reveal her body, reflect a heightened awareness of fashion, as well as a sense of confidence in her sexuality. In fact, Neena's sari, draped in what is known as the Nivi style, was literally revolutionary in its day.

The first record of the Nivi style of draping the saris occurred in 1866, when Jayananda Nandini Devi, an affluent Hindu woman from Calcutta, accompanied her husband, Satyanendra Nath Tagore, to his new post as civil servant in the Bombay presidency, thereby obliging her to enter the public sector. Up until this point, Devi had adhered strictly to Hindu purity laws, which dictate that clothing should be uncut and unstitched (Joshi 1992: 214). For the sake of public modesty, she adopted the Parsi custom of wearing a *choli*, or tailored blouse, and petticoat with the sari; for mobility, she draped the *pallu*, or decorative end of the sari, over her left shoulder to keep her right arm free, thus giving birth to the modern draped sari. The Nivi drape took on political dimensions in the early twentieth century when women involved in the nationalist movement adopted the style (Banerjee and Miller 2003: 254).

In the mid-1930s, as the reality of the Indian nation gained precedence, the Nivi style entered the realm of film (Dwyer and Patel 2002: Illus. 58). By 1949, as is apparent from *Andaz*, the sari develops not only into an element of fashion, but also into a symbol of feminine morality. Thus the Nivi-draped sari was novel on several levels. As an uncut length of cloth, it was

Figure 2.2 Still from the film *Andaz* (1949). Courtesy of copyright owner Mehboob Productions Private Ltd, Mumbai, India.

mindful of Hindu purity laws (Joshi 1992: 215). With the addition of the blouse and petticoat, it took into account a public sense of modesty. The most significant aspect, though, was that the Nivi-drape, while Hindu in character, was free of any regional characteristics. This style, wholly modern yet distinctly Indian, therefore became synonymous with Indian national fashion.

The ease with which Neena transits from Western to Indian attire reflects the increasing mobility of upper-class women in the 1940s, in both an official and social capacity. As one public figure, Kamala Veloso of Bombay, put it, when she was interviewed by *The Illustrated Weekly of India* in 1955, "In the past Indian women were forced to stay in the background, but today we have been accepted as collaborators by men . . . I believe that women should go slowly, however" (Anonymous, December 18, 1955: 34). While the editorial does not further elaborate on Veloso's statement, the film *Andaz* illustrates the dire consequences that women may find themselves in if they attempt to alter age-old customs too rapidly. Dilip and

Rajan's suspicions of Neena's behavior suggest society's perplexity over the new gender relations arising as a result of women's public presence. As one contemporaneous film critic for *Blitz News Magazine* wrote, "the conflict [in *Andaz*] arise[s] out of the subtle difference between friendship and love . . . [a phenomenon which] could only take place in a modern sophisticated setting" (Anonymous, April 9, 1949: 19), inferring that it is only in upper-class society, where Western values are more accepted, that a woman would even consider having a platonic relationship with a man. In essence, while Neena was enjoying the freedom of the international set and shifted easily between Western and Indian attire, she was naive to the social implications her behavior and appearance provoked.

A *Blitz News Magazine* advertisement for *Andaz* warns, "No woman hankering after modernity can afford to miss this film" (Advertisement: April 19, 1949: n.p.). The harsh consequences of Neena's imprudent actions as a youth provide some insight into the late-1940s Indian psyche. As Ashish and Willemen observe, the Indian "filmic identity offered a complex cultural [and] psychological terrain displaying the anxieties of independence and the nostalgias of a pre-Partition childhood" (Rajadhyaksha and Willemen 1999: 123). In placing Neena—or, more pointedly, a woman—in the center of this love triangle, director Mehboob Khan suggests that the responsibility of balancing traditional values with modern advancements rests fully upon women's shoulders. Ironically, Neena's stunning costumes, both Western and Indian, reflect a distrust of the emerging modern Indian woman while simultaneously celebrating her arrival.

Costume and racial identity

In addition to the upper- and middle-class woman who was quick to embrace the sari as the ultimate in modern fashion, there was another type of citizen also refashioning herself, the lower-class urbanite. With independence, villagers, more than ever before, flocked to metropolitan centers with hopes for a better life and perhaps a chance at stardom (Banerjee and Srivastva 1988: 176). While these new migrants were likely to retain critical aspects of their regional and religious identities, the city offered a myriad of stimuli though which they could reimagine themselves, not the least of which was the visual culture of film.[4] In fact, in the larger cities, film productions from Hollywood or London were as accessible as those produced in Bombay. A 1957 advertisement for Cinthol soap best demonstrates the infiltration of film culture into urban women's lives (Figure 2.3). It reads in part, "This Star soap . . . can make a new person out of you too!" In essence, whether urbanites attended cinema halls or not, they were surrounded and influenced by the imagery of both national and international film.

While cinema had a great impact on new urban migrants, they too influ-

Figure 2.3
Advertisement for
Cinthol Soap (1957).
Courtesy of copyright
owner Godrej
Consumer Products,
Mumbai, India.

enced cinema. Beginning in 1954, a new genre of Indian film arose that depicted the working class's dreams for mobility, money, and fame. As one film critic summarized in the *Illustrated Weekly*:

> There have been more successful films [in 1954] than in any corresponding period since independence. The change for the better may be attributed to the new trend toward realism in our films . . . that reflect the real problems of the ordinary people and present life as it is lived by the masses
>
> (Anonymous, November 28, 1954, n.p.)[5]

Taxi Driver, directed by Chetan Anand in 1954, was one such film.[6] Replete with guns, car-chases, and sultry women, it was clearly influenced by Hollywood film noir. As in *Andaz*, the conflict in *Taxi Driver* arises out of a love triangle, but in this case, the main protagonist is a man who must choose between a traditional and a Westernized woman.

Set in Bombay, the film opens on Mangal, a taxi driver. Nicknamed Hero, he is a rakish rebel with compassion for his fellow outcasts of society. Hero has everything a young bachelor could want—a car, money, friends, and a beautiful Anglo-Indian girlfriend named Silvie who works as a cabaret dancer across the street from his flat. Hero's carefree life changes when Mala, an orphaned village girl, gets into his car. Mala dreams of becoming a classical singer and has come to Bombay by invitation from a musical director of questionable ethics. When Mala is nearly raped by the musical director's security guards, Hero saves her and offers to let her stay in his little apartment while he spends evenings at the cabaret.

While Mala sits in Hero's apartment reciting the Mahabharata in her Indian sari, Silvie is at the cabaret singing and dancing in shoulder-baring rumba costumes and Capri pants. Kasbekar identifies the apparent dichotomy between Mala and Silvie as, "a simple bipolarization of women into 'good' and 'evil' … [in which] the vamp's sexual promiscuity, her racial 'otherness' and non-Hindu identity contrasted dramatically with the heroine's own strict adherence to traditionally defined codes of behavior required of the ideal Hindu woman" (Kasbekar 2001: 299). A deeper analysis of the costumes and factors motivating the two characters, however, reveals more similarities than disparities.

When Mala first arrives in Bombay, she wears what appears to be either a half-sari or a *langa*. Both garments are made up of a blouse, a skirt, and a *dupatta*, or veil, that covers the bodice and head. The primary difference between the two is that the skirt of the half-sari is made up of a draped uncut length of cloth and originates among Hindus in south India, whereas the skirt of the *langa* is a cut and stitched garment with roots in northwestern India from the Mughal period. Rather than deciphering exactly where Mala is from, it is more important simply to recognize that her attire identifies her as provincial and therefore "other." As she becomes versed in city ways, as well as emboldened by Hero's attentions, Mala adopts the Nivi-draped sari, reserving her traditional regional dress only for performance. This subtle shift in which Mala relegates her regional identity to that of a role played for specific occasions, marks her transformation from an innocent villager to a modern Indian woman, and from an outsider to a member of society. In the words of Rajeswari Rajan, "The development of an 'Indianness' free of chauvinistic regional markers among its citizenry is, of course, one of the declared aspirations of the Indian State" (Rajan 1993: 133).[7] Within the nationalist agenda, regional dress was looked upon as a hindrance to unification. Within the day-to-day social interactions of the city, it confined women, as well as men, to the margins of society.

While Mala's refashioning fits within the conventions of the ideal national image, Silvie conforms to a subversive Anglo-Indian stereotype. During the nationalist movement, political leaders perceived all Western influence as a threat that needed to be contained. Anglo-Indians, many of whom had been in India for generations, had always lived between the two worlds and thus presented a problem in the new social order. In public and on the stage, Silvie wears revealing garments of Western and other exotic origin. There is, however, one short scene in which Silvie, having just woken from a nap, is not in performance mode, and here she is dressed in a Nivi-style sari. In this scene, Silvie sings the only song which is not technically in performance, about her true yearning desire to be loved by Hero. The subtlety of costuming Silvie in the sari when she is not putting on a show indicates her self-perception as a typical Indian woman. She only wears Western dress when she must assume an exotic sexualized persona in order to guarantee her success as a performer. Silvie's characterization reflects a national nativist sentiment that the Anglo-Indian woman had to "be narratively kept in her separate place lest she endanger the . . . social order" (Uberoi 1997: 155).[8]

The evolution of Mala and Silvie's characters shows that while initially they both exist on the fringes of society and have aspirations as performers, the differences in their race and the choices that they make regarding what is appropriate attire for performance versus daily wear determine the success of their assimilation into society. Whereas Silvie's public and performance personas emphasize her foreignness, Mala's public persona conforms to the new socially accepted standard while her performance persona celebrates, without overemphasizing, her regional origins.

Costume and class disparities

While in *Taxi Driver* social disparities are only subtly touched upon, just three years later class disparities are challenged more directly in the 1957 film *Pyaasa*, directed by Guru Dutt.[9] Set in the urban slums of Calcutta, *Pyaasa*, meaning eternal thirst, is a story about Vijay, an unknown poet struggling for recognition. As in *Andaz* and *Taxi Driver*, the love triangle is also present in here—Vijay is a man caught between two women, an avaricious gentlewoman and a principled prostitute. However, while the love triangle in the previous films is the primary narrative device in which the protagonist must choose between one or the other, in *Pyaasa* the love triangle only illustrates the complex multifaceted characters that result from a directionless, corrupt society.

From the beginning of the film, Vijay is dejected at having just learned that his brothers have sold his poems as waste paper. By fortune, he overhears a young woman, Gulab, singing his poetry. Vijay calls out to her, and as she turns he is aghast upon seeing her garish attire identifying her as a prostitute. Not knowing that he is the author of her songs, she misunderstands his inquiries as sexual advances. When it becomes apparent that he is penniless, Gulab berates him, and only belatedly recognizes him as the poet who has been captivating her attention. Chance encounters bring them together again and again, and eventually Vijay cannot discount Gulab's sincerity and kindness, and he reluctantly accepts her friendship. For Gulab,

Vijay's strict adherence to codes of morality and almost omniscient under-standing of social inequities only increase her love for him. In one of the most poignant and intimate moments in the film, Gulab, making certain that she is alone, stands self-consciously before a mirror and marks her hair-line with vermilion powder, worn only by married women. As she gazes at herself in the mirror, no words are spoken, but the yearning expression on her face clearly indicates that she is dreaming about how different her life could be if she were married to Vijay. For a traditional woman, marriage is the definitive coming-of-age ritual identifying her as a distinguished member of society. Thus, when Gulab dons this accessory of marriage, she is express-ing a desire to be not only Vijay's wife, but also a full-fledged member of society.

The woman whom Vijay imagines as his ideal wife is Mina. Vijay and Mina meet each other in high school and are instantly attracted to each other. Pictured in crisp white Western sporting attire, their romantic rel-ationship develops over a musical montage of badminton games and bicycle rides. Several articles in *The Illustrated Weekly of India* indicate that sports were the rare activity in which respectable unmarried women could wear Western attire and socialize with unmarried men.[10] When the two attend a party together, Mina learns that Vijay does not know how to dance, and her tender expression turns to a look of utter disappointment. In Vijay's anxi-ety, the scene clouds over into a fantasy sequence. Mina, in a taffeta evening dress, cascades down a sweeping staircase to Vijay, who is dressed in a white dinner jacket and bow tie. As their hands meet, Vijay confidently takes Mina into his arms and they waltz among the clouds. Mina's disappointment and Vijay's psychological escape into fantasy mark the end of their relationship, for Mina is unwilling to proceed with a man who is unversed in the pursuits of polite society. Years later, they run into each other again and Vijay learns that Mina has married a worldly and wealthy publisher.

As an affluent married woman, Mina is appropriately dressed in costly saris of Banarsi silk and delicately embroidered chiffons. Mina and Gulab finally meet when Gulab attempts to have Vijay's poems published by Mina's publisher husband (Figure 2.4).[11] Mina looks with disdain at Gulab's tawdry attire, and scornfully says, "How could such a gentleman meet a lady of your background?" Gulab quietly replies, "By good fortune." In the "Home Section" of a 1955 issue of *The Illustrated Weekly*, actress Vinita Butt is featured in an embroidered sari similar to Mina's (Illustration: "Home Sec-tion," December 11, 1955: n.p.). The text accompanying this striking image includes embroidery instructions, demonstrating how middle-class home-makers could also achieve this glamorous look. While Mina is character-ized as a heartless socialite in a stifling marriage, in conjunction with the *Illustrated Weekly* article it would appear that she has at least assuaged her "eternal thirst" for material comforts, which Vijay would have never been able to provide.

Figure 2.4 Still from the film *Pyaasa* (1957). Courtesy of copyright owner Guru Dutt Films Private Ltd, Kolkata, India.

The failures of modern civilization, which ironically pit a narcissistic madonna against a virtuous prostitute, are most keenly expressed in Guru Dutt's cinematography and song lyrics, which emphasize society's utter disregard for spirituality and creativity, which he personifies as women, poetry, and nature. In a montage highlighting female prostitutes and beggars on the streets of Calcutta, Vijay sings, "Here chastity is bargained for and purity is sold . . . These are our sisters, our wives, our mothers . . . These daughters of Eve seek help; these daughters of Radha and Yoshoda; these daughters of Zukha, these children of God." In alluding to figures in Indian history and mythology, Guru Dutt elevates Indian women, regardless of class, to sacred icons of the nation. Virdi states, "Women and feminine values are in fact 'code words for national values and identity . . . [and] the figure of women and feminine values have always been . . . deeply implicated in and utilized by national discourses'" (Virdi 2004: 5). In *Pyaasa* the condition of women becomes a rather disheartening metaphor for the state of the nation, reflecting mounting anxieties about the reality of nation-building after ten years of independence.

Conclusion

As political leaders struggled to establish one unified national identity, increasing social and geographical mobility and exposure to new media and lifestyles presented men and women with a myriad of choices that threatened the leaders' aims. With its widespread popular appeal, film and the melodramatic narrative therefore became the perfect medium to convey national ideals, blurring the lines between region and religion, tradition and modernity, and fiction and reality. The melodramatic narrative was, in fact, so effective that the mediation of "tension between social duty and individual desire" (Uberoi 1997: 155), conspicuously present in Indian films, arose as a central theme of Indian identity. In terms of women's dress, some regional styles became symbols of tradition, while others became stigmas of India's colonial past, and non-Indian dress was practically antinational. As women entered the public sector through various avenues, new styles evolved that were free of all regional identity and were, therefore, considered completely modern. This is most clearly exemplified in the Nivi-style draped sari. On the most sensual level, when women wrapped their bodies in the Nivi style they embodied the sentiments of the nation. At the first Indian Film Seminar in 1955, Devika Rani Roerich, director, identified Hindi film as "a form of creative expression which would serve as a vehicle for the culture of our great land" (*Illustrated Weekly of India*, February 27, 1955: 47). The three films discussed, *Andaz*, *Taxi Driver*, and *Pyaasa*, illustrate how cinema was both a vehicle for and reflection of a culture greatly in flux in independent India. Thus, in this period when India was attempting to assert itself as one autonomous unified entity, "Indianness," constantly defined and redefined, was the pinnacle of fashion.

Notes

1. Film topics were prevalent in all popular magazines, including film-specific publications such as *Filmfare* and general lifestyle magazines such as *The Illustrated Weekly of India*.
2. *Andaz* features actors Nargis, Dilip Kumar, and Raj Kapoor.
3. The love triangle is a classic device in Hindi commercial cinema. Rather than the simple melodramatic formula that pits characters representing extreme good against evil, the love triangle focuses on one principal character and their negotiation of traditional versus modern values.
4. This demonstrates Anne Hollander's idea that "people choose what they will wear and how they will appear . . . according to the way it may suggest certain pictures that they feel they wish to resemble" (Hollander 1993: 315).
5. Indian filmmakers were greatly influenced by Italian cinema in general. The topic and cinematic style of Chetan Anand's film *Taxi Driver* shows the influence of the Italian cinematic movement of neorealism
6. *Taxi Driver* features actors Dev Anand, Kalpana Kartik, and Sheila Ramani.
7. Ravi Vasudevan (1989) makes a similar point.
8. While Silvie's Western costume marks her as an outcast, it also allows her to

express herself as a sexual being—a freedom the Indian muse actresses would not enjoy until the middle of the 1960s. Soon after the release of *Taxi Driver*, Sheila Ramani, the actress who plays Silvie, was featured wearing a sari in a full-color fashion spread. In effect, Ramani asserts her Indian identity rather than quietly accepting the social stereotyping of her character (*Illustrated Weekly of India*, October 5, 1955: 73).

 9. *Pyaasa* features actors Guru Dutt, Waheeda Rehman, and Mala Sinha.
10. Regular news reports on school sporting events in *The Illustrated Weekly of India* suggest that high schools and universities were the few institutions where young men and women were able to meet beyond the family circle.
11. At this point in the film, Vijay is believed to have been killed in a train accident.

References

Publications

Banerjee, M. and Miller, D. (2003) *The Sari*, Oxford: Berg.
Banerjee, S. and Srivastva, A. (1988) *One Hundred Years of Indian Feature Films: An Annotated Filmography*, New York: Garland.
Blitz News Magazine (1949) "Our Review," April 9: 19.
Dwyer, R. and Patel, D. (2002) *Cinema India: The Visual Culture of Indian Cinema*, New Brunswick, NJ: Rutgers University Press.
Hollander, A. (1993) *Seeing Through Clothes*, Berkeley: University of California Press.
Illustrated Weekly of India (1954) "Indian Film Scene," November 28.
—— (1955) "First Film Seminar," February 27: 47.
—— (1955) "Home Section," December 11.
—— (1955) "Woman Claims Her Rights—or Does She?" December 18: 19.
Joshi, O. P. (1992) "Continuity and Change in Hindu Women's Dress," in R. Barnes and J. Eicher (eds.), *Dress and Gender*, New York: Berg.
Kasbekar, A. (2001) "Hidden Pleasures: Negotiating the Myth of the Female Ideal in Popular Hindi Cinema," in C. Pinney and R. Dwyer (eds.), *Pleasure and the Nation: The History, Politics and Consumption of Indian Popular Culture*, Delhi and New York: Oxford University Press.
Rajadhyaksha, A. and Willemen, P. (1999) *Encyclopedia of Indian Cinema*, London: British Film Institute, New Delhi: Oxford University Press.
Rajan, R. S. (1993) *Real and Imagined Women: Gender, Culture, and Post-colonialism*, London: Routledge.
Uberoi, P. (1997) "Dharma and Desire, Freedom and Destiny: Rescripting the Man–Woman Relationship in Popular Cinema," in M. Thapan (ed.), *Embodiment: Essays on Gender and Identity*, Delhi and New York: Oxford University Press, 1997.
Vasudevan, R. (1989) "The Melodramatic Mode and the Commercial Hindi Cinema," *Screen*, 30(3): 25–50.
Virdi, J. (2004) *Cinematic Imagination: Indian Popular Films as Social History*, Delhi: Permanent Black.

Films

Khan, Mehboob (1949) *Andaz*, Mumbai: Mehboob Productions.
Anand, Chetan (1954) *Taxi Driver*, Mumbai: Navketan International Films.
Dutt, Guru (1957) *Pyaasa*, Mumbai: Guru Dutt Pvt Ltd

Chapter 3

Made in America

Paris, New York, and postwar fashion photography

Helena C. Ribeiro

In March of 2003 Richard Avedon headed to the Center for Creative Photography in Tucson, Arizona, where he had kept his "Western Warehouse"—a private storage facility for prints and negatives, ephemera, and correspondence—with the intention of paring down his archive. The month-long process involved separating his "choices"—the photographs and negatives selected for preservation—from the negatives and contact sheets destined for an industrial shredder. Standing before a pile of prints and negatives in his archive, Avedon turned to a student worker and began to talk, suddenly and matter-of-factly, about how he had helped "rebuild" Paris after World War II. He had been "sent over" by *Harper's Bazaar*, he explained, and through his and other New York-based fashion photographer's efforts, while photographing French fashion on French streets, had aided Europe in rediscovering itself (J. Martin, personal communication, March 12, 2003).

Although Avedon's playful claim to "rebuilding" postwar Paris may seem overly nostalgic, if not casually reductive, the way in which he represented the war-ravaged city in the years after the war certainly helped its image on a global scale. His photographs in *Harper's Bazaar* not only redefined fashion photography, but suggested a new narrative for Paris: Avedon's photographs display old "gay Paree" as modern, unblemished, charming, fashionable. His early Paris photographs never hinted that the city was war-torn or tired. Avedon's postwar Paris was impeccable: her seams tightly stitched, her pleats ever pressed, her slip never showing. Indeed, Avedon rebuilt Paris—he reconstructed, in an American magazine, an alternate Paris mythology via an alternate cityscape peopled with lithe American models draped in French couture.

In the introductory essay to his anthology *Landscape and Power*, W. J. T. Mitchell postulates that landscape is a medium, not a genre, and that it "doesn't merely signify or symbolize power relations; it is an instrument of cultural power, perhaps even an agent of power that is (or frequently represents itself as) independent of human interactions" (2002: 2). As a cultural medium, landscape:

has a double role with respect to something like ideology: it naturalizes a cultural and social construction, representing an artificial world as if it were simply given and inevitable, and it also makes that representation operational by interpellating its beholder in some more or less determinate relation to its givenness as sight and site.

(ibid.)

Thus, he explains, "landscape (whether urban or rural, artificial or natural) always greets us as space, as environment . . . An account of landscape understood in this way . . . has to trace the process by which landscape effaces its own readability and naturalizes itself" (ibid.). The sight/site of Marshall Plan-ized postwar Paris, furthermore, becomes what Mary Louise Pratt calls a "contact zone" where "cultures meet, clash, and grapple with each other, often in contexts of highly asymmetrical relations of power" (1991: 34). In the case of the Americans in Paris (however that presence manifests itself: as soldier, as decree, as photographer), the encounter between the global and the local becomes an encounter between two "locals" and two "globals." Of course, we are not used to thinking of the "local" as Western European, or cosmopolitan; when we speak of the "regional" we think of the "primitive" or "exotic." We do not think of Paris. And yet, looking at Paris under the Marshall Plan, we see the presence of globalization as early as the 1940s, a presence that we understand as not only a set of technologies, but also a way of seeing and representing.

The "double role" Mitchell describes, wherein landscape simultaneously represents itself and makes that representation operational by interpellating its beholder, becomes starkly clear in regards to fashion photography. Editorial spreads, for example, must be both "aspirational" (that is, they must give the reader/consumer a consumption goal to aspire to) and accessible; they must hold in tension a portrayal of an idealized product with a desire not to alienate the reader/consumer. Avedon's postwar Paris photos are not only fashion spreads, but also landscapes; when he chose to place his models in the streets and casinos and shops and salons of Paris, the streets, casinos, and so on become not only a backdrop—for he was to abandon backdrops eventually—but part of the sale: Avedon's work does not sell only Dior and Cardin—it sells Paris itself. His photographs are full of Parisian "semes," what Roland Barthes calls the "unit of the signifier" (1974 [1970]: 17),[1] which act as "connotative signifieds" (ibid.: 262) and carry with them the cultural markers which leave the reader with no question as to the location of the photographs.

Of course, the Parisian semes within the photographs are marketed toward an American audience. The leadership of fashion editor Carmel Snow and art director Alexey Brodovitch at *Harper's Bazaar*, according to Rebecca Arnold, "revolutionized its outlook, creating a visually ground-breaking magazine of fashion and culture, which brought its readers a modern, American view of life shaped by the European avant-garde" (2002: 46). *Harper's Bazaar*'s "American view of life" in 1945, however, certainly has Francophile tendencies; a perusal of the September 1945 issue reveals a hosiery product named "Belle-Sharmeer" in "brev," "modite," and "duchess" sizes, available in the equally francophone-esque "demure" color; "exquisite" "Marquise originals" pumps; "Beaudrape" fabric made of rayon; a brief editorial spread on handbags and shoes called "Paris Makes the Most of Leather"; as well as an essay, published posthumously, by Paul Valéry. These texts, ranging from the vaguely French-sounding to the authentically so, imbue what Arnold calls an "American view" with a faux-French accent.

Much like the francophone lexical markers in the *Harper's Bazaar* pages work to lend a "French" air to the magazine, so do the Parisian markers in Avedon's photographs. A 1949 photograph of Suzy Parker at the Café des Beaux-Arts reveals the model leaning, at an almost 90-degree angle, over a pinball machine in a dress by Paris design house Lanvin-Castillo (Figure 3.1).[2] Over her, the high archways, haphazardly hung paintings, and sign advertising "Piscine Deligny . . . Jeux divers . . . PING PONG . . . installation Unique et Moderne . . . Bar Restaurant" (Avedon 2005: 45) work to establish the American mythology of the French ideal. Shabby yet chic, the pinball party's *demitasses* of champagne (resting on the pinball machine!), offset by the stacked café chairs and missing floor tiles, represent the kind of bohemian glamour an American audience could buy.[3] Here is the Old World: copies of Impressionist paintings hang half-framed, salon-style, near the ceiling; the ancient floor crumbles around Parker's heels. But here is also the new, modern, and chic: the pinball machine, the gown with its stegosaurus crest of tulle tumbling down the American's back. Her companions, languidly spread over the side of the machine, look aloof; one looks bored. The bar is empty, the chairs are stacked. Have the Americans overstayed their welcome? These items and gestures, arranged by accident or by a photographer's hand, constitute the message within the photograph. Explaining the signifying capacities of photography in his 1961 essay "The Photographic Message," Barthes explains that "special importance must be accorded to . . . the posing of objects, where the meaning comes from the objects photographed (either because these objects have . . . been artificially arranged in front of the camera or because the person responsible for the final layout chooses a photograph of this or that object)" (Barthes 1978: 22). He goes on to suggest that

> the interest lies in the fact that objects are accepted inducers of associations of ideas (book case = intellectual) or . . . are veritable symbols. Such objects constitute excellent elements of signification: on the one hand they are discontinuous and complete in themselves, a physical

Figure 3.1 Suzy Parker with Robin Tattersall and Gardner McKay, evening
dress by Lanvin-Castillo, Café des Beaux-Arts, August 1956.
Reproduced by permission of the Richard Avedon Foundation.

qualification for a sign, while on the other they refer to clear, familiar signifieds. They are thus the elements of a veritable lexicon.

(ibid.: 23)

The tiles and chairs, the dress and the men, the sign and the pinball machine, then, while existing as "mere" objects on a plane of "reality," exist simultaneously as signs and signifieds; "objects," Barthes continues, "no longer perhaps possess a *power*, but they certainly possess meanings" (ibid.: 23, emphasis original). For Barthes, connotation exists as "the imposition of second meaning on the photographic message proper, [and] is realized at the different levels of the production of the photograph . . . and represents, finally, a coding of the photographic analogue" (ibid.: 20). This analogue, according to Barthes, exists simultaneously with the real-world referent: the live (Queens-born, Texas-bred) Suzy Parker, the smell of chlorine wafting from the basement.

For Barthes, the ways in which photographic connotation functions, then, is necessarily dependent on cultural practice: for him,

the code of connotation was in all likelihood neither "natural" nor "artificial" but historical, or . . . cultural. Its signs are gestures, attitudes, expressions, colors or effects, endowed with certain meanings by virtue of the practice of a certain society: the link between signifier and signified remains if not unmotivated, at least entirely historical.

(ibid.: 27)

The cultural practices which enable the Parisian codes to exist as such, of course, are self-generating. In the case of the American audience, the magazine readers learn "Paris" by exposure to photographs of Paris. "Paris," which may as well be analogous to the "real," geographical Paris, therefore, in the world of *Harper's Bazaar*, is created by and through images; the distinction between "Paris" and Paris begins to erode. The connotative system which enables readers to understand "Paris" is circuitous and performative, a Francophilic ouroboros.

Similarly, the purported denotative capabilities of photography, according to Barthes, depend on an analogous relationship to the flesh-and-blood world being imaged (and imagined); photographs look like life. The photograph professes, according to Barthes, "to be a mechanical analogue of reality, its first-order message in some sort completely fills its substance and leaves no place for the development of a second-order message" (Barthes 1978: 18). The photograph declares itself to be evidentiary, to represent reality. Our persistent belief in the denotative functions of photographs exemplifies the precise mechanism of the photograph-as-evidence; its message becomes denotative because we believe it to be so—the photograph performs the message; it makes its own content referential. What Barthes calls "trick effects"—the manipulation of images—utilizes "the special credibility of the photograph—this, as was seen, being simply its exceptional power of denotation" (ibid.: 21). Paris, then, begins to take shape after its own image. "Paris" becomes, in America, simply Paris.

This re-creation of Paris through an American lens gestures toward another foreigner's gaze upon the Parisian landscape. In the 1939 version of "Paris, the Capital of the Nineteenth Century," Walter Benjamin remarks that "the gaze which the allegorical genius turns on the city betrays, instead, a profound alienation. It is the gaze of the flâneur, whose way of life conceals behind a beneficent mirage the anxiety of the future inhabitants of our metropolises" (Benjamin 2004 [1982]: 21). In the case of postwar fashion photography, the "beneficent mirage" also functions as a salve; the alienation of the imagined metropolis from its geographical counterpart for the "benefit" of American consumers also benefits the rehabilitation of the city; its glamour restored, the shame of occupation ignored, the photographer-as-flâneur becomes an active agent of imaginary restoration. In his book *Appearances*, Martin Harrison describes the historical circumstances which led to New York photographers being shipped out to Paris: "Social and historical factors had combined to place New York at its zenith. Effectively a world capital, it was now in a position to dictate procedure, not least to the world of fashion" (Harrison 1991: 25). Working in Europe after the war, Alexey Brodovitch's assistant, and a photographer in her own right, Lillian Bassman, "had to convey to the Europeans a new expression, a message of optimism founded on the radical changes occurring in New York. It was identified unequivocally as the 'New American Vision' of fashion photography" (ibid.: 25).

That this "New American Vision" depended upon New York photographers alighting on Paris creates a refractive space wherein one "vision" needs to be created, through difference, via another one. The "radical changes occurring in New York" relied completely on radical changes in Paris—the occupation, the fashion industry's isolation, fabric rationing—the "message of optimism" was, in fact, opportunistic. In "Looking American," Arnold describes the circumstances surrounding New York's fashion ascendancy: "New York fashion grew more confident and independent as it took center stage in the absences of Parisian influence" (Arnold 2002: 58). Brodovitch's stark, tidy layouts and the "pared-down photographic style [of *Harper's Bazaar*] fitted well with the functional fashions that were popular" (ibid.). Wartime rationing also figured into design; Arnold explains that

> by the time restrictions on fabric use were introduced under the L-85 scheme in 1943, many New York designers were already showing slim-line silhouettes that required a minimum of fabric . . . such clothes hinted at more independence for women, and, combined with Brodovitchs's stripped-down art direction and photographic style, [and

according to Andy Grundberg] played a role in the transformation of fashion from an essentially aristocratic enterprise devoted to clothes manufactured in Paris into a broad-based . . . preoccupation with personal and cultural "lifestyles."

(ibid.: 58)

If, as Benjamin claims, "fashion prescribes the ritual according to which the commodity fetish demands to be worshipped" (2004 [1982]: 18), then New York's presence in Paris becomes less about optimism and more about "dictating procedure" and usurpation. As Benjamin explains in the 1935 version of "Paris, the Capital of the Nineteenth Century,"

> Corresponding to the form of the new means of production, which in the beginning is still ruled by the form of the old . . . are images in the collective consciousness in which the new is permeated with the old. These images are wish images; in them the collective seeks both to overcome and to transfigure the immaturity of the social product and the inadequacies in the social organization of production. At the same time, what emerges in these wish images is the resolute effort to distance oneself from all that is antiquated—which includes, however, the recent past. These tendencies deflect the imagination (which is given impetus by the new) back upon the primal past. In the dream in which each epoch entertains images of its successor, the latter appears wedded to elements of primal history . . . And the experiences of such a society—as stored in the unconscious of the collective—engender, through interpretation with what is new, the utopia that has left its trace in a thousand configurations of life, from enduring edifices to passing fashions.
>
> (Benjamin 2004 [1982]: 4–5)

The palimpsestic tension Benjamin describes creates an estranging force; the "new," infused with the "old," is a source of both anxiety and desire, while the drive to replace the "antiquated" with the "modern" is alienating—to efface the past, after all, requires also eliding the present. The New York vision of Paris sought to omit four years of occupation while maintaining the old Paris charm that had once led the world of fashion. The photographers and art directors were charged with representing a Paris that had never been through the war: an imaginary city standing in for a wounded one.

Avedon's 1956 photograph of Suzy Parker and Robin Tattersall roller-skating in the Place de la Concorde elucidates his task as a New York photographer in Paris; legs akimbo, their gazes and smiles matching each other's, the models' toes seem to graze the top of the Hotel de Crillon (Figure 3.2). Parker's dress, by Dior, a tweed confection with three-quarter-length batwing sleeves and a high, rolled collar gathered with a tie, is blousy

Figure 3.2 Suzy Parker with Robin Tattersall, dress by Dior, Place de la Concorde, Paris, August 1956. Reproduced by permission of the Richard Avedon Foundation.

enough to allow for movement; the excess fabric billows around her mid-section as her collar tie blows away from Tattersall. The roller skates, like the pinball machine an American invention, propel the couple through the plaza. The modern dress, the roller skates, and the cars parked in the background all infuse the 200-year-old plaza with a sense of the new. The soft focus on the cars, however, envelops them in the same haze as the nearly 200-year-old hotel: here Paris' past and future fuse together as two cheerful Americans frolic through its plazas. And what of those French automobiles? In her book *Fast Cars, Clean Bodies*, Kristin Ross discusses the role of the car in postwar France, explaining that "economic growth was a direct result of having modernized sectors of production that were seen to be vital—and the most vital of these was automobile production. In turn, the augmentation in French buying power after 1949 was used principally to buy cars" (Ross 1995: 19).[4]

The ways in which riding in cars explodes previous notions of space and time for the driver imbues the car with symbolic properties. Consequently, according to Ross,

> any initial glance at the intermediate "moment" of the car—its marketing, promotion, the construction of images and markets, the conditioning of public response, the discursive apparatus surrounding the object, in short, its advertising—reveals a discourse built around freezing time in the form of reconciling past and future, the old ways and the new. This is particularly important in a culture like that of France where modernization, unlike in the United States, is experienced for the most part as highly destructive, obliterating a well-developed artisanal culture, a highly developed travel culture, and . . . a grass-roots national culture clearly observable to French and non-French alike.
>
> (Ross 1995: 21–22)

When the focal depth flattens the automobiles and blurs them into the façade of the Hotel de Crillon, and the crisp wheels of the roller skates in the foreground denote forward action, the "reconciliation" between France's past and future dissolves into tension. Here, the "New York Vision" allows France's own past and future—the hotel and the cars—to dissolve into a landscape to be enjoyed by others: the models, the magazine readers. Geographical Paris is now ahistorical, a spectacle, a Benjaminian wish image.

Paris becomes, through American eyes, an object to be gazed at, a sign composed of bleary signifieds, useful only as signifying "Parisianness," in turn signifying something like "chic" and "culture," and mediated through the magazine and fashion industries. As happens after the war, the ways in which modes of production and national interests collide with modes of representation (and subsequently modes of understanding) are problematized. In his 1967 book *Society of the Spectacle*, Guy Debord proclaims that

> the whole life of those societies in which modern conditions of production prevail presents itself as an immense accumulation of *spectacles*. All that once was directly lived has become mere representation . . . The spectacle is not a collection of images; rather, it is a social relationship between people that is mediated by images.
>
> (Debord 1993 [1970]: 12, emphasis original)

For Debord, within the rubric of modernity the representation replaces the represented, much as the denotated, for Barthes, takes a backseat to the connotated. The division that has "split up into reality on the one hand and image on the other" (Debord 1993 [1970]: 13) inures the gazer to the "real." The geographical land becomes a landscape as it recedes into the image, even as it is marketed as an evidentiary representation of a "real place." Introducing his anthology, Mitchell proposes a study which seeks to understand the way in which

> landscape *circulates* as a medium of exchange, a site of visual appropriation, a focus for the formation of identity . . . landscape is not merely a body of paintings to be interpreted "in historical context" but a body of cultural and economic practices that *makes* history in both the real and represented environment, playing a central role in the formation of social subjects as unreadably "private" identities and determinately public selves figured by regional and national identities.
>
> (Mitchell 2002: 2, emphasis original)

The landscape-as-spectacle and the landscape-as-practice both serve to fix a represented space in place. The collection of images, once circulated, becomes itself social practice, tautologically binding the real to the image. If landscape is, as Mitchell claims, a "technique of colonial representation," then what happens to the Americans in Paris? The carefree skaters, the pinball players, the photographer himself: what work do they do upon the city?

In light of the New York fashion industry's desire to celebrate its good fortune, the need described by Harrison to spread a "message of optimism" seems disingenuous. As Paris is made in New York, so is New York made in Paris. Finally able to twirl on a global catwalk, New York displays its own anxiety: a need for authenticity. It is Paris's aura that photographers like Avedon seek to capture. In "The Work of Art in the Age of Mechanical Reproduction," Benjamin explains that

> the authenticity of a thing is the essence of all that is transmissible from its beginning, ranging from its substantive duration to its testimony to the history which it has experienced. Since the historical testimony rests on the authenticity, the former, too, is jeopardized by reproduction . . . And what is really jeopardized when the historical testimony is affected is the authority of the object.
>
> (Benjamin 1968 [1955]: 221)

Once Paris, reproduced on film, is emptied of its occupation—"the history which it has experienced"—it loses its "aura" as its representation, half-toned and reproduced by the million, falls into the hands of American readers. "Paris" is demystified—it is a vacation locale, a place to play pinball in dramatic dresses. It makes the reader into a tourist: finally, into a flâneuse. Meanwhile, New York usurps Paris's power—the playful way in which the "irreverent" Americans frolic among the monuments effaces the seriousness of the war even while establishing America's cheerful "can-do" attitude. "The desire of contemporary masses to bring things closer spatially and humanly," says Benjamin, "is just as ardent as their bent toward overcoming the uniqueness of every reality by accepting its reproduction" (ibid.: 223). In this way, the American magazine and fashion industries colonize Paris through the control and mediation of its images. The "rebuilding" described by Avedon, then, functions doubly: as an American reimagining of Paris, and as a way to assert American power. The distribution of lovely pictures of Paris into American hands not only reminds readers of who liberated Paris, but also of who beautified it. More importantly, even while preserving those marks of Parisian chic and sensibility, the Americans leave their own marks: their own *joie-de-vivre*, their tourist dollars, their pinball machines. The distinction between the Old World and the new one begins to collapse as Paris is mined for its loveliness.

Notes

1. Richard Avedon and Roland Barthes held each other in high regard: Barthes featured Avedon's work prominently in his *Camera Lucida*. Avedon once proclaimed that "Roland Barthes writes like I take pictures," explaining the affinity between their aesthetic philosophies. He expressed regret for having never met nor photographed him (R. Avedon, personal communication, March 15, 2003).
2. The limited-edition volume *Made in France*, published in 2001, reproduces twenty-eight engraver's prints, as if mounted on boards, that typify Avedon's photographs of the postwar period. Reproducing the prints as they were submitted to magazine publishers—complete with notes, markings, stamps of authenticity, even cellophane tape—the book not only concretizes the intellectual labor (and commodification) of the image-as-object, but also catalogs the *Harper's Bazaar* version of Paris.
3. Suzy Parker, in fact, was the inspiration for Audrey Hepburn's "bohemian" character in *Funny Face*; fresh-faced and erudite, the accidental model fell in with Richard Avedon when she accompanied her older sister, the model Dorian Leigh, on a photo shoot.
4. It is worth noting that before World War II the European auto industry was essentially staffed by skilled workers, but the postwar years saw the importation of Fordism to Europe's auto factories, as well as a subsequent car boom (Harvey 1990: 129).

References

Arnold, R. (2002) "Looking American: Louise Dahl-Wolfe's Fashion Photographs of the 1930s and 1940s," *Fashion Theory*, 6(1): 45–59.

Avedon, R. (2005) *Woman in the Mirror*, New York: Abrams.

Barthes, R. (1974) [1970] *S/Z*, R. Miller (trans.), New York: Hill and Wang.

—— (1978) *Image-Music-Text*, S. Heath (trans.), New York: Hill and Wang.

Benjamin, W. (1968) [1955] *Illuminations*, H. Zohn (trans.), New York: Schocken Books.

—— (2004) [1982] *The Arcades Project*, H. Eiland and K. McLughlin (trans.), Cambridge, MA: Belknap Press of Harvard University Press.

Debord, G. (1993) [1970] *Society of the Spectacle* (trans. unknown), Detroit: Black and Red.

Harper's Bazaar (1945) September.

Harrison, M. (1991) *Appearances*, London: Jonathan Cape.

Harvey, D. (1990) *The Condition of Postmodernity*, Cambridge: Blackwell.

Mitchell, W. J. T. (2002) *Landscape and Power*, Chicago: The University of Chicago Press.

Pratt, M. L. (1991) "Arts of the Contact Zone," *Profession*, 91: 33–40.

Ross, K. (1995) *Fast Cars, Clean Bodies*, Cambridge, MA: MIT Press—October Books.

Chapter 4

Framing the Self, staging identity

Clothing and Italian style in the films of Michelangelo Antonioni (1950–1964)

Eugenia Paulicelli

Most critics have agreed that Antonioni's films create a new cinematic language and visual poetry in which his characters, their identities, and their narratives dissolve. Clothing plays an integral part in this project. At first sight, this might seem an insurmountable contradiction since it is impossible not to acknowledge intimate links between dress and the formation of identity. It is, however, only an apparent paradox because what clothing does in Antonioni's films is, on the one hand, to articulate the relationship between clothing and identity, and, on the other, to reveal, through fashion and cinema, how clothing becomes an integral part of cultural mediation. These two mechanisms are complementary since clothing, and especially how it appears in cinema, does not have a straightforward relationship with identity. The clothed body is always made up (in the many senses of the expression). Dressing implies a sort of masquerade that is in turn a semiotic act. It is this process that ensures that the Self enters the social scene and becomes, through clothing, culturally visible. Self and identity are also engaged in a fluid process of becoming as an examination of some of the characters in Antonioni's films will show. The clothed Self in cinema illustrates in the strongest of ways the presence of an external gaze, the gaze of the Other who redefines one's own identity (Bakhtin 1990). This process, which is always open-ended, never done once and for all, is emblematic in cinema, and, I would say, even amplified, insofar as the gaze, the role of the camera, and spectatorship are key in creating a multifaceted dialog with characters. Furthermore, the typical lack of continuity in Antonioni's films, the way they defamiliarize, and his use of the long take are all integral parts of an innovative cinematic language in which clothing plays a vital and leading role.

Let us dwell briefly on the dual function of clothing in Antonioni. Like any artist, he uses clothes to comment on and illustrate his characters' roles and status. This is a process that I would identify as narrative, and close to fashion, and as a macronarrative structure (Barthes 1983 [1967]). In this context, clothing is linked to individual feelings and aesthetic tastes and does more than merely tell the story of a given character. Rather, in Antonioni's films clothes have a vital role in an opposite process, that of dissolving both the very identities they attempt to capture and the narratives that hold together the complexity of their emotions and fears. If the narrative mode might correspond to fashion, the dissolution of narrative coincides in Antonioni with style, a distinct feature of his visual language. This is similar to what Barthes calls the "punctum" in his essay on photography, in which he distinguishes it from "studium." This latter is a mode close to narrative and to what is codified, whereas punctum stands for that which ruptures, a detail that affects emotions (Barthes 1982 [1980]). It is around this ever-present ambivalence, which is far more than a binary opposition or dichotomy (but is in a way complementary), that I would like to frame my own approach to clothing and Italian style in his films.

As a starting point and example, let us think of how in a film like *L'avventura* (1960) clothes take on this double mode. In the very beginning of the film we see how the class contrast between Anna and Claudia, the film's two main female characters, is made clear by their dress and appearance. Of the two, Claudia is the outsider of the group of friends and acquaintances setting out on a cruise together in the seas north of Sicily. She is more the bohemian type and clearly is not as well-off as her friends. In the film's opening sequence, set in Rome, Anna, wearing a classy silk shantung dress, accessorized with a Gucci bag and shoes, approaches her father against a background in which we can see the dome of St. Peter's. (Figure 4:1, the sketch by the costume designer Adriana Berselli, shows the notes where we see that Anna must carry a Gucci bag, and the dress should be in shantung, and so on.) In the foreground we see some new construction near Anna's family villa, which her father, a retired diplomat, even mentions in his conversation with his daughter. These are visible signs of the economic boom that was then spreading over most parts of Italy, bringing with it corrupt building practices. Anna's friend Claudia arrives, wearing an ensemble with a dark top and a pencil Prince of Wales check skirt, apparently a pattern very much loved by Antonioni (Berselli 2007). Anna is in the mainstream of high fashion, Claudia of style. Claudia, who will become the central character of the film, is attractive and beautiful, but is not wearing the designer accessories that Anna wears; she is an outsider among the group of socialites and aristocrats who are the other guests on the cruise. The contrast between the two is further accentuated through skin color and hair: Anna is a dark-skinned brunette dressed in white, Claudia is a pale-skinned blonde dressed in dark colors. Anna's dress is cut at the waist and has an ample skirt; Claudia's straight skirt allows the camera to capture the movement of her legs as she walks. In fact, we see her walking and wandering while she waits for Anna, who has gone up to her boyfriend Sandro's apartment. The contrast between the two women, however, will be dissolved in the course of the film and in the act of capturing the aesthetic and affective sides of clothing that define its linguistic and visual style.

Figure 4.1
Sketch by Adriana
Berselli: Anna's
costume (Lea Massari),
left, and Giulia's
(Dominique Blanchard)
right. Courtesy of
Adriana Berselli.

So clothes in Antonioni's films are never simply an obvious and unambiguous representation of his characters' inner or outer self. Rather, in his films, dress is instrumental to the impact his cinematic language conveys elsewhere through landscape, architecture, and the framing of objects that, when they appear on-screen, lose their utilitarian function in favor of an aesthetic perception of the image. Think, for instance, of how walls both of interiors and exteriors, in *Il deserto rosso* (1964), the first film in color made by Antonioni, are unrecognizable as such and thus become a canvas on which color is the only subject and protagonist. Walls in some sequences take up the whole screen, defamiliarizing the viewer who expects elements of narrative continuity. A painterly quality is recurrent in Antonioni's films, a modernist, metaphysical style *à la* De Chirico where even everyday objects appear as pieces of abstract art through the lens of his camera. Clothing participates in this aesthetic process and journey with its texture, design, fabric, and cut. Indeed, characters are almost embraced by the clothes they wear, caressed by them, both visually and cinematically. Clothes express either a suffuse and aesthetic chromatism of whites, grays, and blacks, as in the case of *L'avventura*, or beautiful earthy tones as in *Il deserto rosso*. More than illustration, they become an integral component of the painterly quality of Antonioni's films. This is the very act of "fashioning . . . a framework" (White 1978: 111) in filming that transforms an object, a landscape, a wall, as well as the identity of a character always in the process of becoming, and caught in a grey zone of in-betweenness.

Fashion both as an industry and more generally as a macro structure of signification (Barthes 1983 [1967]), with all its mediatic and symbolic apparatus, plays a prominent role in all of Antonioni's films. Many of his characters are linked directly to the world of fashion, as is the case of Clelia in *Le amiche* (1955) or the photographer known as Thomas in *Blow-Up* (1966), and are involved in professions that deal with appearances, media culture, and cinema. Rohdie is right when he says that "the world of fashion has always fascinated Antonioni" (1990: 121) and that "it is the world of almost all of Antonioni's main characters: film stars, fashion photographers, directors, architects, journalists, novelists, and, perhaps to be included as well, stockbrokers (*L'eclisse*)" (ibid.: 88). It is far from surprising, then, that Antonioni is one of the most quoted sources of inspiration for fashion photography in contemporary fashion magazines, such as American *Vogue*. Often they set their high fashion shoots in the context of the Italian *dolce vita* where sexiness, sophistication, beauty, and warmth are blended with the kind of ideal lifestyle that has so lulled foreign travelers to the peninsula.

A geography of forms, emotions, and architecture is to the fore in Antonioni's films and in his choice of what the characters wear on film. The choices of location as well as clothing were crucial elements of the visual composition of Antonioni's shots. As the costume designer for *L'avventura* recalls (Berselli 2007), after carefully choosing the location of the island "Lisca Bianca," the director had a long conversation with her explaining how crucial it was for him that the clothing would blend into that particular landscape. What they wear has almost the function of a chronotope in a novel where location, place, and landscape are key in the temporal unfolding of the story, but also in its visual perception.[1] It is interesting to note Antonioni's involvement with the choice of clothing for the films. Not completely satisfied with the sketches he was shown, he wanted a more concrete idea of clothing, seeing and touching the fabric prior to giving the OK for the making of the clothes (Berselli 2007: 17).

Otherness or feelings that are impossible to comprehend or contain in a frame are the very stuff of Antonioni's films. The wandering, suffering, joy, and playfulness of seeing, as well as the fragility of his characters, do not solely pertain to their inner selves. Rather, these moments and events are always treated as "opportunities for cinema" and the aesthetic act in general (Rohdie 1990). It is the poetic, affective power of clothing that interests Antonioni, its ability to signify through the effects and texture of fabric and color, and how this all works visually in the composition of the shots, similarly to the twists and turns of folds and details of dress. The breeze, the uncertain light of dawn, the darkness of night or of a sudden eclipse, the whiteness of a desert island in the Mediterranean, the grayness of a northern industrial town, all work to establish, along with clothing, an autonomous language, multifaceted in its nuances. The cut and fabric of a skirt have a say in the particular movement of the legs; the footsteps in an almost deserted city or in a crowded street are often the only sound we hear when women in high-heeled pumps walk, wander, dream, explore. Walking—the *passeggiata*—has a structural function in Antonioni's films, ever since his first feature film *Cronaca di un amore* (1950) (Cuccu 1973: 35).

In this process of staging and framing, clothes too have both a structural and an aesthetic function. In his 1950s films, dress and accessories have a more overtly theatrical function than in those of the 1960s, where clothing seems to blend in more with the visual language of landscape and architecture.

Staging women through dress: the 1950s

Female characters, like Paola in *Cronaca di un amore* (1950) and Clara in *La signora senza camelie* (1953), both played by the then newly elected Miss Italia, Lucia Bosè, would not exist cinematically without the painstaking attention devoted to their clothes and accessories and the performances they make possible. Paola and Clara, for different narrative reasons, seem to be always on stage. Paola, a beautiful young woman from Ferrara, is married to a much older industrialist from Milan, Enrico, who hires a detective agency to know more about the past of his wife. Right at the beginning of the film, we see the detectives he has hired looking at several pictures of Paola and noting the transformations she has been through, from her high-school days to the diva-like appearance of the present as a high-society lady in Milan. We see her going to a fashion house, on her way to meet her lover, her past flame Guido, in a hotel room, dressed in a glamorous black suit with a tight jacket and a fur-trimmed pencil skirt, accessorized by a fur bag and a hat. While at the fashion house, she chooses an evening gown that she will wear at the very end of the film. These details are crucial in staging an identity that twists the genre of the film noir and produces the refashioned Paola in the role she plays in the film.

It is as if some of Antonioni's characters, in the act of staging their public personas, see themselves as they take on a role that is not entirely theirs, as do Paola in *Cronaca* and Clara in *La signora*. After plotting the car accident in which Paola's husband Enrico is killed, the two lovers do not stay together. The film ends with Guido, who has witnessed the accident from a distance, going to Paola's house (she is dressed for a party they were holding) (Figure 4.2). There is nothing more theatrical than the moment when

Figure 4.2
Lucia Bosè and
Massimo Girotti in
Cronaca di un amore
by Michelangelo
Antonioni (1950).
Photograph by
Osvaldo Civriani.

we see Paola first waiting at the window wearing a stunningly sophisticated white gown and then going down to see Guido. We are left with a sense of lack of fulfillment, a feeling that belongs to the characters themselves. They decide to take opposite paths. They are unable to cope, unable to be together. The camera shows us the duplicity of the gaze within the same woman who watches her own performances and roles within a codified narrative that is always being disrupted. Although *Cronaca* has all the components of a film noir, the last thing Antonioni is interested in is revealing the mechanics of plot and solving the mystery.

Paola, without the couture wardrobe designed by Count Ferdinando Sarmi, would be just a beautiful young lady without any of the theatricality that makes up her character and activates the different levels of perception. Sarmi, an aristocrat from Ravenna who in the film plays the role of the prominent textile industrialist Enrico Fontana, Paola's husband, created the costumes for Lucia Bosè. The film is full of images like those of a fashion shoot, with angles and obliqueness of perspective. Some of Paola's evening gowns are stunning, especially when she appears dressed in white when at the beginning of the film Guido sees her again from a distance in the street outside a theater, and at the very end of the film when he goes to her after the car accident to say goodbye. Interestingly, in 1950, the same year the film came out, Sarmi moved to New York City and started to work as head designer for Elizabeth Arden, for whom he designed until 1959, when he opened his own Sarmi fashion design house on Seventh Avenue in New York, dressing many celebrities, New York socialites and foreign dignitaries. Sarmi was also among the Italian designers appreciated by the influential Carmel Snow, editor in chief of *Harper's Bazaar* in the 1950s (Milbank 1989).

Along with Paola's dresses, her accessories, especially her hats, also play a great role in staging her screen persona. They are theatrical, and sometimes almost as surreal as in a Schiaparelli design. The four hats that Paola wears in different key sections of the film mark the framing of turns in the narrative. Paola is an eager consumer of high-fashion clothes, but the film as a whole is concerned with the performance and theatrical side of fashion, its ephemeral presentness, its beauty, its transience.

In Antonioni's 1955 film *Le amiche*, the world of fashion is explored even more closely through the protagonist Clelia. She is the manager of a Rome-based fashion house that is opening a branch in Turin, her hometown. A successful example of a self-made woman, she finds herself at odds with the spoilt and corrupted men and women she accidentally encounters in the city. She happens to be involved, in fact, in their lives only because she is an accidental witness to the attempted suicide of the young Rosetta, one of these new acquaintances, whom she attempts to help. Clelia is an outsider, even in her former hometown, which she decides to leave again at the end of the film to go back to Rome. She is in transition, expressing the desires and doubts of conducting an independent life in the midst of a society that is also experiencing deep transformations. She even refuses to sacrifice her career for a promise of love and marriage with Carlo, the only positive male character of the film, as we might expect in a traditional narrative. Clelia works in the world of fashion, in the kind of 1950s Italian atelier that helped to launch Italian fashion globally, especially through cinema. The Fontana sisters from Rome provided all the costumes and some of the models for the fashion show in the film where we see a parade of fashion, Italian style (Figure 4.3, the fashion show, and Figure 4.4). Even the designer from Rome, who in the film appears for the official opening night of the *maison*, has an incredible resemblance to one of the three Fontana sisters. She even reminds Clelia of all the work she has done to reach her position and how she cannot jeopardize what she has achieved for personal reasons. One can legitimately surmise that the three Roman sisters provided more than one hint for the way these characters were represented.[2] The Fontana sisters were major players in establishing Italian style and fashion internationally and greatly contributed to what has been called the period of "Hollywood on the Tiber," when American directors and Hollywood actors

Figure 4.3 Maria Gambarelli, Eleonora Rossi Drago, and Yvonne Fourneaux
in *Le amiche* by Michelangelo Antonioni (1955). Photograph by
Francesco Alessi for *Foto Dial.*

animated the Roman *dolce vita* while filming in the Cinecittà studios. At
the same time actors populated the Rome-based fashion houses (especially
Fontana's and Gattinoni's), and not only for the costumes of the film. They
discovered that Italian couture was beautiful and stylish and above all much
cheaper than its French rival. In the 1950s and 1960s Gattinoni, along with
the Fontana sisters, dressed many Hollywood stars and designed costumes
for many films. Gattinoni reglamorized in Italian style Ingrid Bergman as
well as the American ambassador to Rome of the time, Claire Booth Luce,
who both became testimonials for the global status of Italian fashion.[3]

Women like Clelia and Clara, against the backdrop of Catholic Italy, do
not buy the dream of a perfect marriage and family, a dream that does not

Figure 4.4 Michelangelo Antonioni during a pause while filming *Le amiche.* Photograph by Francesco Alessi for *Foto Dial.*

match their desire to do something independently with their lives. Clara, the protagonist of *La signora senza camelie*, is an attractive shopgirl turned movie star who gets married to Gianni, one of her two producers. It seems like the usual trite fairy tale. However, she does not seem to fit in with any of the environments, even her own beautiful "doll's house," nor with the roles assigned to her. She has, indeed, no say even in the marriage decision, which she would have liked to postpone, and because of her looks she is manipulated according to the needs and circumstances of a film industry led by males who are pushed either by the need for money or by possessiveness, as in the case of her husband.

In the beginning of the film, we see Clara walking at night in semi-deserted streets while she goes to a movie theater where they are showing the film in which she first appeared, singing and dressed like Rita Hayworth. Throughout, *La signora senza camelie* stresses the cinematic, fictional dimension of the protagonist and how the process of refashioning and restyling her responds to the need to fulfill others' desires. Indeed, the film succeeds in showing how Italian moviegoers in the 1950s craved romance and spicy stories. The film industry, for its part, craved commercial gain, while her mother, for her part, wanted her daughter to be a star, no matter the price, even that of remaining unhappily married to the producer. Similarly, the Roman socialites and aristocrats are eager to be part of stardom and have their houses used in the shooting of the film, and to be able to mix and mingle with the glitterati of the fashion and film industries. Nardo, too, the diplomat with whom Clara has a squalid affair, is not excluded from the hypocrisy of a world of appearances.

In *Le amiche* fashion acts as a window and a theater for framing the actions of both insiders and outsiders. But Clelia is neither blinded by the glittering phantasmagoria of the world of fashion nor blind to the emptiness and hypocrisy of the upper-class people she meets in Turin who simply do not know how to face life and death, as happens with the suicide of one of their friends, Rosetta. However, if Clelia can be said to belong to herself, Clara Manni in *La signora* does not have the strength or the ability to detach herself from a world that uses her as an object to be displayed and consumed. She is, indeed, defeated when at the end of the film we see her once again in the Cinecittà studios. After failing to become a serious actress, she has accepted a part where she plays a sexy queen and is photographed while hiding her tears. She is again on stage wearing a luxurious leopard fur, queen of a deserted island with a puppet show over which she has no say.

Outsiders, doubles, travelers

It is typical of Antonioni to signal the out-of-placeness of his characters, especially those we can call foreigners. Sometimes they are foreigners to themselves, like Claudia in *L'avventura* or Vittoria in *L'eclisse* (1962). There was, however, an eminent forerunner in depicting the wanderings of the woman traveler, namely, Roberto Rossellini's film of his Ingrid Bergman period, *Viaggio in Italia* (1953). The film establishes through Katherine, the protagonist played by Bergman, a cinematic recounting of a portrait of an artist, and is also a reflection on the process of filmmaking, similar to what happens in Antonioni's films, but this time through Katherine's wanderings and walkings in the streets of Naples and its surroundings. There is, however, a major difference between how Katherine is dressed and deals with feelings and Antonioni's female characters in the 1960s films. During her sightseeing, Katherine dresses as the typical upper-class English tourist. She does her sightseeing in flats and a suit, holding an umbrella and a camera.

The tight jacket is all buttoned up, she wears a scarf wrapping her neck, she is beautiful and yet expresses a sort of prudishness, an uptightness that is emphasized by an outfit that makes her look older than she is. We see this clearly when Katherine goes to the Museo Archeologico Nazionale in Naples in the sequence involving the classical Greek and Roman statues. She is overcome by emotions and toward the end of the sequence appears on the screen dwarfed by the magnitude of the muscular bodies of the sculptures and the overflowing of an almost undefined passion and overt sexuality.

Antonioni's women in his 1960s films are not overcome by their passions and fears. They wander through the films, they walk and drive through fogs. Take Claudia and Anna, the two female characters in Antonioni's *L'avventura*, in the scene in which they are getting dry and undressing after a swim. They are shot in a sort of opposite and contrasted setting, a technique that Antonioni will use time and again to depict a sense of a thin and yet insurmountable barrier that pulls the two women apart, as happens later with the two lovers. And yet Claudia and Anna are somehow joined, not only in the intimate space of the cabin where one can even grasp a thinly disguised sexual attraction between the two. Although presented as opposites, Claudia and Anna seem to be two sides of the same coin. They are both outsiders. But because of their being on the border of an undetermined area of an in-betweenness, they are, like all women in the 1960s films, more experimental, more able to travel, than their male counterparts (and thus similar in this to Katherine in *Viaggio in Italia*), and more able to feel what they cannot express or see, or cannot see yet. Claudia sees Anna vanishing, but also sees a part of herself disappearing, dying. She cannot and does not want to retrieve what she has lost, but at the same time she cannot see things clearly.

It is when the two women are still in the cabin that Anna, pulling two shirts, one dark and one light, from her bag, asks Claudia: "Which one should I wear?" Claudia has no doubt, picks the darker blouse, and wears it, asking her friend's opinion. Anna says that the shirt looks so much better on her and decides to give it to her. Indeed, as soon as Claudia leaves the cabin, Anna puts the shirt in her friend's bag without being seen by her. This simple gesture is a prelude to the exchange of identity between the two women. A similar gesture, although in a completely different context and narrative, appears in Antonioni's *The Passenger* (1975) when David Locke, played by Jack Nicholson, exchanges his chequered shirt for the light denim one of Robertson, now dead, taking over his identity and appropriating his life.

Later in *L'avventura* Anna will vanish from the island, never to be found again. The following day Claudia, having spent the night in a hut, on awakening goes toward the window. Claudia is seen from the back, it is dawn, and we see on the horizon the sea and the white rocks of Lisca Bianca. Then from her backpack she takes Anna's shirt. She puts it on over a pair of skinny pants and goes to meet Sandro. Later, when Anna's father arrives at the island and notices Claudia's shirt, she answers his question with "Yes, it's Anna's. She gave it to me. I found it in the bag." This is a shirt, as with many of the clothes in *L'avventura*, that chromatically and thematically blends in with the landscape, the rocks, and the nature around it. We see Claudia wandering on the island almost enveloped by her surroundings, becoming an integral part of the landscape and almost swallowed by it. Indeed, it was Antonioni himself who chose this particular shirt. Apparently it was originally a shirt-dress, a chemisier purchased by the film's costume designer, Adriana Berselli, who had followed the crew on the shoot. Antonioni liked it because of the ethnic print of the fabric, its brown and copper color combination, which he thought would work well with the chromatic tones of the film as a whole, but in particular for the sequence after Anna's disappearance. It was decided then to cut the dress and transform it into a shirt for Claudia's character (Berselli 2007). From the moment in which Claudia puts on Anna's shirt she becomes the new partner of Anna's lover, Sandro. When Locke puts on Robertson's shirt in *The Passenger* he takes over his identity.

In *La notte* (1961) we have, as in *L'avventura*, an intimate moment and a conversation between Lidia and Valentina Gherardini that takes place during the all-night party at her father's villa. A sudden thunderstorm has drenched many partygoers, some of whom take a swim under the rain in the open-air pool, and Lidia takes a car ride with one of the guests, who had been courting her. Her husband Giovanni, meanwhile, has been flirting with the young Valentina. When Lidia appears all wet, Valentina gives her dry towels, while she gets undressed, appearing in black lingerie to dry her hair and clothes. Here the two women, who should be "rivals," appear instead to be accomplices, dressed in the same style, both wearing an impeccable "little black dress." They are the only two at the party dressed in black; their styles are very similar, both dresses exposing their bare backs. Lidia, after the rain, seems almost to be reborn, a liberation similar to that in T. S. Eliot's *The Waste Land*. Costumes for the film came from the Milan-based designer Biki, famous for dressing international celebrities including Maria Callas. As so often in Antonioni's films, there are several shots where women are shown from the back: observing a landscape, wandering in the streets, or obliquely looking out of a window. We see them from the back, going, vanishing, where? We do not know. There is a very special attention to hairstyle, to cut of dress, and to where the cleavage ends. Antonioni's wanderers are always sexy, women and men alike. There is a keen stylistic care in choosing the cut and color of dress: a low-cut neckline, a bare back as in the case of Lidia and Valentina's black cocktail dresses. We see close-ups of Giuliana's necklines in *Il deserto rosso*, when the group of friends are in the hut near the port, as well as of Vittoria in *L'eclisse* (1962). Lidia in *La notte* wears only two dresses. One has floral motifs, a sophisticated sun dress with back cleavage and a white jacket with a three-quarter-length sleeve that she wears open and unbuttoned while she walks in Chanel sandals, carrying a clutch. In the second part of the film, after her long walk and a bath upon her return home, she wears her black dress until the end of the film. Her two dresses mark the temporal beat of the film.

In contrast to neorealism, in Antonioni's films there are no miracles, only perhaps revelations and surprises. Miracles are not to be found in the plot or narrative. Rather, they are to be found in the creation of a new cinematic language. Even expectations in a narrative path, as we have seen in *Cronaca*, are somehow unattended; they are, so to speak, watched. From this perspective, *La notte* is particularly striking. Think, for instance, of how Lidia plays the part of the unhappy wife. When she wanders in the streets of Milan and its outskirts, she appears elegantly dressed, a classy sophisticated elegance that makes her stand out wherever she is and whoever she meets in the street. She appears at ease with her body; we often see from the back how she walks, her high heels clicking on the asphalt; the only sound we hear accompanies the harmonic and sexy rhythm of her walk.

She wanders through the film, either in the streets or during the party in the millionaire industrialist's villa. She is never still, only at the end when at dawn, sitting on the grass, she tells her husband Giovanni that she does not love him anymore. He is a successful writer, but is stuck and predictable in his attempts at semi-casual sexual encounters. He is also the typical false intellectual. He often mentions in his conversations, in fact, his inability to find new words for his fiction. He simply recycles. At the end of the film, in one of the most striking sequences, he cannot even remember what he had written as Lidia reads to him a passionate letter of his, which he thinks has been written by one of Lidia's would-be lovers, and follows the story he has told himself about the reason why Lidia wants to end their relationship. After finishing the letter Lidia tells him that what she read was his letter, a letter he wrote to her when their relationship was not strangled by routine.

Lidia is never predictable in any of her actions. In her walk she even goes to the outskirts of Milan—Sesto San Giovanni—a place certainly not suitable for a *signora*. Here she watches some boys, who look like local thugs, as they fight. She tries to stop them; there is a moment of tension, as an elegantly dressed bourgeois *signora* is surrounded by muscular young men. They are all staring at her, especially one of them who, while putting on his shirt, stares at her and then follows her. At any moment we expect him to rape her, all the clues and ingredients are there. Instead, nothing happens. The guy loses track of her. The gazes of the youths here recall a scene in *L'avventura* when Claudia and Sandro are in the main piazza of the Sicilian town of Noto. While waiting for Sandro, Claudia finds herself surrounded by local males who whisper in Sicilian dialect: "Forestiera questa, che bedda femmina, deve essere francese!" ("This one's a foreigner, what a beautiful woman, she must be French!") Here Claudia wears, for the only time in the film, a "*signora*" outfit, consisting of a black and white small-print suit with a string of pearls. Apparently this was the only outfit not completely approved of by the film costume designer, who thought the suit, chosen by Monica Vitti herself, conveyed a different and more bourgeois perception of Claudia's character. The suit, however, works chromatically well against the stunning Noto baroque architecture.

A new visual texture and chromatism is achieved in *Il deserto rosso*. Giuliana, the protagonist, a neurotic, suffers on account of her excess of vision; she sees too much, too many things. She does not know how to deal with and contain the things she sees without making her mind or the objects themselves explode, as they will do in the final scene of a later film, *Zabriskie Point* (1969). Giuliana's questions, however, share similar concerns with visual artists who might ask themselves how the canvas, the frame, can contain what one sees and feels.

The textures and combination of colors between the way the characters appear and the way they are dressed vis-à-vis the landscape are rendered in such a way that one can almost touch the walls, feel the fogs, feel the green woolen coat Giuliana wears while she walks with her son at the beginning of the film. Gritt Magrini, who had also collaborated on the costumes in *L'eclisse*, designed the costumes for this film. In the opening shot, we follow Giuliana wearing a knee-length green coat, her blondish copper hair seeming almost to emerge from the screen, as she walks against the grayness of the factory. We see in the film several close-ups of detritus, resembling debris after a catastrophe, the visible damage to the environment contrasted to other sequences of the sea, the rhythmic movement of the waves, leaves rustled by the wind (a similar shot was already present in *L'eclisse*, although representing a different kind of tree, and reappears later in *Blow-Up* (1966) when Thomas the photographer is in the park).

Although never given by watches or clocks, time plays a crucial role in Antonioni's films, especially in its intimate links with space both imaginary and real. Let us think, for instance, of the sequence when Corrado Zeller, a friend and associate of Giuliana's husband Ugo, joins her in her unfinished shop in Ravenna. At the beginning of the sequence the frame is entirely occupied by a grey wall, after which we see Corrado's head emerge from his car. The interior of the shop is still empty, with patches of different colors on the walls, paint left in some corners. Giuliana, dressed in purple, moves from one wall to the other and gives a painterly quality to the whole sequence. Indeed, it is like a visual tour de force that is carried over when the two go outside onto the sidewalk and a newspaper page falls slowly from the sky. Wearing a beautifully crafted high-heeled pump, of which we see a close-up, Giuliana traps the newspaper page on the ground with her foot (Figure 4.5 and Figure 4.6). She tells us that it is today's paper, reminding us of time, and how she is the measure of time. In reminding us of contingency she becomes timeless, weightless like the floating page or the overflowing thoughts couched in her visionary mind. In the absence of

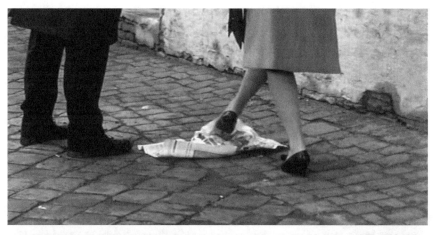

Figures 4.5 (top) and 4.6 Monica Vitti and Richard Harris in *Il deserto rosso* by Michelangelo Antonioni (1964).

music it is shoes, the high-heeled shoes with their tick tack, that establish a rhythmic tempo, following the footsteps of women wanderers (Lidia in the streets of Milan, Vittoria in the streets of Rome, Giuliana in Ravenna and its vicinity). Each one of them has a distinct way of being in the world articulated by the rhythms of their heels touching the ground, in their restless search, their desire for a somewhere and a something that is not always identified. Desire is what drives these characters. But on-screen they also become objects of desire. They seem almost suspended in their search, their paths neither predictable nor predetermined. "I do not know," Vittoria keeps repeating in *L'eclisse*.

The characters, however, are always positioned in a precise space–time relationship. The geography of passions and emotions acts in a relational mode with social and cultural geography. This mode, however, is never deterministic and straightforward. Indeed, the modernity and the lack of moralism, albeit not of moral integrity, in Antonioni reside in his ability to convey social, political, and cultural issues in a very experimental form, all the time creating a new cinematic language.

Style in Antonioni does not make him lose sight of the crucial political issues that are present discreetly in his films. The issue of class, especially at a time when Italy was going through a radical transformation which would gradually propel the country onto the global stage and market, is always present in Antonioni's films. It is present, however, in the subtlest of ways, avoiding the too obvious or moralistic representations of which classic neo-realism was sometimes guilty. In the 1960s films he addresses very specific issues, namely the boom in the building trade and the contrast between natural and historic landscape in *L'avventura*; the Stock Exchange and the fear of a new nuclear conflict during the Cold War in *L'eclisse*; Milan and the relationship between industrialists, intellectuals, and media culture in *La notte*; alienation, damage to the environment and pollution in *Il deserto rosso*. These were all issues affecting the Italian peninsula during the boom years, a period in which Italy came to be recognized, especially abroad, as a modern country. During this period, Italy produced an attractive, new, and modern self-image of itself that went on to become an icon of what was considered to be the best that Italy had to offer the world, Italian style. Along with the Vespa, a long-lasting icon that was a tribute to style and physical mobility, Italy exported art cinema, fashion, and design.

Think too about how the notion of "progress" vis-à-vis "*sviluppo*" (development), to borrow Pasolini's terminology, is played out in *Il deserto rosso*. All the signs of "capitalist" alienation, pollution, and serious damage to the environment are seen here along with the attempt made by Corrado Zeller to launch his corporation into a global venture in Argentina, another promised land, for both global capitalism and Italian workers (from the north) in search of a better future. Corrado, who is attracted to Giuliana, establishes with her an intimate relationship, something missing between Giuliana and Ugo. Corrado too seems a character in transition. He is the only one with a foreign family name; he is an industrialist not by choice but by family inheritance. He says that he does it under protest, despite his misgivings. He also travels, not sure where to stop, where to take roots. These are some of the reasons why he connects with Giuliana. He says to her in one of their conversations, "You say, how do I have to look? I say, how do I have to live. Basically, they are the same things." These are issues and concerns that Antonioni, differently from his characters, solves and dissolves in his cinematic language. By way of this language, Antonioni is able to establish a sense of intimacy that seems to be missing in the malaise of his characters' relationships.

Figure 4.7 Monica Vitti in *L'avventura*, by Michelangelo Antonioni (1960).

There is a scene in *L'avventura* with which I would like to conclude. Claudia is with Sandro. As he is about to leave their *pensione* in Noto, we hear a popular song with the lyric "You will never leave me." Claudia is dancing in the room to the rhythm of the song. We see her tracing a series of shadows on the walls following her movements. Sandro watches her on his way out. During her sexy performance, Claudia asks him to tell her that he loves her. Then, toward the end, Claudia's cheerful face becomes sad and thoughtful while she looks at Sandro, whose mind seems to be elsewhere. Then Sandro finally goes out. It is at this point that we see a close-up of Claudia sitting on the floor with the balcony door open, through which we can see the town behind her. She is wearing a house robe, funny and housewifely-looking compared to the other dresses she has worn in the film. She looks at the camera, puts her hands in the front pockets, which are detachable like little wings with fringes, and lifts her hands while they are in the pocket and makes a funny gesture with her face (Figure 4.7). With this simple gesture of her hands and face, she almost mocks all the drama: Anna's disappearance, her love story with Sandro, her attempts to under-stand his feelings or measure his emotional involvement with her. All of this is dissolved in a gesture that also dissolves narrative itself. The result is a light playfulness that could not have been achieved cinematically without the complicity of the house robe (*vestaglietta*) Claudia is wearing.[4] In Clau-dia's gesture we see Barthes's punctum in photography, a detail that has the power to disrupt any sense of linearity or conventional expectation and that affects and exceeds the logic of identity. Perhaps what Barthes says about photography and his interest for the still can also be said about Antonioni's cinematic style:

Photography must be silent (there are resounding pictures that I do not love): this is not a question of "discretion," but of music. Absolute subjectivity can be achieved only in a state striving towards silence (close your eyes to make the image speak in silence). The photograph strikes me if I pull it away from the usual bla-bla: *"Technique," "Reality," "Reportage," "Art,"* etc. Do not say anything, close your eyes, let the detail alone come to the surface, to the affective conscience.

(Barthes 1982 [1980]: 56)

In Antonioni's film style, single gestures and details enable us to look at the world with new eyes and with a deeper sense of intimacy, strengthening the perception of our emotions and feelings. Gestures and their recollections through the camera become powerful mnemonic devices that activate in a Proustian mode the involuntary mechanism of memory, just as an old shirt accidentally found in a forgotten corner of our closet can activate a chain of images. Interwoven with music and images, clothing becomes the very fabric of memory.

Acknowledgments

I wish to thank Hazel Clark, David Ward, and Sam Rohdie for their comments and feedback on this essay. Many thanks also to Laura Di Bianco for facilitating the contact with the photographic archive of the Centro Sperimentale di Cinematografia in Rome, and Antonella Felicioni, Viridiana Rotondi. Thanks also to Laura Mancinelli from the CSC Library and the enthusiasm and kindness of costume designer Adriana Berselli for talking to me about her work with Antonioni. My deepest gratitude goes to Leonardo Rivera who graciously, as always, helped me to reproduce the screen grabs from *L'avventura* and *Il deserto rosso*.

Notes

1. Interview with Adriana Berselli, December 2007.
2. Interview with Micol Fontana. Parts of this interview have been published in Paulicelli (2004).
3. In an interview in Rome in the summer of 2001, Ferdinanda Gattinoni talked about her role in restyling the American ambassador to Rome, as well as stars like Ingrid Bergman who became clients of her maison. Gattinoni made Bergman's costumes for the film *Viaggio in Italia*. The interview is unpublished.
4. This was one of the questions I was eager to ask when I had the chance to interview Adriana Berselli, the costume designer of *L'avventura*. She told me that she presented two kinds of dress to Monica Vitti, the actress who plays Claudia, who chose the more playful one because she was dying to do a little comical piece in the film.

References

Publications

Bakhtin, M. (1990) *Art and Answerability*, Austin: University of Texas Press.

Barthes, R. (1982) [1980] *Camera Lucida*, New York: Hill and Wang.

—— (1983) [1967] *The Fashion System*, New York: Hill and Wang.

—— (1988–1989) "Cher Antonioni," in *Cher Antonioni: 1988–1989*, Rome: Ente Autonomo di Gestione per il Cinema.

—— (2006) *The Language of Fashion*, Oxford: Berg.

Berselli, A. (2007) interview with the author, December.

Bruzzi, S. (1997) *Undressing Cinema: Clothing and Identity in the Movies*, London: Routledge.

Cuccu, L. (1973) *La visione come problema*, Rome: Bulzoni.

Fondazione Centro Sperimentale di Cinematografia (2005) *Carte, colori e tessuti. Ritratto di una costumista: Adriana Berselli*, Rome.

Mancini, M. and Perrella, G. (eds.) (1986) *Michelangelo Antonioni: Architetture della visione*, Rome: Coneditor.

Milbank, Caroline Rennolds (1989) *New York Fashion*, New York: Harry N. Abrams.

Paulicelli, E. (2004) *Fashion under Fascism: Beyond the Black Shirt*, Oxford: Berg.

Pidduck, J. (2004) *Contemporary Costume Film*, London: British Film Institute.

Rohdie, S. (1990) *Antonioni*, London: British Film Institute.

—— (2001) *Promised Lands: Cinema, Geography, Modernism*, London: British Film Institute.

White, H. (1978) *Tropics of Discourse: Essays in Cultural Criticism*, Baltimore: The Johns Hopkins University Press.

Films by Michelangelo Antonioni

Cronaca di un amore (Story of a Love Affair) (1950)

La signora senza camelie (The Lady without Camelias) (1953)

I vinti (The Vanquished) (1953)

Tentato suicidio (Attempted Suicide) (1953); episode of *L'amore in città (Love in the City)*

Le amiche (The Girlfriends) (1955)

Il grido (The Cry) (1957)

L'avventura (The Adventure) (1960)

La notte (The Night) (1961)

L'eclisse (The Eclipse) (1962)

Il deserto rosso (The Red Desert) (1964)

Prefazione: Il provino (Preface: The Screen Test) (1965); episode of *I Tre volti (The Three Faces)*

Blow-Up (1966)

Zabriskie Point (1970)

The Passenger (Professione: Reporter) (1975)

Il mistero di Oberwald (The Oberwald Mystery) (1980)

Identificazione di una donna (Identification of a Woman) (1982)

Al di là delle nuvole (Beyond the Clouds) (1995), co-directed by Wim Wenders
"Il filo pericoloso delle cose" ("The Dangerous Thread of Things") (2004) in *Eros* omnibus film

Documentaries directed by Michelangelo Antonioni

Gente del Po (People of the Po Valley) (1947)
N.U.—Nettezza urbana (Sanitation Department) (1948)
Superstizione—Non ci credo! (Superstitions) (1948)
L'amorosa menzogna (Lies of Love) (1949)
Sette canne, un vestito (Seven Reeds, One Suit) (1949)
La villa dei mostri (The Villa of the Monsters) (1950)
La funivia del Faloria (The Funicular of Mount Faloria) (1950)
Chung Kuo Cina (Chung Kuo China) (1972)
Ritorno a Lisca Bianca (Return to Lisca Bianca) (1983); segment of *Falsi ritorni (Fake Returns)*
Kumbha Mela (1989)
Roma (1990); segment of *12 Autori per 12 Città (12 Authors for 12 Cities)*
Noto, Mandorli, Vulcano, Stromboli, Carnevale (1992)

Chapter 5

The art of dressing

Body, gender, and discourse on fashion
in Soviet Russia in the 1950s and 1960s

Olga Gurova

This chapter is devoted to the reconstruction of discourse on fashion in
socialist Russia in the 1950s and 1960s. It is common to consider fashion a
phenomenon of capitalist societies and to question the existence of fashion
in socialist societies. The view is that Soviet industry did not attempt to
constantly launch new goods as in Europe and North America, where the
view was that Soviet "people looked like a grey mass."[1] I believe that Soviet
fashion was not that grey and dull. In many ways it can be compared with
Western fashion, although it had its own peculiarities, with state control
over appearance being one of the most significant.

The main point of the chapter is to identify how and why fashion and
dress became state concerns via media publications in the post-Stalin era in
the USSR. I argue that fashion became important as part of the process of
civilizing the Soviet people, which started right after the Revolution of 1917
as an anthropological project of creating of the New Soviet man.[2] Back
in 1917, the "revolutionary overturn of cultures" occurred, which meant
that the "high culture" of the nobility and intelligentsia gave way to "low
culture" of workers and peasants, the social classes the authorities of the
young state relied on. As a consequence, the main topics in media publications were the issues of how to civilize, and bring culture to, the relatively
uncultured social classes.

In the 1920s hygienic issues were of the utmost significance. The media
discussed norms of hygiene such as washing the hands, brushing the teeth,
and spitting into a spittoon. By the 1930s, when elementary rules had been
internalized by the majority of people, publications took the next step, to
issues of "cultureness" (*kul'turnost'*), explaining how to behave in public,
how to use perfume and makeup, and how to dress. Then, in the second
part of the century, the discourse started to cover the more sophisticated
and complicated topics of choosing accessories, matching clothes, and creating a personal style which would fall into the category of "Soviet taste."

The promotion of discourse concerning Soviet taste coincided with relatively close interactions between Soviet Russia and the West. From that
point, on the one hand, the strong influence of the Soviet state continued

to dominate in fashion discourse. On the other hand, Western influence has meant that many similarities can be found between socialist and bourgeois cultural processes, such as the importance of consumption and consumer values, attention to the female body, the growth of youth culture, and so on.

I begin the chapter with the concept of Soviet fashion and its peculiarities. Then I continue with a discussion of the "Westernization" of Soviet fashion and cultural context in the 1950s and 1960s. After that, I examine in detail the dominating concept of Soviet style, which was under both Soviet state control and Western influence. In conclusion, I discuss the official attitude, and the people's response to the Western influence in fashion.

The concept of Soviet fashion

Scholars have emphasized several characteristics of socialist fashion that make one consider Soviet fashion an oxymoron. First, fashion supposes changes in style from season to season and is closely connected to the concept of time. According to British scholar Djurdja Bartlett, Soviet fashion existed in the form of "official socialist dress," constructed in the discourse of magazines. It was closer to uniform than to fashion itself. Bartlett wrote that time was differently inscribed on official socialist dress than on Western fashionable dress. Official socialist dress was a prisoner of time, as socialism mainly neglected changes in favor of stability, which is why it always looked a bit out-of-fashion (Figure 5.1) (Bartlett 2005: 141–142).

Second, being the prisoner of time, Soviet dress lived an eternal life, which was almost impossible for fashionable dress in the West. Socialist society is often called the "repair society," with the aim of emphasizing the duration of the life cycle of clothes (Gerassimova and Tchouikina 2004). In Western societies the life cycle of clothes is short; the "death" of dress is stimulated by advertisement, by the marketing strategies of garment producers, by celebrity culture, and so on (Baudrillard 1998). In the Soviet Union, on the contrary, the life cycle of things was long and the arts of making and remaking clothes, sewing, and embroidering were a meaningful cultural activity (Crowely and Reid 2000: 14). This activity was popular due to structural conditions such as shortages, lack of appropriate things, and so on. Therefore, regardless of fashion, the appropriate things could be used over and over again.

The third point refers to the basic functions of fashion, such as differentiation and unification. The official Soviet discourse rejected differentiation and considered unification the only norm: "We don't mind the resemblance in clothes, because in socialist society dress shouldn't reveal one's class position. We want people of different social positions, city dwellers and countrymen, to be dressed equally well in the USSR" (*Sovetskaia zhenshchina* 1956: 46–47). Despite this, the role of clothes as symbols of status, age, and profession certainly remained a part of daily life.

Figure 5.1 Official fashion—1953—in *Rabotnitsa*, 12 (1953): 18.

Fourth, the official attitude to fashion changed significantly during Soviet times. In the 1920s fashion was under harsh criticism, it was excluded from the lifestyle of working-class people. The word "fashion" appeared in media discourse in quotation marks, as if it referred to something unserious, worthless, and bourgeois. In the 1930s the attitude to fashion changed to a more positive one. The change of attitude was proven by the opening of the House of Fashion (Dom modelei) in Moscow and, after that, in several big cities such as Leningrad, Novosibirsk, Yekaterinburg, and Rostov-na-Donu (Gurova 2006).

In the 1950s and 1960s the official attitude to fashion remained positive. In 1967 *Rabotnitsa* (Working Woman) magazine put a questionnaire to young women in a column called "Podruzhka" (Female friend). Answers included the following:

> "I go along with fashion. But this should have reasonable limits!" (Sveta, 18 y.o., Rubezhnoe).
> "I like fashionable things" (Vika, 18 y.o., Leningrad).

"When to dress up if not when you're young? After 25 one doesn't need it" (Lida, 16 y.o., Kemerovo).
"It is considered that to be dressed fashionably is to be dressed appropriately" (Natasha, 16 y.o., Volgograd).

(*Rabotnitsa* 1967)

In 1968 *Rabotnitsa* wrote that "Fashion concerns everyone. Grandmothers and granddaughters, husbands and mothers-in-law—everyone" (Maliovanova 1969: 31). In general, these citations show positive attitudes to fashion. There are several significant points in the citations which allow understanding of the ideological attitude to fashion in the 1950s and 1960s. First, fashion was a necessary part of the lifestyle of Soviet girls. Second, one could be fashionable regardless of where one lived—be it countryside, small town, or big city. Third, fashion was an immanent part of youth culture, though everyone was allowed to be interested in fashion regardless of age or gender. Fourth, fashion easily correlated with appropriateness and reasonability. This prudent, accurate, and timid attitude to fashion represents the essential feature of the ideology of fashion in Soviet culture in the 1950s and 1960s.

Western influence on Soviet fashion

Discussion of fashion in the media was contextualized in the rebirth of society after World War II. The state established a new official ideology according to which Soviet women should be involved not only in spheres of production and reproduction, as before the war, but also in other forms of social activities like consumption (Zharmukhamedova 2007). Therefore consumption was legitimated as an important part of the life of the Soviet middle class.[3]

Why was consumption recognized as a significant sphere for Soviet women? Several hypothetical reasons should be taken into account. First, consumption became a potent political force in the peaceful competition between the Soviet Union and the West. In general, the 1950s and 1960s were characterized by the intensification of cultural contacts between Soviet Russia and the West. Examples of the cooperation include the International Festival of Youth and Students, the International Congress of Fashion, the Moscow Movie Festival of 1961, and other events. From the mid-1950s onward, economic and cultural networks between the Soviet Union and foreign countries were rebuilt. International contacts promoted cultural and commodity exchange, which was carried out at the level of state institutions as well as in daily life.

British scholar Susan E. Reid called the Soviet–Western competition "Operation Abundance" or the "Nylon War," with the aim of emphasizing the deliberate strategy of the US of exporting its lifestyle patterns to the USSR in the time of the Cold War. The purpose of the strategy was the following:

if Russians were allowed to taste the riches of America (nylon stockings, vacuum cleaners, and so on), they would no longer tolerate masters who gave them tanks and spies instead of vacuum cleaners and beauty parlors. This strategy would help consumption to become a real political force (Reid 2007: 54–55). Even if it was more satire than truth, such a strategy had reasons to exist. America might have experienced success in exporting since the Soviet middle class was interested in consuming patterns of lifestyles similar to those of America's middle class. These patterns included financial security and the "suburban dream"—a private house in the suburb of a city. In the USSR, instead of a private house, people hoped for a separate apartment rather than rooms in communal apartments. In the US consumer values flourished, in the USSR structural conditions were changing as well as values: fashion and the possession of consumer goods ceased to be perceived in a negative way (Gurova 2006).

To remain loyal to the regime, the Soviet middle class needed change, which was provided by the state. Sociologists and historians emphasized the shift that occurred in the nature of the regime; this shift included the change in ideological orientation from a totalitarian mode of control, i.e. terror and purges, which dominated in the 1930s, to a symbolical mode of control of the post-Stalin epoch (Bartlett 2004). Not terror but symbolical manipulations became the basis for state power in the post-Stalin era. The Soviet middle class needed symbolical legitimating and, to remain loyal, it needed a good life, which it was able to acquire through consumption and lifestyle which included ex-bourgeois elements such as fashion, glamour, luxury, coziness, and pleasure (Dunham 1979; Fitzpatrick 1999; Gronow 2003).

In the context of the Soviet–US competition and the changing base of the regime, the sphere of consumption grew. A number of magazines on fashion proliferated, as well as an increase in the number of booklets on the art of looking good. These booklets had titles such as *Iskusstvo odevat'sia* (The Art of Dressing), *O kul'ture odezhdy* (On the Culture of Clothing), *Moda i my* (Fashion and Us), *Vkus i moda* (Taste and Fashion). Between 100,000 and 375,000 copies of these books and booklets were usually printed. The target audience for this discourse was women of different ages, professions, and social status, from young girls to old ladies, from city dwellers to women of the countryside, from party leaders to ordinary non-party members.

In general, the audience of the discourse should be loyal to the regime since the booklets devoted to appearance and fashion often contained politicized statements. Despite the fact that these books were meant for women, they often contained information without specifying gender: "The development of taste is one of the most important forms of struggle for the raising of Soviet socialist culture, for cultural growth of all Soviet people" (Zhukov 1954: 159–160). This lack of emphasis on gender means that the taste and art of dressing are considered as a construction of Soviet man rather than a building of gender identity. Russian feminist historian Yulia Gradskova has mentioned that in the context of media discourse the Soviet woman was considered primarily as a person, and after that as a woman (Gradskova 1998). Victoria Bonnell has suggested that it was class rather than gender that provided the fundamental conceptual framework for the Soviet authorities in classifying individuals, and that gender distinctions occupied a markedly secondary position (Bonnell 1997: 84). Anyway, the target audience of the magazines and booklets were women, and, as Susan E. Reid has put it, despite the ideology of overall equality, consumption continued to be naturalized as a female concern (Reid 2007).

The women's magazines of the 1950s and 1960s, for example *Rabotnitsa*, started to publish more items on fashion and beauty, providing a general discursive shift toward increasing the significance of issues related to consumption. For example, *Rabotnitsa* established a column called "Posmotrite na sebia, pozhaluista!" (Look at Yourself, Please!) at the beginning of the 1960s. The column contained advice on taking care of the body, learning etiquette, and, in general, acquiring Soviet taste. Art critics, artists, and designers from houses of fashion were considered experts and invited to provide comments on the topics. The comments were often made in an authoritarian way, so readers would take them seriously. Sometimes the comments were satirical, which was very effective in reaching the audience and getting attention.

In addition to *Rabotnitsa* there was *Krest'ianka* (Peasant Woman), *Sovietskaia zhenshchina* (Soviet Woman) or magazines devoted to fashion and sewing, such as *Modeli sezona* (Fashions of the Season), *Zhurnal mod* (Magazine of Fashions). Fashion magazines published abroad were also part of the discourse on fashion. Magazines from the West were extremely rare, though magazines from friendly socialist countries like *Kobeta* (Woman) from Poland, and journals from Soviet republics like *Banga* from Lithuania, *Silhouette* from Estonia, and *Rizhskie mody* (Riga's Fashion) from Latvia were affordable and accessible to the Soviet woman. Later journals from the German Democratic Republic (GDR), such as *Burda Moden*, appeared but continued not to be easily available, although they could be obtained through subscriptions to the workplace.

In general, Soviet media and women's magazines had two significant features in Soviet culture. First, the number of magazines was very limited, and second, all of them were under the control of state institutions. Therefore women's magazines were the medium by which the State wrote its ideology as text on the surface of women's bodies. It was also the easiest way to reach the audience, because public opinion considered magazines one of the most significant ways of spreading fashion in Russia.[4]

A survey conducted in the second part of the 1960s showed that the most influential sources of the diffusion of fashion were:

TV and movies—31.2%,
Newspapers and magazines—26%,
Exhibitions and fashion shows—21%,
Radio—19.5%

(Zhilina and Frolova 1969: 151–152)

Comparing Soviet and non-Soviet sources, 98 percent of parents and 88 percent of children among two generations supposed that Soviet media were the
most important sources of fashion. It is interesting that only 39.2 percent of
parents and 80 percent of children thought that non-Soviet sources were the
main channels for diffusion of fashion (ibid.: 152). Obviously, parents were
more conservative, patriotic, and sensitive to ideology, whereas youth were
more liberal, pro-Western, and sensitive to international influence.

In the 1950s and 1960s international movies and magazines had a great
influence on the look of the Soviet woman. The media wrote about celebrities; for example, *Rabotnitsa* devoted an article to the popular Argentin-
ian actress Lolita Torres during her visit to sailors on a boat, and ran a
picture of her with the following text: "Sailors present Lolita Torres with a
bunch of flowers, 'Kransaia Moskva' perfume and a Palekh casket" (Figure
5.2) (*Rabotnitsa* 1957: 32). The actress was charming, she was dressed in
an elegant white Atlas dress, her neck was decorated with a necklace, and
she had graceful bracelets and earrings. One of my informants recalled,
"We watched movies from Western Europe, from abroad. Lolita Torres
and her movie *The Age of Love*, everyone wore beautiful clothes. Life in
the movie was totally different from ours . . . This was so astonishing! . . .
And then we compared . . . We didn't know before that there is a different life somewhere. Just in movies."[5] Not only Western actresses but also
domestic celebrities were the models for the Soviet woman. From the 1950s
clothes and fashion ceased to be a "blind spot" in Russian movies, therefore
Soviet divas like Liudmila Gurchenko were role models in style and fashion
(Dashkova 2007).

Official discourse in the 1950s and 1960s stressed the importance of not
following Western-style fashion. In 1962 E. Semenova, the chief designer
of the Department of Fashion of GUM (the main department store), wrote
about international influence:

Where did this so-called "fashion" come from to our Soviet youth?
Such an unhealthy influence has been brought to our youth by some foreign movies, which appeared on our screens, blatant cosmetic ads from
foreign magazines, and, finally, one's hunger to imitate a best female
friend, who looks "smart," "exactly like in a fashion magazine."

(Semenova 1962: 30)

Figure 5.2
Lolita Torres on board
the motor ship *Rionges*
in *Rabotnitsa*, 10
(1957): 32.

The binary oppositions, such as we/they, domestic/foreign, capitalist/social-
ist, communist/bourgeois came to the scene, and totally corresponded to the
idea of the "Nylon War," or Cold War in general. In the second half of the
1960s to be too trendy or to follow Western fashion meant one "has poor
taste, can't think independently and make one's own decisions" (Maliovanova 1969: 31). As a consequence, in the 1950s and 1960s the discourse
was focused on the frame of the Soviet style (*sovetskii stil'*). The Soviet style
was identified by the following key categories: simplicity, modesty, and a
sense of moderation. These categories were opposed to the trendy look
associated with Western culture and, at the same time, with bad taste.

The concept of Soviet taste

The dominating concept which determined the discourse on body and
appearance in the 1950s and 1960s, was Soviet taste: "What is necessary
today is taste" (Mertsalova 1964: 30). An actualization of the concept of
taste had at least two meanings. On the one hand, the category of taste
was supposed to raise individualization and reflexivity toward one's body
in the context of the civilizing process. On the other hand, taste played an
important role in the regulation of "irrational consumer behavior." Taste
formed common symbolical fields for different social groups in Soviet culture. The question of how to recognize and acquire good taste occurred
many times on the pages of newspapers and magazines: "What are the

attributes of good taste?" The answer was: "Good taste represents the combination of simplicity and a sense of moderation." "Too much is too bad" (ibid.: 30). Several sets of rules for acquiring good taste were identified. The first set included rules related to the shape of the body and its surface. The second set included rules regulating the style of dress. The third set described rules setting up norms and practices for using dress in everyday life. The fourth set consisted of rules regarding the adoption—or not—of Western dress practices and their relation to Soviet fashion.

Rules related to the shape of the body and its surface

In the 1950s and 1960s the "figure" became a key category in the discourse on the body, and appearance became one of the key points in the presentation of self and the estimation of women in Soviet culture. Discourse constructed hierarchies of women's bodies. Body shape and obesity were criticized: "no doubt, obesity doesn't suit you" (*Rabotnitsa* 1966: 30–31). Russian scholar Olga Vainshtein points out that besides textual frames there was a significant difference in pictorial representations of plump and slender women in Soviet magazines. Plump women were pictured with their eyes downcast, as if they were ashamed, whereas slender women almost always looked directly into the eyes of the spectator (Vainshtein 1995).

The struggle against obesity or a "tyranny of slenderness" influenced the cultural meanings of clothes, which were supposed to correct the defects of the body, as mentioned in the following line: "the right choice of dress can help to eliminate the defects of a woman's body" (Ponomareva 1961: 30). In an article entitled "How a Plump Woman Should Dress" N. Golikova, a designer for the All-Soviet Union House of Fashion, wrote,

> It is so pleasant to watch a woman who looks good! . . . Clothing can help you to hide your weight problems, though it can't help you to change the body itself. That is why it is still important to follow a diet, to do gymnastics, to walk a lot in the fresh air—these will help you keep your body in good shape. If you're overweight, you should choose an outfit of a simple style. A dress shouldn't fit too tightly to the body and, at the same time, it shouldn't be too wide. It shouldn't have frills and flounces. A dress should suit your body well . . . Talking about colors, we can say that a plump woman shouldn't wear bright colors, they should avoid big patterns. Dresses in deep blue or black colors help to hide the plumpness visually better than dresses in other colors.
>
> (Golikova 1958: 30)

This extract reveals different techniques of normalization of a woman's body; a woman should manage her body with diet, physical exercise, or gymnastics. Surprisingly, this discourse appeared in the Soviet Union as early as in the 1950s and 1960s in the context of the discourse of good taste. Thus a lady with good taste should correct her body with clothes that cannot change its form but can visually improve it. According to magazine experts, there were several rules for improving the body: a plump woman should avoid dresses dividing her silhouette into two parts; she should not wear dresses with stripes, bright-colored dresses, wide clothes, or dresses with bows (Figure 5.3).

At first sight the recommendations have a lot of in common with the discourse of women's magazines from the West and from Eastern Europe, which articulated the same things and went in the same direction as to how to make a silhouette slender (Bartlett 2004; Stitziel 2005). Regardless of cultural peculiarities, the development of the discourse on the body of taste can be considered a sign of the penetration of consumer-society values into Soviet culture. However, even if general trends are similar, their meanings can be different. For example, the set of rules had its hidden meaning in Soviet culture, and to follow rules meant to reveal one's loyalty to the ruling regime. Olga Vainshtein points out that it was important for the Soviet state to have people dressed according to particular rules, because it was easy to classify them. Theoretically, each person had to be easily classified according to one's age, gender, and social position, i.e. their place in a particular social group (Vainshtein 1996).

Besides weight, the other body characteristic considered problematic in discourse was age: "the most important skill is to dress appropriately to one's age" (Polikovskaia 1962: 31). In the Soviet discourse there was a connection: obesity came when a woman got older. A glance at fashion magazines helps to uncover the following rule: plump women look much older than their young colleagues. Slenderness was considered an attribute of youth. Therefore, for example, a young and plump girl had no right to exist, neither in discourse nor in reality. She was excluded by producers of clothes as well as by producers of media discourse.

Rules regulating the style of dress: a case of clothing color

The choice of the appropriate color of an outfit was considered a skill related to good taste: "taste is most obvious in choice of colors" (*Rabotnitsa* 1969: 32). A woman should know which colors suit her age, complexion, and hair: "One should be jealous of a woman who knows 'her colors' (colors which suits her best), and who has the ability not to change them according to the latest fashion. However, we often meet women who wear colors totally inappropriate for their age, complexion, eyes, and hair color" (ibid.: 32).

All the colors were divided into two groups: "warm" (red, orange) and "cold" (blue, burgundy). There was also a group of neutral colors like white, black, grey, and beige. It was supposed that cold colors make a figure visibly more slender whereas warm colors make the same figure appear plumper.

Figure 5.3
"If you've got plumper" in
Rabotnitsa, 7 (1966): 31.

Warm colors suit blondes, and cold colors suit brunettes; bright colors work well for youth, and don't work for elderly women (Ponomareva 1961: 30). In general, the system of color allows a woman with a young and slender body to be a bit more expressive than a woman who is slightly plump. Bright colors were under suspicion since they were considered more emancipative, whereas neutral colors had a more reliable reputation.

The colors of clothes were also regulated by the concept of "ensemble." A designer from the House of Fashion in Leningrad clarified: "the unity of costume's parts in style and colors was called the 'ensemble'."[6] A truly elegant woman with good taste should be an expert in making ensembles,

choosing accessories like gloves, necklaces, brooches, and hats, and matching the colors of clothes and accessories.

> For colors, if an outfit consists of so-called neutral colors like grey, beige,
> white, and black, the accessories could be in bright colors, and vice versa.
> It was not recommended to match many colors. An ensemble with too
> many colors was perceived as too mannered and gaudy, and this revealed
> bad taste. Good taste depended on matching up to three colors. It was
> also not recommended to make all the parts of an outfit in one color, as it
> would look boring and monotonous.[7]

The ensemble should be neither too bright nor monotonous; it should include
accessories but not too many, just as an accent. Elegance, the choice of colors
and accessories, attention to detail, all these norms allow a comparison between Soviet dress and the petty-bourgeois dresses of pre-Revolutionary Russia,
therefore Djurdja Bartlett calls this style "pseudo-classical" (Bartlett 2004).

In Soviet culture several specific social meanings of colors can also be
found. For example, bright colors were considered flamboyant, and were
under critique since a woman should be modest and her style should be
simple. For the same reason, paillettes, rhinestones, and big bright patterns were considered vulgar and flaunting. Some colors like yellow had a
really bad reputation as a sign of Western fashion. In the 1950s, when the
youth subculture *stiliagi* came to the scene, its followers wore yellow neckties, so the reputation of yellow was ruined (Vainshtein 1996; Kharkhordin
1999; Kimmerling 2007; Yurchak 2006). In schools there was "a rule of
three colors," which meant that everybody had to wear a uniform in black,
brown, and white. The common style for the workplace was a white top
and dark bottom. If in the GDR black was considered a color of intellectuals,[8] in the USSR black, beige, white, and grey were considered as neutral
colors and widely used in fashion design. In general, the relevant term to
describe the ideology or social construction of colors, with its emphasis on
neutral colors, is "invisible visibility." Russian scholar Tat'iana Dashkova
applies this term to Soviet fashion, and explains its meaning as "simplicity,"
"purity," and loyalty to the collective (Dashkova 2007: 154).

Rules setting up norms and practices of using dress in everyday life

The next set of rules insisted that clothes should be appropriate to particular everyday situations: "the culture of clothes consists not only of the right
understanding of what to put on, but also of knowledge of where and how
to put it on" (Kireeva 1970: 12–13).

Generally, clothes were classified according to three groups: for house,
for work, and for holiday, as in the following headline: "Your Clothes: At

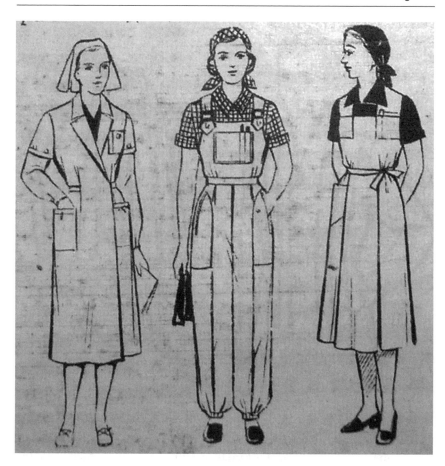

Figure 5.4 "Dress for work" in *Rabotnitsa*, 4 (1954): 30.

Home—at Work—at the Theatre" (*Rabotnitsa* 1968: 24). The classification was strict, and good taste required one to follow it. A body at work should not be expressive; it was not recommended to wear fancy dresses, décolleté, or jewelry, nor, in general, to dress up when going to work. Instead, dressing for work should be comfortable, practical, and modest (Figure 5.4).

Besides clothes for work, Soviet women had to have clothes "to go out." An outfit "to go out" should be new or one which is not used every day and keeps a sense of novelty. It is interesting that items of clothing worn to go out to different places could be used for several years until they lost their novelty. Here is a quote which describes a confusing situation with a dress that suddenly lost its novelty after ten years:

> Each holiday required something to dress up, and we didn't have that something. There was a story, N. came back to our place . . . He used

to pay attention to me, so he came back and we met. So, he . . . well
. . . Once at a friend's birthday he had shot a picture of us. And there
he was, he met me and said he had a surprise for me . . . We went to his
place and he showed me those ten-year-old shots. And me, while I was
preparing to meet him, dressed up. I wore a costume and a blouse . . .
We started to watch and I realized I am in the same blouse now. It was
very unpleasant.[9]

Having lost the effect of newness, dresses usually passed to the category of
everyday clothes and then to the category of clothes for home. There was
also a special kind of dress for the home called *khalat* (a robe). The robe signified home, it was an essential part of living in both private apartments and
communal ones. In the communal apartment it helped to keep one's body
hidden in shared spaces. In this sense it can be considered as "unintentional
social invention" (de Certeau 1998: 37).

Rules discussing Soviet and Western fashion

According to an existing cultural stereotype, appearance reflects one's inner
self, and bad taste means bad inner self. Since the imperatives of good taste
in the Soviet Union were simplicity and the sense of measure, the imperatives of bad taste were the reverse. To have bad taste meant to be eccentric,
to have kitschy clothes, to be too trendy, or, in general, to follow Western
fashion. Soviet design theorist I. A. Ter-Ovakimian wrote, "Fashion design
in the USSR fundamentally differs from the capitalist countries. Many Western designs are extravagant, with disturbing asymmetry, unbalanced and
eccentric lines" (Ter-Ovakimian 1963: 7). Not only fashion, but Western
lifestyle in general, including music, dance, and movies, was under criticism
(Figure 5.5).

At the same time, many Western designs, produced for ordinary workers,
not for the bourgeoisie, were perceived positively and were warmly welcomed:
"However, many Western designs were produced not only for the bourgeois
classes, but also for the working classes. These designs should receive a welcome in our country. The Soviet consumer treats them positively" (ibid.).

In 1970 *Rabotnitsa* provoked a discussion on the controversial issue of
the relationship between clothes and behavior. One of the journal's rubrics
was devoted to questions and answers, the typical form of getting and giving
feedback in the Soviet media and a very effective way to teach the rules and
promote officially approved values. Here is a quote from a reader's message:
"It is well known that personality develops with the growth of modesty.
How can we talk about modesty if a woman shows her knees? No way, a
pure inner self could never coexist with a skirt above knees" (Maria Babuk,
Kiev) (Efremova 1970: 30–31). The quote shows that ideology was learned
well and internalized by Soviet women.

Figure 5.5
"On a dance floor" in
Rabotnitsa, 7 (1966): 19.

At the same time, ideology was changing. In the 1960s in the context of international interactions, Western patterns came to the Soviet Union and needed to be redefined and politically approved. This is an example of such redefining:

Many people think that short clothing reflects bourgeois society morals ... But what about physical training classes, public competitions in gymnastics or swimming, when girls' bodies are covered with maillots, and billions of spectators watch them? No, dear comrades. If we evaluate the inner self according to the length of the skirt, we would be much closer to bourgeois morals than to our socialist high-moral qualities of the individual.

(Efremova 1970: 31)

The miniskirt was not the only controversial phenomenon; another was women's trousers, which also needed to be politically legitimated when women, mostly foreigners, appeared in trousers in the streets of Soviet cities. Here is another quote from *Rabotnitsa*: "I think there is a connection between fashion and behavior. Our fashion is obliged to educate our youth to have modesty, simplicity, rationality, in other words, a sense of beauty. A woman in a shirt and trousers, with a short boyish haircut, is unnatural" (V. Savchenko, Nsk) (ibid.: 30–31). The answer from an expert was,

> Western fashion in recent years is extremely persistent about women's trousers and ensembles with trousers. Strangely enough, the trousers were always criticized harshly . . . particularly in the case of attitudes to trousers by the older generations, who see in them the reason for dissoluteness. Despite this, trousers are still a part of women's wardrobes. Even the All-Soviet Union House of Fashion recommends outfits with trousers.
>
> (Kireeva 1970: 14–15)

This discussion shows how the emphasis was shifting from material objects themselves to their symbolic meanings in the ideology of fashion. If the Soviet woman dresses in a miniskirt or women's trousers, this does not allow us to consider these clothes as bourgeois or non-Soviet objects, and the woman as non-loyal, with a bad inner self. This means that the miniskirt and trousers themselves didn't represent the bourgeois values. The meaning of clothes was determined by their use and the context in which they were used.[10] Thus, it was important to define a miniskirt as a "socialist skirt" and to rehabilitate naked knees. This shift in discursive interpretation allowed Soviet fashion to go along with Western fashion and politically approve global fashion patterns and trends.

Conclusion

The sets of rules discussed above refer to the ideology of fashion in Soviet Russia in the 1950s and 1960s. One of the main discursive ideas was that of Soviet taste. On the one hand, the idea of Soviet taste was part of a civilizing discourse, which taught the Soviet woman how to care for her body, from simple rules of hygiene to more sophisticated issues of personal style and taste. On the other hand, this discourse can be explained as a reaction to intercultural interactions, to the ideological competition with America and other so-called "bourgeois" countries, to the penetration of patterns of Western culture and fashion into Russia, and to the distribution of consumer-type values in the daily life of Soviet people. Therefore the discourse was built around the opposition of Soviet lifestyle versus bourgeois or capitalist lifestyle. Such discourse became even more intense when Western fashion went out onto the streets of the Soviet cities (particularly women in trousers or miniskirts).

Actualization of the concept of taste could have the following sociological meaning: taste played an important role in the construction of the Soviet lifestyle and social groups. In the 1950s consumption became a powerful tool for the symbolic making of the Soviet middle class, which was interested in well-being, fashion, and consumer goods. In this sense, the Soviet middle class shared the values of the Western middle class and was interested in Western-style fashion patterns. As a result, Soviet fashion and ideology were not as separated from their Western counterparts as the Soviet media persistently used to depict. Along with peaceful competition, the rhetorical enemy pushed Soviet fashion toward global patterns.

Acknowledgments

I would like to thank the Center for Russian, East European, and Eurasian Studies at the University of Illinois, Urbana-Champaign, which supported my participation at the Fabric of Cultures: Fashion, Identity, Globalization conference, and the Carnegie Corporation of New York, which supported my stay at the University of Michigan in Ann Arbor, where this article has been completed. I would also like to thank Eugenia Paulicelli and Hazel Clark for their valuable comments, and Lucie Pokorná for her generous help.

Notes

1. Finnish sociologist Jukka Gronow mentioned this stereotype of Soviet fashion and disproved it (Gronow 2003: 1).
2. The category "civilizing process" was discussed by German sociologist Norbert Elias (Elias 1994).
3. The term "middle class" sounds problematic because it has sociological connotations that pertain to non-communist societies. In this paper I rely on the definition of American historian Vera S. Dunham. Dunham applies this category to a diversity of people, including intellectuals; professional, technical, and managerial specialists; white-collar workers; and others. These groups have in common their position among the educated elites and privileged groups of Soviet society. The middle classes also had common lifestyles and were interested in material goods and well-being in exchange for loyalty to party leaders. The middle class was the base for the ruling regime, and the party relied upon it (Dunham 1979: 13–14; Bartlett 2004; Reid 2007).
4. The survey devoted to attitudes toward material objects was conducted in the city of Chelyabinsk in the 1960s—1,740 families were interviewed (Zhilina and Frolova 1969).
5. Interview with a male, born in 1937.

6. Interview with a female, born in 1947.
7. Ibid.
8. Russian historian Anna Tikhomirova mentioned that in the GDR the color black was perceived as a sign of bohemian circles (Tikhomirova 2007). In the USSR the problem of black was solved by calling it a neutral color, which was appropriate for socialist women.
9. Interview with a female, born in 1959.
10. British anthropologist Victor Buchli in his book *An Archaeology of Socialism* gives several examples of changing attitudes to different material objects in the 1920s and 1930s in Russia. He based his thesis on the idea of shifting cultural interpretations of material objects from the denotative model of understanding of things that was characteristic of Lenin's culture, to the contextual model of Stalin's culture. According to Buchli, the denotative model supposes attributing meaning to a material object itself whereas the context model supposes that judgment is made on the basis of the context of use of the object (Buchli 2000).

References

Bartlett, D. (2004) "Let Them Wear Beige: The Petit-Bourgeois World of Official Socialist Dress," *Fashion Theory*, 8(2): 127–164.

Baudrillard, J. (1998) *The Consumer Society: Myths and Structures*, London: Sage.

Bonnell, V. E. (1997) *Iconography of Power: Soviet Political Posters under Lenin and Stalin*, Berkeley and London: University of California Press.

Buchli, V. (2000) *An Archaeology of Socialism (Materializing Culture)*, Oxford: Berg.

de Certeau, M. (1998) *The Practice of Everyday Life*, Minneapolis: University of Minnesota Press.

Crowely, D. and Reid, S. E. (2000) "Style and Socialism: Modernity and Material Culture in Post-war Eastern Europe," in D. Crowely and S. E. Reid (eds.), *Style and Socialism: Modernity and Material Culture in Post-war Eastern Europe*, New York: Berg.

Dashkova, T. (2007) "Nevidimye miru riushi: moda v sovetskom dovoennom i poslevoennom kinematografe," *Teoriia mody: Odezhda, telo, kul'tura*, 2007 (3): 149–162.

Dunham, V. S. (1979) *In Stalin's Time: Middleclass Values in Soviet Fiction*, Cambridge: Cambridge University Press.

Efremova, L. (1970) "Moda i my," in *Rabotnitsa*, 1970 (11): 30–31.

Elias, N. (1994) *The Civilizing Process: The Development of Manners, Change in the Code of Conduct and Feeling in Early Modern Times*, Oxford: Blackwell.

Fitzpatrick, S. (1999) *Everyday Stalinism. Ordinary Life in Extraordinary Times: Soviet Russia in the 1930s*, New York and Oxford: Oxford University Press.

Gerassimova, K. and Tchouikina, S. (2004) "Obschestvo remonta," *Neprikosnovennyi zapas*, 2004 (2): 70–77.

Golikova, N. (1958) "Kak odevat'sia polnym zhenshchinam," *Rabotnitsa*, 1958 (8): 30.

Gradskova, Y. (1998) *"Obychnaia sovetskaia zhenshchina": obzor opisanii identichnosti*, Moscow: Sputnik plus.

Gronow, J. (2003) *Caviar with Champagne: Common Luxury and the Ideals of the Good Life in Stalin's Russia*, Oxford and New York: Berg.

Gurova, O. (2006) "Ideology of Consumption in the Soviet Union: From Asceticism to Legitimating of Consumer Goods," *Anthropology of East Europe Review* (Autumn): 91–102.

Kharkhordin, O. (1999) *The Collective and the Individual in Russia*, Berkeley: University of California Press.

Kimmerling, A. (2007), "Platforma protiv kalosh. Stiliagi na ulitsakh sovetskikh gorodov," *Teoriia mody: Odezhda, telo, kul'tura*, 2007 (3): 81–99.

Kireeva, L. (1970) *O kul'ture odezhdy: Kostum, stil', moda*, Leningrad: Obshchestvo "Znanie."

Maliovanova, I. (1969), "Novaia moda novogo goda," *Rabotnitsa*, 1969 (1): 31.

Mertsalova, M. (1964) "Chto chereschur—to plokho," *Rabotnitsa*, 1964 (11): 30.

Polikovskaia, E. (1962) "Posle soroka," *Rabotnitsa*, 1962 (7): 31.

Ponomareva, V. (1961) "Dlia polnykh zheshchin," *Rabotnitsa*, 1961 (9): 30.

Rabotnitsa (1957) "V gostyakh u sovetskikh moriakov," 1957 (10): 32.

—— (1966) "Esli Vy raspolneli," 1966 (7): 30–31.

—— 1967 (3).

—— 1968 (1).

—— (1969) "Kakoi tsvet vam idet?" 1969 (5): 32.

Reid, S. E. (2007) "Gender and Destalinization of Consumer Taste in the Soviet Union," in E. Casey and L. Martens (eds.), *Gender and Consumption: Domestic Cultures and the Commercialisation of Everyday Life*, Aldershot: Ashgate.

Semenova, E. (1962) "Kosmeticheskoe povetrie," *Rabotnitsa*, 1962 (8): 30.

Sovetskaia zhenshchina, 1956 (4).

Stitziel, J. (2005) *Fashioning Socialism: Clothing, Politics, and Consumer Culture in East Germany*, Oxford and New York: Berg.

Ter-Ovakimian, I. (1963) *Modelirovanie i konstruirovanie odezhdy v usloviiakh massovogo proizvodstva*, Moscow: Legkaia industriia.

Tikhomirova, A. (2007) "'Modno odevat'sia—eshche ne znachit byt' sovremennoi.' Sotsialisticheskii proekt 'al'ternativnoi sovremennosti' i zhenskaia odezhda kak ob'ekt proektsii v GDR (na primere zhurnala Sybille)," *Teoriia mody. Odezhda, telo, kul'tura*, 2007 (3): 233–250.

Vainshtein, O. (1995) "Polnye smotriat vniz, Ideologiia zhenskoi telesnosti v kontekste rossiiskoi mody," *Khudozhestrenny zhurnal*, 1995 (7): 49–53.

—— (1996) "Female Fashion, Soviet Style: Bodies of Ideology," in Helena Goscilo and Beth Holmgren (eds.), *Russia, Women, Culture*, Bloomington: Indiana University Press.

Yurchak, A. (2006) *Everything Was Forever, Until It Was No More: The Last Soviet Generation*, Princeton: Princeton University Press.

Zharmukhamedova, Z. (2007), Ideologiia v obrazakh: vizual'naia reprezentatsiia zhenshchiny v zhenskikh zhurnalakh 50–60h godov. Online. Available at http://takaya.by/texts/essay/sov_magazin/ (accessed September 20, 2007).

Zhilina, L. and Frolova, N. (1969) *Problemy potrebleniia i vospitaniia lichnosti*, Leningrad: Mysl.

Zhukov, N. (1954) "Vospitanie vkusa. Zametki khudozhnika," *Novyi mir*, 1954 (10): 159–179.

Chapter 6

Fashioning appropriate youth in 1990s Vietnam

Ann Marie Leshkowich

In February 1997 the cultural celebrations marking the Lunar New Year (*Tet*) in Ho Chi Minh City included a Spring Fashion Contest (*Hoi Thi Thoi Trang Ngay Xuan*) for youth. Held at the Youth Cultural House (*Nha Van Hoa Thanh Nien*) run by the Ho Chi Minh Communist Youth League, the event drew several hundred spectators, including friends and family of the contestants, representatives of the media, and curious onlookers, such as myself. The contest had been organized by members of the Youth League's Fashion Club. As the house lights dimmed, the evening's MC informed the crowd that the event was not a beauty contest. Instead, a panel of judges—the head of a popular clothing company, a fashion reporter, and a well-known Vietnamese designer and director of the state-run national design institute—would determine how well contestants had chosen clothing that was attractive and appropriate for their life circumstances.

Over the next several hours, thirty-two contestants, all students or workers in their late teens to mid-twenties and approximately two-thirds of them women, modeled outfits of their own selection or design in two categories: office or school attire (*trang phuc di lam hay di hoc*), and eveningwear (*trang phuc da hoi*). For the first section, most of the young women wore white *ao dai*, the long tunic and wide-legged pants that constitute Vietnam's national costume and are the required uniform for most female secondary students. The young men wore light dress shirts and dark pants or suits (Figure 6.1). For the eveningwear portion, many of the young women donned elaborate, but rather banal, evening gowns (Figure 6.2). The young men tended toward trendy, slightly grunge (*bui*) styles juxtaposing different patterns and colors.

As the audience awaited the results, the famous designer took the microphone. I expected her to congratulate the contestants or expound on the role of fashion as Vietnam strove for prosperity under the market-oriented policies known as *Doi moi* (Renovation) that had begun a decade earlier. Instead, she delivered a pointed rebuke:

> I thought that spring fashion and this contest were supposed to open up a new atmosphere and a new lifestyle. But there's a problem with

Figure 6.1 Contestants model clothing for school or work. (Photograph by Ann Marie Leshkowich.)

the fashion that makes me feel hopeless. The outfits chosen by the female contestants aren't appropriate for their age, or for the life-style of Vietnamese people . . . It's strange . . . a young woman of sixteen who wears an evening outfit looks old . . . I'm wondering what kind of vehicle they'll use, to go where? [Turning to the female contestants] You young women have gotten old; you've become supermodels and lost your innocence.[1]

When the designer asked the audience whether they agreed that young people needed to represent the next generation by "comporting themselves appropriately" (an mac mot cach phu hop), the crowd responded with vigorous applause.

The assertion that clothing needed to be "appropriate" (phu hop) had surfaced quite often in my conversations with Ho Chi Minh City market sellers, boutique owners, designers, and consumers over the course of nearly two years of research on the sociocultural effects of economic transformations.[2] Excitement about how "open-door" (mo cua) policies had made new styles available, albeit primarily to well-heeled urbanites, was tempered by concern about whether appropriation of foreign fashions would erode a sense of Vietnamese-ness, particularly among impressionable young people.

Figure 6.2
An evening gown
selection. (Photograph
by Ann Marie
Leshkowich.)

The designer echoed this prevalent concern, but she did so with a vehemence and in a setting that raise several questions. Why were the fashion choices of some contestants so upsetting? Why did audience members, most of them contestants' friends and family members, applaud her critique? Finally, given that the event took place under the auspices of the youth organization of the Vietnamese Communist Party and the designer represented a state-run company, how and why was the party or state involved in the fashion choices of youth? In short, why did young people's clothing matter (Tarlo 1996) to their elders and state officials during the late 1990s?

This chapter addresses these questions by examining the youth fashion contest as a diagnostic event (Moore 1987: 730) that dramatized official and popular concerns about the roles, behavior, and attitudes of urban Vietnamese youth. First, I examine the moral panic about youth created and expressed in reports by state-run media. While the overwrought tone of the moral panic hardly matched the realities of most young people's lives and attitudes, I argue that this rhetoric nonetheless needs to be taken seriously as a means through which state organs such as the Ho Chi Minh Communist Youth League use media, expert knowledge, and cultural activities to interpellate (Althusser 1971) youth as particular kinds of citizen–subject–consumers.

Second, I consider how the mode and object of such interpellation has shifted since the "Liberation" (*Giai phong*) of the south by northern-led communist forces in 1975. Formerly hailed as a vanguard to lead workers in radical socialist resistance to oppression and hierarchy, youth under *Doi moi* are exhorted by a Youth League turned media and marketing conglomerate to build the nation by becoming model middle-class consumers, cosmopolitan yet judicious in maintaining cultural traditions in the context of globalization. The rhetoric of moral panic constructs youth as vulnerable and insecure and hence justifies intervention into individual consumer choice as part of attempts to preserve state and party authority under the developmentalist agenda of *Doi moi*.

Finally, I consider the relationship between materiality and morality under both postwar socialism and contemporary *Doi moi* to show why fashion is an important site for interpellating and constructing this new model youth. Rather than a mode of creative, performative play, clothing tends to be viewed as an obvious signifier of one's moral and material status. These are linked, with moral virtue hinging on material position. Economic reforms have shifted this relationship from the straightforward association in which virtue was defined through the position of one's labor in relation to the means of production, to a more freewheeling and ambiguous regime of display through forms of consumption. Immature and vulnerable to alluring commercialized images, youth are thus said to require guidance in how to recognize and enact morally correct consumption. At the same time, the social problem of emerging class inequality under *Doi moi* becomes recast as one of individual morality.

My goal throughout this discussion is to interrogate the discourses surrounding the fashion contest in order to situate debates about youth and clothing within the broader dynamics of social, economic, and political change in Vietnam during the 1990s. This focus and the constraints of space mean that I must neglect other issues raised by the contest. These include (1) why it was the young women, rather than the young men, who failed to meet judges' expectations; and (2) the intentions and goals of contestants in putting together their outfits. With respect to the first issue, elsewhere I compare the contest to other fashion events in Ho Chi Minh City in order to consider dilemmas of gender and mimicry in the use of clothing to construct Vietnamese-ness under *Doi moi* (Leshkowich n.d.). Here I focus on the category of youth as including men and women, all of whom were expected to use clothing in ways that the judges and audience would find appropriate. As for the fascinating and significant issue of contestants' intentionality, I found that their agency was effectively erased within the domain of the contest, as experts seized control over the signification of participants' outfits in a moralizing discourse that constructed youth as recipients, rather than creators, of fashion meanings. My task here is to understand why this happened, and what this reveals about shifting modes of governmentality vis-à-vis youth.

Moral panic

The late 1990s was a time of both optimism and anxiety for many in Ho Chi Minh City. *Doi moi* had resulted in economic prosperity and desire for personal accumulation, the latter recast as an act of patriotism: "*dan giau nuoc manh*" ("wealthy people, strong country"). An increasing number of city residents drove late-model motorbikes, wore designer fashions, and patronized upscale restaurants. Whereas an earlier generation had embraced ideals of struggle and independence with the slogan "*an no mac am*" ("eat enough, dress warmly"), *Doi moi* youth talked about "*an ngon mac dep*" ("eat deliciously, dress beautifully"). The anxiety stemmed from a concern that the consumption craze would become excessive. Were well-heeled urbanites becoming materialistic at the expense of concern for others, including their own family members? Was the desire to be fashionable becoming an obsession?

In media discussions of the allure and corruption of the "new," youth figured centrally. This focus stemmed in part from the demographic fact that by the mid-1990s more than half of the Vietnamese population had been born after the war ended in 1975. While an older generation knew firsthand the sacrifices necessary to secure independence or to move from dressing warmly to dressing beautifully, a younger generation accustomed to privilege might "lose its roots" (*mat goc*) (see, e.g., Drummond 2003: 158). Journalists and academics sketched harrowing portraits of bad youth: lazy, drug-addicted, sexually active, provocatively or sloppily dressed, prone to motorcycle racing, criminal, spendthrift, or irresponsible (Hang Chuc Nguyen 1995; Le Minh 1997: 76; Marr and Rosen 1998: 149–150). The government specifically targeted youth in media and educational campaigns designed to combat the "social evils" (*te nan xa hoi*) of prostitution, drug abuse, and AIDS (Nguyen Phuong An 2007: 288). In some accounts, the blame for this wayward generation fell upon the decadent influence of foreign culture, or what the minister of culture and information called "the flow of garbage from foreign degraded, reactionary culture which is strange to our tradition of humanities, and benevolence" (Nguyen Khoa Diem 1997: 56). Other accounts called upon parents and teachers to provide greater guidance to confused young people (see, e.g., Nguyen Thi Oanh 1995; Rydstrøm 2001: 398).

In the midst of moral panic, clothing provided a convenient measure of youthful morality. An English-language newspaper published by the

Vietnamese News Agency proclaimed, "Many HCM [Ho Chi Minh] City youngsters are crazy about fashion." Their "extravagant" tastes were evident in their shopping habits: "Rather than shop at local markets, the city's newly rich buy stylish clothes and accessories at expensive fashion boutiques" (Cu Mai Cong 1996: 16). If the price of youthful fashion was not cause for alarm, the styles were. Social commentators attempted to decode the meanings of *bui*, an interpretation of grunge that involved T-shirts, unbuttoned plaid shirts, baggy jeans, or miniskirts, all donned with an attitude of ennui. *Bui* became the harbinger of what one journalist worried would be a soulless generation (Cu Mai Cong 1995). As part of a series of articles in the *Tuoi Tre* (Youth) newspaper produced by the Ho Chi Minh Communist Youth League, well-respected sociologist Nguyen Thi Oanh speculated that the grunge styles of youth "obsessed with fashion" signified a quest for identity by those lacking in self-esteem (Nguyen Thi Oanh 1995). Another scholar worried that grunge fashion, perhaps harmless as simply a style, would serve as a point of entry to a delinquent, disaffected subculture alienated from other youth and from elders (Nguyen Minh Hoa 1995: 7). The foreign press quickly picked up these generation-gap concerns with speculations that youth might be staging a quieter, gentler revolution through consumption (Mydans 2000) or more negative depictions of them as "young and insolent" (*The Economist* 1996: 38).

Such accounts of materialistic, disrespectful, rebellious, or ennui-ridden youth match anxieties voiced by elders around the world (see, e.g., Hebdige 1979; White 1993; Valentine et al. 1998; McRobbie 2000 [1991]; Mead 2001 [1928]; Cohen 2002 [1972]; Cole 2007). The tone of moral panic seems to have increased over the past several decades, as the growing availability of mass media targeting youth has intersected with broader anxiety about cultural and social reproduction in the wake of rapid socio-economic change (Comaroff and Comaroff 2001; Graeber 2002; Cole 2007; Durham 2007). In an environment of uncertainty, youth can serve as a convenient symbol of liminality on which to project anxiety (Maira and Soep 2005). As a result, youth studies scholars who might originally have been interested in the disruptive potential of spectacular, irreverent subcultures (Hebdige 1979; Willis 1981 [1977]) have more recently considered the gap between, on the one hand, hyperbolic images of moral panic, deviancy, and shocking styles, and, on the other hand, the more mundane, mainstream realities of young people who are not just active participants in and shapers of mass culture, but are also students, workers, family members, and citizens (White 1993; Thornton 1996; Valentine et al. 1998; McRobbie 2000 [1991]; Miles 2000; Comaroff and Comaroff 2001; Maira 2002; Cole 2007; Cole and Durham 2007). Such scholarship argues that a generation gap is not an inevitable biological fact, but the result of a social process through which groups interact and come to see age as a determining factor of their differences (Cole and Durham 2007).

Consistent with this broader trend, scholars interested in Vietnamese youth over the past decade have tempered accounts of what Marr and Rosen call a "yawning generational gap" (1998: 145) with attention to the actual attitudes of young people. Surveys and qualitative interviews suggest that most young people in Vietnam tend to be rather traditional or conservative. They respect elders' authority over career and other life choices, hope to form families, want political and economic stability, and plan to take care of their parents as they age (see Marr and Rosen 1998; Nilan 1999; Mensch et al. 2003; Nguyen Phuong An 2006; King et al. 2008). When we look beyond the rhetoric of moral panic, youth reveal their most pressing concern to be neither fashion nor rebellion, but education and employment (Nguyen Phuong An 2002; Mensch et al. 2003). At the same time, young people increasingly link their identities to the use of fashion and consumption as tools for articulating issues of sociality and status (Nilan 1999, King et al. 2008). They may be a consumer generation, but materialism does not consume them.

That the moral panic about youth and their dress was more perceived than real does not mitigate the fact that these concerns seemed credible and pressing to officials, academics, journalists, and the broader public. If anything, the situation becomes even more puzzling: in the face of little concrete evidence, why did people view youth as a danger requiring immediate attention? Answering this question requires attending to the source of hyperbolic claims about youth and tracking their effects to determine whose interests the rhetoric served. David Oswell argues that moral panics reflect two impulses:

> The *othering* of young people is, we might argue, constituted within an ambivalence which leads both to the desire to expel these dangerous youths from the realms of decent society (to exclude them from the boundaries of citizenship) and also to the desire to protect them from further harm (to lead them out of the wilderness back into the fold).
>
> (Oswell 1998: 38, emphasis in original)

Oswell's statement implicitly connects both of these desires to issues of power and control over the social and political body. In Vietnam the sources of the panic discourse all had some connection to the state: the minister of culture, a youth newspaper published by the Communist Youth League, and researchers affiliated with state-run institutes. Depictions of the problem of youth were by no means uniform, and they certainly did not result from a central directive. But they do suggest official investment in particular modes of apprehending and correcting transgressions on the part of youth. The moral panic was thus a vehicle through which organs of the state interpellated youth as either good or bad citizens in the midst of rapid economic, social, and cultural change. Although the context of the 1990s moral panic may have been new, this mode of interpellation was consistent with a much longer history of party and state reliance on youth to advance the project of socialism.

Hailing youth under socialism and late socialism

Louis Althusser defines interpellation as an ideological process through which the state, via its agents, hails an individual. In responding, the individual becomes a subject identified according to the terms by which he or she was hailed and hence tacitly consents to the ideology that constructed the hailing (Althusser 1971: 174–175). While Althusser's model depicts power relations monolithically, it nonetheless can prove helpful in thinking about how processes of defining and constructing categories of persons said to be endowed with particular attributes might be a strategy of governmentality through which the state attempts to engage and manage its citizens.

Throughout its history, the Vietnamese Communist Party has interpellated youth as a cornerstone of its strategy of mass mobilization. According to Helle Rydstrøm, Vietnamese tend to think of youth as blank slates, or "like white pieces of paper" (*nhu mot to giay trang*) (Rydstrøm 2001: 394). As such, they need to be inscribed with moral values through education and socialization. Their "whiteness" makes them vulnerable to bad influences, but this can be offset by surrounding them with role models, such as their parents or exemplary peers, whom they can "imitate" (*bat chuoc*) (ibid.: 398).

These notions of socialization and imitation guided communist youth organizing and educational activities throughout the twentieth century. In 1925, Ho Chi Minh founded the Viet Nam Revolutionary Youth League (Viet Nam Thanh Nien Cach Menh Dong Chi Hoi) (Duiker 1972: 475). The League included a Communist Youth Group (Thanh Nien Cong San Doan) which organized and agitated from its exile base in Canton through its official journal, *Thanh Nien* (Youth) (ibid.: 481). Later renamed the Ho Chi Minh Communist Youth League, the group served as a vanguard for anti-French mobilization. Following the establishment of a communist-led government in the north in 1954, the league's political connections and educational training provided a means of upward mobility (Marr and Rosen 1998: 146). Youth also played a central role in the Democratic Republic of Vietnam's fight against the American-supported southern regime. For example, the sacrifices and hardships endured by Thanh Nien Xung Phong (Volunteer Youth) in keeping the Ho Chi Minh Trail open have become legendary (Turner 1998; McElwee 2005; Phinney 2005; Werner 2006). When the victorious regime sought after 1975 to implement its policies of restructuring economic and social relations in the south, it was youth brigades who were mobilized to confiscate private property and proselytize about new policies (Leshkowich 2008: 21).

During the 1990s, the state and party had to reinvent themselves as their policies shifted from radical mobilization in service of centrally planned socialism to neoliberal embracing of market forces to promote national development. Once again, however, officials hailed youth as central to these goals. One party pronouncement declared:

Whether the cause of *doi moi* will be successful or not, whether the country . . . will gain a deserving position in the world community or not, whether the Vietnamese revolution will firmly follow the path of socialism or not, it depends largely on the force of youth, and on the educating and training of young generations. The matter of youth is a matter of life and death for the nation, and one of the decisive factors for the success or failure of the revolution.

(Vietnamese Communist Party 1993: 82, quoted in Nguyen Phuong An 2006: 330)

In a book establishing youth as a field for academic research, Dang Canh Khanh portrayed this sentiment as scientific fact: "Social research and sociological surveys [on the Vietnamese youth] in recent times have shown that the remarkable successes of the reform process have created a confident and energetic generation of youth who are looking forward to the future" (Dang Canh Khanh 1996: 24, quoted in Nguyen Phuong An 2002: 225). As an antidote to the wayward youth depicted in the moral panic, the party continued to use mass organizations such as the Young Pioneers to identify and reward virtuous role models (Rydstrøm 2001: 399).

Images of youth as central to revolutionary goals may have been an effective hailing technique to mobilize young people against French or American troops, but there was evidence that this rhetoric wore thin once the national mission shifted from independence to wealth and consumerism. Although Dang Canh Khanh asserted that more youth than ever wished to join the Youth League and Communist Party (Dang Canh Khanh 1996: 24, quoted in Nguyen Phuong An 2002: 225), most observers reported declining membership in the 1990s (see, e.g., Marr and Rosen 1998; Nilan 1999; Nguyen Phuong An 2006). The party's broader influence was also said to have decreased. For example, Nguyen Phuong An found that most young people in Hanoi, the seat of state and party power, were not aware of the various campaigns supposedly directed at them (Nguyen Phuong An 2006: 333). A reporter for *Time* magazine summed up the prevailing sense that the party had become irrelevant to the younger generation:

It's a whole new world. Vietnam's younger generation has escaped from under the very eyes of the government, which didn't even see them going. The Party's authority no longer reaches across the generation gap, and a huge empty space has opened up in society for youngsters to prosper—or self-destruct.

(McCarthy 2000)

The influence of traditional mass mobilization techniques may have been waning, but to conclude from this that the state or party was losing its ability to manage youth would be to neglect the ways in which *Doi moi* had inaugurated a shift in its mode of interpellation. The state and party were not just the architects of market-oriented policies, they were key economic players. Throughout the 1990s the dominant form of enterprise was in state hands, either through direct ownership of factories or retail outlets, or through joint ventures between foreign companies and state entities such as the army (Gainsborough 2003). Add to this the state's continued direct management of a growing range of media, and it becomes clear that the government was the major producer and distributor of consumer goods, and also a generator of consumer desire for those products through advertisements and media coverage of key trends.

Consistent with this development, the Ho Chi Minh Communist Youth League during the 1990s became a major presence in the fashion industry. In collaboration with Ringier Switzerland, the league produced a popular fashion magazine, *Thoi Trang Tre* (New Fashion). The Youth League developed a joint venture to produce and market styles designed by a young Vietnamese American, while an additional league-run company provided advertising and marketing consultants. The league's more traditional publications, such as the newspaper *Tuoi Tre* (Youth), analyzed fashion and lifestyle trends. Finally, the league provided direct programming on elements of mass culture and popular trends, such as the Fashion Club that sponsored the New Year's fashion contest.

In urban areas, state lifestyle marketing constructed the ideal middle-class consumer as "civilized" (*van minh*) and "cultured" (*co van hoa*); conversant with cosmopolitan trends, yet judiciously maintaining select elements of traditional Vietnamese style and values. Women were the most obvious symbols in these campaigns, either as decorous housewives managing their families' emotions and finances, or as disordered subjects liable to behave crassly or wantonly (Pettus 2003; Drummond and Rydstrøm 2004; Leshkowich 2005). Thu-Huong Nguyen-Vo finds these campaigns to deploy both disciplinary and coercive tactics: magazine features (in publications run by the Women's Union), courses on domestic arts (sponsored by the Women's Union), and manuals on conjugal happiness (from government-employed researchers) shaped middle-class women, while incarceration and reeducation tried to mold prostitutes and other undesirables into a docile working class (Nguyen-Vo 2002). Although programs targeting youth have not received as much attention from scholars, the Youth League followed similar strategies. Symbolically, the housewife and the prostitute find their youthful counterparts in the model student or worker and the delinquent engaged in social evils. Just as the Women's Union sought to guide women in developing taste and domestic management skills through instruction and media, the Youth League deployed a combination of pedagogy and reform through recreational programming, newspapers, magazines, and educational campaigns.

Rather than retreat from involvement in individuals' daily lives, the transformation of the party's mass mobilization organizations into diversified production, retail, and marketing conglomerates suggests that the state shifted the arena in which it engaged youth. Revolutionary politics morphed into cosmopolitan style. In the process, commerce became an ideological tool. In her study of teenaged girls' readership of fashion and lifestyle magazines, Angela McRobbie describes media as part of a Gramscian private sphere of civil society in which "teenage girls are subjected to an explicit attempt to win consent to the dominant order—in terms of femininity, leisure, and consumption, i.e. at the level of culture" (2000 [1991]: 73). What McRobbie describes in England as an *"unspoken* consensus" (ibid.: 75, italics in original) between state ideologues and private publishing, becomes in Vietnam, because of the direct involvement of state entities in commerce, an explicit attempt to hail particular kinds of citizen-consumers whose activities affirm party leadership. According to Nguyen Bich Thuan and Mandy Thomas, "The state is developing a new relationship with consumers, testing the ground of possibility by simultaneously authorizing and disallowing. Working in tandem with mass culture, a new mass-oriented state has become the mark of the postsocialist era" (2004: 135). Fun, fashion, and taste become matters of politics and patriotism.

For their part, the young people I encountered, all of them self-identifying as upwardly mobile and responsible, seemed receptive to this guidance. Although many described party leaders as behind the times and eschewed direct membership in the Youth League, they welcomed expert advice. The imbrication of the Youth League, Women's Union, or other party organs into production, retail, and marketing meant that they provided the platform through which expertise was filtered to the general public. As a result, the values that most young people held in fact paralleled those emphasized by the party (see, e.g., Nguyen Phuong An 2006).

While urban youth may not have overtly accepted the guidance of the "party," they did respect the expertise deployed by that party. This became clear to me when a university student in her twenties who had accompanied me to the fashion contest assured me that the designer's critical rebuke was accurate, necessary, and appropriate. This young woman, who considered herself independent-minded and iconoclastic, patiently told me, "With status comes the responsibility to instruct those below you. The designer has to teach us how to understand fashion." In their desire to become models of middle-class decorum and responsibility, this woman and others like her were heeding the hail of a state apparatus.

Moralizing clothing

Clearly, the open-door policies of *Doi moi* had generated anxiety about cultural identity that coalesced into attempts to mold proper Vietnamese young people. Why, however, was clothing a key element of these efforts? What exactly was the understanding of fashion that contestants at the Youth

Cultural House needed to acquire? The answer has to do with the ways in which outward appearance reflects inner goodness—a correspondence between materiality and morality that the Vietnamese Communist Party has reinforced since Liberation in 1975 as part of a broader effort to link national goals to individual subjectivity.

At the end of the war in 1975, the victorious regime attempted to restructure the southern part of the country by determining the economic status and political affiliations of individuals and families. Consistent with Marxist materialism, one's identity and character hinged on one's relation to the means of production. Workers and peasants were held up as moral exemplars; by not owning property, they had not been corrupted by oppressing or dispossessing someone else. The simple purity of the working classes or masses was represented in their dress: inexpensive, utilitarian styles without artifice.

In the logic of the revolutionary vanguard, a larger number of exemplary socialist worker-citizens could be created through imitation of the model peasant or proletariat. Officials thus explicitly rejected the transnational youth culture of the 1960s and 1970s by promoting an ethic of discipline in body and spirit common to socialist revolutionary movements throughout the world (see, e.g., Burgess 2002: 288). Donning socialist clothing styles would build a new citizen from the outside in—an inverted version of the "fake it 'til you make it" dictum. Because they were still deciding what they wanted to be, youth were particularly urged to make careful clothing choices. Just before the New Year in 1978, Ho Chi Minh City's *Tuoi Tre* (Youth) newspaper provided a full-page feature on proposed new outfits for various kinds of young people. The text emphasized the importance of clothing:

> Choosing for yourself an outfit/uniform (*dong phuc*) also means that you are choosing for yourself a career service, a position in order to implement your ideals, obligations, and dreams. Have you chosen a position for yourself yet? If you haven't, then you should ascertain it soon.
>
> (*Tuoi Tre* 1978: 17)

Accompanying the article were drawings of simple, modest, and functional styles for different professions and mass organizations, including office workers, laborers, and volunteer youth brigades (see Figures 6.3a and 6.3b).

By the 1990s the content of fashion styles had clearly changed. In fact, a key part of the allure of the fashion craze was the opportunity, particularly for women, to experiment with more elaborate styles that departed from the austere, androgynous look of the postwar decade. At the same time, the fashion contest suggests that clothing continued to be viewed as a straightforward projection of identity that reflected the close association between socioeconomic status and individual morality.

Figure 6.3a Attire for vocational students (*Tuoi Tre* (Youth) 1978: 17).

The day after the fashion contest, I interviewed the designer who had been so disturbed by the young participants' outfits. She told me that she was worried that young Vietnamese were becoming dangerously obsessed with foreign fashion. In her view, fashion is both a product of economic status and a means to express personal and cultural identity. This explained her comment that the contestants were wearing clothing that was not appropriate for the lifestyles of Ho Chi Minh City residents. How, she wondered, can you maneuver a motorbike through city traffic in a white gown with an elaborate train? The choices were not just impractical, she told me, they were immoral. The goal of fashion was to help Vietnamese forge a unique sense of style that was individual, yet part of a broader national identity. As with other Youth League programming, the contest organizers intended the event to promote exemplary youth who could serve as fash-

Figure 6.3b
Attire for Youth Union
office workers and
administrators (*Tuoi Tre*
(Youth) 1978: 17).

ion role models. Instead, the designer had witnessed confusion: "Because of waves of different cultural influences, the girls don't know how to choose for themselves, they don't know how to create a 'character' [she used the English word] for themselves." Her mission was to chart Vietnam's fashion course by guiding people in acquiring powers of discernment and critiquing missteps. Without expert guidance, Vietnam might become what she decried as the "second Hong Kong." She explained, "Although Hong Kong clothes are pretty and cheap, I think that they're only copies cribbed from the other nations around the world. They don't have their own style."

That the designer used the English word "character" to describe the distinct Vietnamese identity that she believed the young fashion contestants lacked poses an irony reminiscent of the dangers of mimicry identified by Homi Bhabha (1997). Yet the term also permits an instructive double meaning: character can be both a persona projected outward, as in a play, and one's own inner moral worth. In the designer's view—one consistent with broader opinion in Vietnam, including among party officials—these should be consistent: surface should reflect substance. The fashion choices in the contest were problematic not just because they were uninspired or unattractive, but because the sartorial confusion betrayed a vulnerability to external influences stemming from an uncertain inner character. Sociologist Nguyen Thi Oanh made this logic explicit in her assessment of the *bui* (grunge) trend: "Excessively following fashion is in fact an inclination to look for one's identity, to look for a foothold in the midst of insecurity" (1995: 6). Although such confusion was an understandable part of maturation, it was not acceptable at an event explicitly designed to provide exemplars for young people to follow.

To draw together the threads of this analysis, the fashion contest revealed that despite massive shifts in political goals and styles of dress, the party continued to attempt to ground moral personhood in materialism. The pure peasant or proletarian may have been replaced by the civilized middle-class urbanite, but clothing remained a key signifier of one's virtue. Dress has often been interpreted as what Terence Turner (1980) termed the "social skin," but this characterization tends to emphasize fluidity: the performative potential to change identity or status by donning a different look (see, e.g., Hansen 2000: 4–5). As economic reforms accelerated processes of class differentiation in urban areas, it was precisely this kind of fluidity that worried state leadership. While many Vietnamese sought to dress aspirationally and fashion magazines in the 1990s advised them about how to do so, there was nonetheless tremendous anxiety about a shift similar to that noted by Richard Sennett in his account of the aftermath of the French Revolution: presentation in a system of fixed statuses had given way to representation in an environment of new socioeconomic differentiations (Sennett (1992 [1977]: 39–42, quoted in Hansen 2000: 4).

Under *Doi moi*, the shift in the locus of meaning from position in production to status through consumption threatened to disrupt the equation between class status, morality, and outward appearance. Whereas an individual's position in production was obviously social, in that it depended on a broader economic system subject to government oversight, consumption could be an individualistic, anarchic affair. Individuals and media outlets affiliated with the state tended to respond to this dilemma by reinterpreting individual style choices as anchored in a broader social morality and cultural identity, through such concepts as "appropriate" (*phu hop*), "modern" (*hien dai*), and "civilized" (*van minh*). In her analysis of Vietnamese television shows during the 1990s, Pam Nilan notes a tendency to treat "social issues as *moral* issues in the private lives of the characters" (Nilan 1999: 366, italics in original). Nilan implies this conflation to be a smokescreen: an attempt to absolve the state of responsibility for the problems of rapid socioeconomic change by shifting blame to individuals. The youth fashion contest suggests a different interpretation: defining social issues as problems of individual moral character might allow the various apparatuses of the state to interpellate citizens on the new terrain of the market. Through deploying a moral discourse of appropriateness and engaging in pedagogical efforts to establish its parameters through the fashion media, design and retail businesses, and recreational activities, the Ho Chi Minh Communist Youth League defined the individual problem of what to wear as a public moral concern that required the guidance of experts, many of whom were conveniently in its employ.

Conclusion

The Spring Fashion Contest illuminated a controversy about what clothing would be appropriate for Vietnamese teenagers and twenty-somethings that was part of a reconfiguration of state–youth relationships in the wake of economic changes from centrally planned socialism to a market-oriented economy. In contrast to representations of youth as rejecting the party, and the state as retreating from control over daily life, this chapter has highlighted how an activist state fomented such controversy as part of a shift in the modes through which it organized citizens (see also Zhang 2001; Gainsborough 2002; King et al. 2008). In the 1990s, the Vietnamese Communist Party moved from organizing a vanguard of urban working-class and revolutionary youth to developing a skilled, savvy middle class of consumers whose fashion choices would embody the success of the state developmentalist and civilizing agenda. It attempted to do so in part by reinterpreting issues of social status and economic transformation as questions of individual moral character in ways that would make citizens receptive to expert guidance. Clothing became central to these efforts because it was widely presumed to be an outward projection of inner character. Youth, for reasons related to their symbolic association with the future, their active participation in broader circuits of popular culture, and their receptiveness to moral inscription, became objects of state attempts to hail and fashion them as appropriate Vietnamese consumers by drawing them into a nexus of discourse and instruction overseen by an increasingly entrepreneurial Ho Chi Minh Communist Youth League. Vietnamese youth in the 1990s may have increasingly eschewed party membership, but the applause that greeted the designer's critique of the participants at the Spring Fashion Contest suggests that they, their parents, and the broader public willingly answered the hail of consumerism issued by a party that had reinvented itself as a savvy arbiter of style.

Notes

1. Unless otherwise indicated, all translations from Vietnamese are my own.
2. I conducted ethnographic fieldwork in Ho Chi Minh City for twenty-one months between 1995 and 1997, with follow-up visits in 2003–2004 and 2007–2008. My research focused on cloth and clothing sellers in the city's central market-place and consisted of daily participant observation and extended life-history interviews. To get a broader sense of how changing fashion tastes affected stallholders' businesses, I conducted research on the fashion industry which included interviews with prominent designers and boutique owners, attendance at fashion shows and beauty contests, and analysis of fashion publications. All research was conducted in Vietnamese.

References

Althusser, Louis (1971) "Ideology and Ideological State Apparatuses," in *Lenin and Philosophy and Other Essays*, New York: Monthly Review Press.

Bhabha, Homi (1997) "Of Mimicry and Man: The Ambivalence of Colonial Discourse," in Frederick Cooper and Ann Laura Stoler (eds.), *Tensions of Empire: Colonial Cultures in a Bourgeois World*, Berkeley: University of California Press.

Burgess, Thomas (2002) "Cinema, Bell Bottoms, and Miniskirts: Struggles over Youth and Citizenship in Revolutionary Zanzibar," *International Journal of African Historical Studies*, 35(2): 287–313.

Cohen, Stanley (2002) [1972] *Folk Devils and Moral Panics: The Creation of the Mods and Rockers* (3rd edition), Oxford: Basil Blackwell.

Cole, Jennifer (2007) "Fresh Contact in Tamatave, Madagascar: Sex, Money, and Intergenerational Transformation," in Jennifer Cole and Deborah Durham (eds.), *Generations and Globalization: Youth, Age, and Family in the New World Economy*, Bloomington and Indianapolis: University of Indiana Press.

Cole, Jennifer and Durham, Deborah (2007) "Age, Regeneration, and the Intimate Politics of Globalization," in Jennifer Cole and Deborah Durham (eds.), *Generations and Globalization: Youth, Age, and Family in the New World Economy*, Bloomington and Indianapolis: University of Indiana Press.

Comaroff, Jean and Comaroff, John L. (2001) "Millennial Capitalism: First Thoughts on a Second Coming," in Jean and John L. Comaroff (eds.), *Millennial Capitalism and the Culture of Neoliberalism*, Durham and London: Duke University Press.

Cu Mai Cong (1995) "Thoi Trang 'Bui'" [Grunge Fashion], *Tuoi Tre* [Youth], September 21: 6.

—— (1996) "Fashion Obsession Hits HCMC," *Vietnam News*, November 22: 16.

Dang Canh Khanh (1996) "Khi Thanh Nien Tro Thanh Doi Tuong Nghien Cuu Khoa Hoc" [When Youth Becomes a Subject of Science Research], in Dang Canh Khanh et al. (eds.), *Nghien Cuu Thanh Nien: Ly Luan Va Thuc Tien* [Studying Youth: Theory and Practice], Hanoi: Nha Xuat Ban Thanh Nien.

Drummond, Lisa B. W. (2003) "Popular Television and Images of Urban Life," in Lisa B. W. Drummond and Mandy Thomas (eds.), *Consuming Urban Culture in Contemporary Vietnam*, London and New York: Routledge Curzon.

Drummond, Lisa and Rydstrøm, Helle (2004) "Introduction," in Lisa Drummond and Helle Rydstrøm (eds.), *Gender Practices in Contemporary Vietnam*, Singapore: Singapore University Press.

Duiker, William J. (1972) "The Revolutionary Youth League: Cradle of Communism in Vietnam," *China Quarterly*, 51: 475–499.

Durham, Deborah (2007) "Empowering Youth: Making Youth Citizens in Botswana," in Jennifer Cole and Deborah Durham (eds.), *Generations and Globalization: Youth, Age, and Family in the New World Economy*, Bloomington and Indianapolis: University of Indiana Press.

The Economist (1996) "Young and Insolent," April 27: 38.

Gainsborough, Martin. (2002) "Political Change in Vietnam: In Search of the Middle Class Challenge to the State," *Asian Survey*, 42(5): 694–707.

—— (2003) "Slow, Quick, Quick: Assessing Equitization and Enterprise Performance Prospects in Vietnam," *Journal of Communist Studies and Transition Politics*, 19(1): 49–63.

Graeber, David (2002) "The Anthropology of Globalization (with Notes on Neomedievalism, and the End of the Chinese Model of the Nation-State)," *American Anthropologist*, 104(4): 1222–1227.

Hang Chuc Nguyen (1995), "Khi Vat Chat Che Khuat Dao Ly, Nhan Tinh" [When Things Obscure Principles, Human Feeling], *Tuoi Tre Chu Nhat* [Sunday Youth], November 5: 7.

Hansen, Karen Tranberg (2000) *Salaula: The World of Secondhand Clothing in Zambia*, Chicago and London: University of Chicago Press.

Hebdige, Dick (1979) *Subculture: The Meaning of Style*, London and New York: Routledge.

King, Victor T., Phuong An Nguyen, and Nguyen Huu Minh (2008) "Professional Middle Class Youth in Post-Reform Vietnam: Identity, Continuity, and Change," *Modern Asian Studies*, 42(4): 783–813.

Le Minh (1997) "Some Problems about the Family and Women Advancement," *Vietnam Social Sciences*, 1(57): 71–80.

Leshkowich, Ann Marie (n.d.) "Making Modernity Appropriate: Dress, Mimesis, and Gender in Ho Chi Minh City," article in preparation.

—— (2005) "Feminine Disorder: State Campaigns against Street Traders in Socialist and Late Socialist Vietnam," in Gisèle Bousquet and Nora Taylor (eds.), *Le Vietnam au Féminin*, Paris: Les Indes Savantes.

—— (2008) "Wandering Ghosts of Late Socialism: Conflict, Metaphor, and Memory in a Southern Vietnamese Marketplace," *Journal of Asian Studies*, 67(1): 5–41.

McCarthy, Terry (2000) "The Kids Are All Right: A Generation of Vietnamese, Born after the End of the War, Set their Eyes on the Future," *Time*, 156(2), available at http://www.time.com/time/asia/features/ontheroad/vietnam.kids.html (accessed October 4, 2007).

McElwee, Pamela (2005) "'There is Nothing that is Difficult': History and Hardship on the Ho Chi Minh Trail in Ha Tinh, North Vietnam," *Asia Pacific Journal of Anthropology*, 6(3): 197–214.

McRobbie, Angela (2000) [1991] *Feminism and Youth Culture* (2nd edition), New York: Routledge.

Maira, Sunaina Marr (2002) *Desis in the House: Indian American Youth Culture in New York City*, Philadelphia: Temple University Press.

Maira, Sunaina and Elisabeth Soep (2005) "Introduction," in Sunaina Maira and

Elisabeth Soep (eds.), *Youthscapes: The Popular, the National, the Global*, Philadelphia: University of Pennsylvania Press.

Marr, David and Rosen, Stanley (1998) "Chinese and Vietnamese Youth in the 1990s," *The China Journal* 40: 145–172.

Mead, Margaret (2001) [1928] *Coming of Age in Samoa*, New York: Harper Perennial Modern Classics.

Mensch, Barbara S., Clark, Wesley H., and Dang Nguyen Anh (2003) "Adolescents in Vietnam: Looking beyond Reproductive Health," *Studies in Family Planning*, 34(4): 249–262.

Miles, Steven (2000) *Youth Lifestyles in a Changing World*, Buckingham and Philadelphia: Open University Press.

Moore, Sally Falk (1987) "Explaining the Present: Theoretical Dilemmas in Processual Ethnography," *American Ethnologist*, 14(4): 727–736.

Mydans, Seth (2000) "Vietnam's Youth Stage a Gentler Revolution," *New York Times*, November 12: WK6.

Nguyen Bich Thuan and Thomas, Mandy (2004) "Young Women and Emergent Postsocialist Sensibilities in Contemporary Vietnam," *Asian Studies Review*, 28: 133–149.

Nguyen Khoa Diem (1997) "Some Problems of Culture and Urban Lifestyle in our Country at Present," *Vietnam Social Sciences*, 6(62): 50–58.

Nguyen Minh Hoa (1995) "Co The Chap Nhan Thoi Trang Bui?" [Can We Accept Bui Fashion?], *Tuoi Tre* [Youth], October 17: 6.

Nguyen Phuong An (2002) "Looking Beyond *Bien Che*: The Considerations of Youth Vietnamese Graduates when Seeking Employment in the *Doi moi* Era," *Sojourn*, 17(2): 221–248.

—— (2006) "State–Society Relations in Contemporary Vietnam: An Examination of the Arena of Youth," *Asia Pacific Viewpoint*, 47(3): 327–341.

—— (2007) "'Relationships Based on Love and Relationships Based on Needs': Emerging Trends in Youth Sex Culture in Contemporary Urban Vietnam," *Modern Asian Studies*, 41(2): 287–313.

Nguyen Thi Oanh (1995) "Model Bui—Nhung Ban Tre Dang di Tim Minh" [Bui Style—Young People in Search of Themselves], *Tuoi Tre* [Youth], October 10: 6.

Nguyen-Vo, Thu-Huong (2002) "Governing Sex: Medicine and Governmental Intervention in Prostitution," in Jayne Werner and Danièle Bélanger (eds.), *Gender, Household, State: Doi moi in Vietnam*, Ithaca: Cornell University Southeast Asia Program.

Nilan, Pam (1999) "Young People and Globalizing Trends in Vietnam," *Journal of Youth Studies*, 2(3): 353–370.

Oswell, David (1998) "A Question of Belonging: Television, Youth, and the Domestic," in Tracey Skelton and Gill Valentine (eds.), *Cool Places: Geographies of Youth Culture*, London and New York: Routledge.

Pettus, Ashley (2003) *Between Sacrifice and Desire: National Identity and the Governing of Femininity in Vietnam*, New York and London: Routledge.

Phinney, Harriet (2005) "The Shifting yet Conventional Logic of Sex and Reproduction in Northern Viet Nam: Post-war Refashioning of Single Women's Reproductive Space," *Asia Pacific Journal of Anthropology*, 6(3): 215–230.

Rydstrøm, Helle (2001) "'Like a White Piece of Paper': Embodiment and the Moral Upbringing of Vietnamese Children," *Ethnos*, 66(3): 394–413.

Sennett, Richard (1992) [1977] *The Fall of Public Man*, New York: Knopf.

Tarlo, Emma (1996) *Clothing Matters: Dress and Identity in India*, Chicago: University of Chicago Press.

Thornton, Sarah (1996) *Club Cultures: Music, Media, and Subcultural Capital*, Middletown, CT: Wesleyan University Press.

Tuoi Tre [Youth] (1978) "Ngay Xuan Chon Cho Minh Bo Quan Ao Dep Nhat" [This Spring, Choose the Prettiest Outfit for Yourself], So Mau Ngo [Mau Ngo New Year's edition]: 17.

Turner, Karen Gottschang, with Phan Thanh Hao (1998) *Even the Women Must Fight: Memories of War from North Vietnam*, New York: Wiley.

Turner, Terence (1980) "The Social Skin," in Jeremy Cherfas and Roger Lewin (eds.), *Not Work Alone: A Cross-cultural View of Activities Superfluous to Survival*, London: Temple Smith, 110–140.

Valentine, Gill, Skelton, Tracey, and Chambers, Deborah (1998) "Cool Places: An Introduction to Youth and Youth Cultures," in Tracey Skelton and Gill Valentine (eds.), *Cool Places: Geographies of Youth Culture*, London and New York: Routledge.

Vietnamese Communist Party (1993) *Van Kien Hoi Nghi Lan Thu 4 Ban Chap Hanh Trung Uong Dang Khoa VII* [Documents of the 4th Session of the 7th Central Executive Committee of the Party], Hanoi: Nha Xuat Ban Chinh Tri Quoc Gia.

Werner, Jayne S. (2006) "Between Memory and Desire: Gender and the Remembrance of War in *Doi moi* Vietnam," *Gender, Place, and Culture*, 13(3): 303–315.

White, Merry (1993) *The Material Child: Coming of Age in Japan and America*, New York: The Free Press.

Willis, Paul (1981) [1977] *Learning to Labor: How Working Class Kids Get Working Class Jobs*, New York: Columbia University Press.

Zhang, Li (2001) *Strangers in the City: Reconfigurations of Space, Power, and Social Networks within China's Floating Population*, Stanford: Stanford University Press.

Chapter 7

Youth, gender, and secondhand clothing in Lusaka, Zambia

Local and global styles

Karen Tranberg Hansen

"Watch Lusaka," argued Samuel Ngoma, a feature writer for one of the daily newspapers in Zambia. "All who are gorgeously attired mostly get their clothes abroad." The capital's so-called boutiques, he went on, "have become rather like museums . . . Neither Lusaka's Cairo Road nor Kamwala shopping area is the place to look. You have a better chance at the second-hand clothes dealer, the flea market or even the city centre market dealer who jaunts between Lusaka and Johannesburg" (Ngoma 1995). To be sure, people in Zambia have shaped their material culture, including their dress, with commodities and ideas from far away. Their lively interest in clothing is not a new thing. The anthropologists who conducted research on urban life in Zambia during the colonial period were struck by the active interest Africans took in dress (Wilson 1941–1942; Mitchell 1956; Mitchell and Epstein 1959; Powdermaker 1962). Their preoccupations were with Western-style dress, a matter that many scholars examining dress practice in Africa have understood only through its Western origin rather than with reference to local use.

Today in Lusaka, influences "from outside," as Zambians refer to the world away from home, are more present, and more visibly evident, than they have ever been. Five shopping malls have opened since 1995 when Samuel Ngoma wrote this feature article. Increasing interaction across space and the consciousness of such processes are due to globalization understood broadly in Ida Susser and Jane Schneider's words, as an "integrated phenom-enon bringing all the world's cities into a single interconnected life" (2003: 2). In this view, cities like Lusaka are stages for the translation of globalization into local terms. When we trace the secondhand clothing commodity chain all the way to places like Lusaka, as I have done in my work (Hansen 2000b), we will realize that it is African consumer demand and specifically the desire to be well dressed that drives this industry. In short, we must bring the local geography of consumption, with its spaces, agents, and performances, into the global story in which dressed bodies become the point of contact between local knowledge and the broader global context. It is from this angle that I approach my discussion of dress practice, including of secondhand clothing, in Lusaka, with specific focus on young people (Figure 7.1).

Figure 7.1 Sign painting on small-scale fashion shop, 2003. Photograph by Karen Tranberg Hansen.

The international secondhand clothing trade is a part of the global circuit of garment production, although it is rarely explained in that way (Gereffi and Korzeniewicz 1994; Rivoli 2005). This circuit moves Western-style clothing, much of it manufactured in developing countries, into markets and stores in the developed world. Since the early 1990s in the West, high-level consumerism facilitated by declining prices of apparel and footwear, especially women's, has ensured the creation of a vast amount of clothing we no longer wear and which we donate from time to time to charitable organizations. The vast surplus of unsold donated clothing collected by such organizations constitutes a commodity chain in the global garment production circuit in its transfer to textile graders and processors who sort and bale the clothesdestined for export. The consequences of this trade are manifold and controversial (Hansen 2004a). As scholars of material culture, we must not take their Western significance for granted. For secondhand garments do not travel with ready-made meanings attached to them, but rather, their meanings change at different stages of the process (Kopytoff 1986). In the view of consumers in Zambia, the only Western thing about such clothes is their origin.

This is why globalization does not produce uniformity in dress practice even though we all wear many of the same garments and accessories, for example jeans and sneakers, shirts and dresses, and suits and ties. It is also why the term "Western dress" is a misnomer (Eicher 1995:4) that ought to be referred to as "world fashion" (Eicher and Sumberg 1995) or "global fashion" (Hansen 2004c, Maynard 2004). The meaning of dress does not inhere in the garments themselves, but is created in the practices through which they are put to use. It is in clothing performance, I argue, that meanings are lodged and constructed by wearers and viewers, and therefore meanings are a product of distinct dress practices in specific situations (Hansen 2003). These observations apply perforce to the import of secondhand clothing to Africa in the analysis of which the association of the West is so hegemonic that it is a challenge to argue—as I do here—for creative localization. The few Western observers who have paid passing attention to the flourishing secondhand clothing markets in many African cities have viewed the dress practices such markets are giving rise to as a faded and worn imitation of the West; that is, as the flip side of Western fashion (Haggblade 1990). In such accounts, the special significance of dress—its unique ability to mediate between the self and society—becomes entirely incidental. As dress scholars we must ask what, aside from their utilitarian value for money, in fact accounts for the attractions of imported secondhand clothing?

In Zambia, dressing, and dressing up, are both an end and a means. Dress is a resource as well as a technique. There is a genuine pleasure to be gained from being dressed well which in the view of local observers is a sign of well-being. It is a very long time—during the early colonial period—since rural and urban Zambians eagerly accepted Western-styled garments and made them their own. But while preoccupations with the dressed body are of long standing, specifically styled garments have come and gone. This preoccupation constitutes an aesthetic sensibility that implicates discerning skills from a variety of sources in creating an overall look resulting in pride, pleasure, and experiences of feeling good. In this way, clothing is part of the aesthetic of everyday life. Mediating between self and society, the dressed body also construes desires, including global imaginaries. As a cultural and material resource, secondhand clothing does all of these things.

In their engagements with the West's used clothing, consumers in Zambia reconstruct these garments as "new" or "fresh" and transform them by notions of taste and selection to fit the embodied dress norms of their local clothing universe. It is by crafting themselves through dress that Zambian wearers of secondhand clothing achieve the look they call "the latest," that fluid appearance of change and novelty that we tend to associate with fashion (Finkelstein 1998). But even if the effect of such appearances is rarely precise or explicit but fluid and volatile, appearance itself is not arbitrary. Rather it is the product of a set of clearly identifiable, interacting practices the effects of which converge in the moment of display. Behind the commanding appearances of "the latest" lies a series of practices that entail competence in dealing with garment fabrics, as well as strategy and rehearsal of the ways in which people dress. I call the critical skill that is central to consumers' clothing savvy "clothing competence."

This chapter describes how the West's discarded clothing becomes fashion for young people in Zambia's capital, Lusaka, in a process expressing a vibrant aesthetic sensibility in its cultivation of appearances that make people take notice, with admiration or opprobrium as the case may be. As background information, I first provide a brief overview of the secondhand clothing markets in Zambia. Then I explore how fashion works in some specific cases. I begin with examples of young men's dress preferences, turning then to young middle- to upper-income women's preoccupation with their dressed self-presentation in public settings. I argue that the meanings of "new" or "fresh" and "the latest" do not inhere in the garments themselves but are constructed anew in each context. While the crafting of "the latest" hinges both on the material properties of garments and on identifiable "techniques of the body" (Entwistle 2000; Mauss 1973), the process also has an affecting hold that makes heads turn. When this occurs, the problematic reference to the Western origin of these clothes has long vanished.

Secondhand clothing markets in Zambia

Zambia is one of the world's least-developed countries. This was not always the case, but the economy has been on a downward slide since the mid-1970s. Between 1980 and 1994, Zambia received numerous structural adjustment loans from the World Bank and its sister agency, the International Monetary Fund. Although the country's gross national product has improved in recent years, today Zambians are poorer, on a per capita basis, than they were at independence from British colonial rule in 1964. Yet the enormous cross-over appeal of secondhand clothing cannot be explained merely in terms of its affordability to poor people, but above all by reference to the importance people attribute to dress and appearance.

In both past and present Zambia, people have been eager to cut a fine figure. Dressing in secondhand clothes has been part of this active engagement with clothing for a long time. In the 1940s and 1950s such clothes were brought across the border from the Belgian Congo into Northern Rhodesia, as Zambia was then known. Since the mid-1980s, secondhand clothing has been imported directly from the United States and Europe into Zambia. Importers truck container-loads of secondhand clothes from ports in South Africa, Mozambique, and Tanzania to Zambia's capital, Lusaka, where they wholesale bales. Small-scale vendors and itinerant traders in turn retail the clothes in local markets and distribute them across the country. After a period of rapid growth during the first half of the 1990s, the import and local trade in secondhand clothes appears to have become an established part of the clothing scene that no longer causes public debate. With the growth of imported new garments from China in recent years, secondhand clothing's share of total clothing imports has actually declined.

Since the mid-1980s imported secondhand clothing in Zambia has been referred to as *salaula*, which in the Bemba language means approximately "selecting from a pile by rummaging" or, for short, "to pick." The term describes vividly the process that takes place once a bale of imported second-hand clothing has been opened in the market and consumers select garments to satisfy both their clothing needs and their clothing desires. The shop window of Zambia's secondhand clothing trade, the big public markets, creates an atmosphere much like the West's shopping malls where consumers pursue almost unlimited desires with an abandon not possible in the formal stores, where they are often dealt with offhandedly or are pressured to purchase.

The value consumers in Zambia attribute to *salaula* is created through a process of recommodification that involves several phases. In the United States and Europe, the sorting and compressing of secondhand clothing into bales in the clothing recycler's warehouse strip used garments of their prior social life. The decommissioned value of the West's unwanted but still wearable clothing is then reactivated on local terms in transactions between overseas suppliers and local importers. Through subsequent transformations the meanings shift in ways that help redefine used clothing into "new" garments. These transformations begin in communications between exporters and importers and in on-site visits, continue at the wholesale outlet and in public markets, and are made visible in how consumers put themselves together with *salaula*. In addition to these processes through which the register of meaning of clothing shifts, there are also physical and material changes involving alteration, mending, and recycling.

On first sight, the *salaula* markets meet the non-local observer's eye as a chaotic mass of secondhand clothing hung up on flimsy wood contraptions, displayed on tables or dumped in piles on the ground. But that view is deceptive. There is in fact a variety of informal rules that organize vending space and structure sales practices. Both vendors and customers know these practices. A prospective customer looking for a specific garment will go to a particular part of the market. The vendors of men's suits, for example, one of the most expensive items, tend to be located in a part of the outdoor market that is near to major thoroughfares such as a main road passable by automobiles. So are vendors of other garments in high demand, such as women's skirts and blouses, and the best-selling item of all, at least in Zambia, baby clothes. There are spatial clusters of vendors selling shoes and, during the winter in the southern hemisphere, cold-weather clothing such as sweaters, jackets, and overcoats. Yet these spatial demarcations are not static, as vendors sometimes change inventory.

The display on most secondhand clothing stands is carefully designed (Figure 7.2). High-quality items are hung on clothes hangers on makeshift walls. A clothing-line or a wood stand may display a row of cotton dresses. Everything that meets the eye has been carefully selected with a view to both presentation and sales strategy. Lively discussions and price negotiations accompany sales. The piles on the ground include damaged items

Figure 7.2 Display of shirts and other garments in a *salaula* market, 1993.
Photograph by Karen Tranberg Hansen.

and garments that have been around for a while. Such items are sold "on order"—that is, several pieces at a discount—and they are often purchased by rural customers who take them to the villages to resell.

Near the high end of the secondhand clothing display, and near the major roads of the market section, cluster the "boutiques." Boutiques in these markets sell specially preselected items, coordinated to form matched outfits that are stylish. They tend to be operated by young vendors who "pick," in the language of the market. Once other traders open secondhand clothing bales, the pickers descend on them, selecting garments they buy on the spot. Then they make up, for instance, women's two-piece ensembles, men's suits, and leisure wear. Most of the boutique operators I met were young men who were very skilled at choosing quality stock with a fine eye for what might sell, a great sense of style, and a flair for making stunning combinations. I also met boutique operators who were women. Some of them had tailoring skills and they sewed clothing to order from their own homes.

Consumers in Zambia go to secondhand clothing markets for many reasons. White-collar workers of both sexes in Lusaka's city center often spend their lunch hour perusing the secondhand clothing stalls, sometimes making purchases at whim. Others go in order to look for just the right item to match a particular garment. Some women who tailor in their homes search the markets for interesting buttons, belts, and trim to accent garments. And some go to purchase garments with the intention to resell. But the vast majority shop from *salaula* in order to obtain clothing for themselves and their families. Secondhand clothing does not serve only poorer consumers. Consumers come into the city center from residential areas like those in which I examined clothing consumption and where roughly two-thirds of all households supplied most of their members' clothing from secondhand clothing markets. Only the very tiny high-income group in Zambia has an effective choice in the clothing market. This group, called *apamwamba*— a term in the Nyanja language that means approximately "those on the top"—purchases clothing everywhere, including from secondhand clothing markets. People from these better-off households spend more money on tailor-made clothing than do poor households (Hansen 2000b). Recent years have witnessed the emergence of entrepreneurs who have launched themselves as local clothing designers and are beginning to make a mark with "African designs" in *chitenge* (colorful print) fabrics that is adding new value to the local fashion scene (Mukota and Phiri 2005).

Clothing competence

Clothing consumption is hard work. A vital dimension of the demand side concerns issues about cultural taste and style that come together in the creation of a "total look." Concerns with fabric quality, texture, and construction precede that creation which in turn revolves around the anticipated dress needs of the specific situation. When shopping from secondhand clothing markets, consumers' preoccupation with creating particular appearances is inspired by styles and trends from across the world. Through this exposure, *salaula* fashions bring consumers into a bigger world: the world of awareness, the world of now.

Consumers draw on these influences in ways that are informed by local norms about bodies and dress. The desired clothing silhouette for both adult women and men is neat and tidy. It is a product of immaculate garment care and of wearing clothes in ways that are not considered to be too revealing. Even then, female and male garments are understood differently. The cultural norms about how to dress weigh down on women more heavily than on men, with the result that women feel restrained in their freedom to dress so as not to provoke men (Hansen 2004a). Women should not expose their shoulders. Above all, they must cover their "private parts," which in this region of Africa includes their thighs. This means that dress length, tightness, and fabric transparency become issues when women interact with men and elders both at home and in public. With such dress norms as background, it is perhaps not surprising that controversies that date back to the 1960s over women's wearing of miniskirts continue to occur (ibid.).

The desire for uniqueness, to stand out, while dressing the body on Zambian terms entails considerable skill in garment selection from the abundance of *salaula*; in making discriminating decisions concerning quality, style, and value for money; in garment coordination to fit specific occasions and contexts; and in the overall presentation and comportment of the dressed body to produce a "total look." Many consumers are extraordinarily savvy when it comes to clothing purchases aimed to produce particular effects. In order to highlight that shopping from *salaula* does not mean that anything goes, I have called the skill that is critical to the successful work of consumption "clothing competence." The underlying sensibility is a visual aesthetics that on first sight cultivates endless variation of dress yet on closer analysis is also in the service of continuity. In this creative process, consumers are active in putting together an attractive and unique look for themselves.

Suit aesthetics and provocative wear: young men's dress dilemma

Unlike young women, who carefully monitor the way they dress in public, young men like to draw attention to themselves, in different ways to be sure, depending on their socioeconomic circumstances and regional location. They actively seek to present a smart appearance that is both fashionable and neat. Young men's self-conscious preoccupations with suits and jeans illustrate different constructions of these attributes of dress.

Suits are worn very widely across the civil service ranks and other white-collar jobs in Zambia and are sometimes referred to as corporate wear. Formal suits index young urban men's desire to become adult, hold jobs, and head households. Consider George Chulamanda—in 2005 the youngest ever minister of sport, youth, and child development—whom fashion pundits characterized as a very trendy and fashionable guy. Wanting to be an inspiration to young people, he told a reporter that dark pinstriped suits were his favorite, the dress for today's leaders: "We are leaders of today and tomorrow and we should lead by example" (*Post* 2005). In effect, cutting a fine figure in a smart suit conveys something important about personal background, respectability, and responsibility. In this view, suits are identified with patriarchal social power that is widespread throughout Zambia.

Most of the young men in their late teens or early twenties in a secondary school in Lusaka who in 1995 described for me where they bought their clothes and how they liked to dress aspired to this dress practice and the ideal it conveys. "Suits are the clothes I like most," explained Simon, "because they make me look decent and soon I will be joining the society of workers." Morgan, his classmate, described a pair of trousers and a jacket he had recently received: "I was full of joy . . . I like these clothes because a lot of people say that I look like a general manager and not only that, they also say that I look like a rich man." And Moses's delight in a double-breasted jacket his father had given him is evident: "I like jackets because they suit me like a second skin."

Other classmates liked jeans, particularly because of their durability but also because "they are in style now." But wearing jeans had a flip side that too readily called forth the image of scruffy youths and street vendors, who in the popular view are readily associated with illegal activities. According to Moses, "I hate wearing jeans because people may fail to distinguish between cigarette sellers and myself." Lusaka's downtown streets are full of young male traders in all kinds of goods. They put much effort into being seen, and many of them dress in a striking manner.

If suits and jeans frame young urban men's desires for a better life, young men in rural areas have similar desires but are more circumscribed by the conditions in which they live. Secondary-school students in Mansa, a provincial town in Luapula Province, explained this clearly. Joshua explained, "Of all the clothes, I like strong ones which can serve me longer such as jeans. I like them because it is not easy for me to buy soap, and most of the time I do manual work in order to earn my living." The suit figures in the desires of these young rural men mostly by its absence. Describing why the suit combination did not fit his situation, Nicholas explained, "Such clothes can easily be torn and I think they are for office working people, so they don't suit me." Yet he added as an afterthought, "If I had a choice, I would really like to wear suits."

Jeans are a must in the evolving street vendor style. In addition to the style explanations I describe below, the preference of street vendors for denim has an obvious practical reason. Jeans, one of them explained, "are durable; they are nice and easy to keep especially for bachelors like me who have no one to look after our clothes." What the young vendors my assistant interviewed in 1997 did for their own pleasure was to dress up in public in variations on the baggy-jeans look. The layered look was in vogue that year, as were knitted caps referred to as head-socks and shoes with thick rubber soles, often worn without stockings.

The secondary-school students and the young street vendors purchased their clothes from a variety of sources. Some bought imported clothing from "suitcase" traders who bring in garments from abroad, some went to the tailor for specific wear, and all of them scoured the *salaula* market for just the right items. As one of the street vendors explained, "In *salaula* you will find things you can't believe how good they are." When shopping for clothes, the young vendors look for garments that will contribute to the overall creation of a particular style, which in the late 1990s was "the big look," rather than for brand-name items. "I wear the big look, because it is fashion," one of them said while another explained how he liked to "move with time." Yet another said he did not like "common clothes and imitations."

Making associations between specific articles of clothing and behavior, young people construct an understanding of their world and how they inhabit it. Young male secondary-school students with high economic aspirations for themselves do not want to be mistaken for the school drop outs-turned-street-vendors. They desire suits. The vendors for their part wear clothes they

Figure 7.3
Young man wearing
his first ready-made
suit, 1993. Photograph
by Karen Tranberg
Hansen.

equate with the power and success achieved by popular performers both in Africa and beyond. Putting themselves together with clothing the major part of which is from *salaula*, both groups of young people are dressing to explore who they are and who they would like to become (Figure 7.3).[1]

Dress codes and choices: *apamwamba* women's dress practices

If suits are the garments to wear for young men who wish to be upwardly mobile, "decent dress" that does not reveal too much is the clothing style for young women, including young women of better means who have real options in the clothing market because of their economic background. The dress presentation of male and female announcers of the daily evening news on national television in Zambia, the government-controlled Zambia National Broadcasting Corporation (ZNBC), illustrates the almost iconic status of the suit and decent dress in Zambia.

I tracked these dress presentations over the course of my two-month stay in Lusaka during the southern hemisphere's cold months of July and August both in 2003 and 2004. Back in 1995 I had interviewed then-popular television announcer Mary Phiri about dress protocol for the news announcers. There was none, she said, other than "decent." Unlike on South African television, where clothing firms sometimes dress announcers and have their names appearing in the credit line, clothing firms do not (to my knowledge) dress the news announcers on Zambian television.[2] The announcers themselves purchase their clothes, including garments from *salaula*. Without exception, men announcers wore suit and tie. While the severity of their suits varied from striped and check, to single colors of very dark grey and beige, ties and handkerchiefs offered variation. By contrast, the women announcers' clothes were more diverse. Some women announcers were more likely than others to wear *chitenge* suits or dresses; that is, very ornamented outfits, tailored with much elaboration and attention to detail from colorful printed fabric. This dress presentation sometimes included complicated head-ties constructed in the "Nigerian fashion." A global fashion fusion is evident here, as Zambian women refer to such headdresses as *dukas*, a term that derives from the Afrikaans word *doek*, or "scarf." More women news announcers wore *chitenge* dresses in 2003 than in 2004 for reasons that may have to do with the temporary absence of some very popular announcers. The rest of the women news announcers wore world or global dress, most frequently jackets with contrasting shirt or blouse with a variety of decorative trim.

In male-dominated Zambian society, the considerable scrutiny women's bodies receive in public extends into the television production studio. A highly profiled event in 1997 involved popular television announcer Dora Siliya, who was suspended by the ZNBC for "insubordination arising from her wearing miniskirts" (*Post* 1997a). Storming out of the office, Ms. Siliya claimed that "dressing is personal and has nothing to do with my work." Letters to the press by women ridiculed the management's decision. In the words of three such women letter writers from Lusaka: "This is the 20th century for God's sake and not the Elizabethan era! Young women have to move with times and keep up with fashion. Besides, women should not have their right to dress as they please stifled by old hags" (*Post* 1997b).[3]

Some segments of Zambian society continue to attribute highly charged sexual meanings to women's dressed bodies. Controversies over miniskirts (Hansen 2004a) keep recurring, not in a *déjà vu* sense but in accentuated versions in the time of HIV/AIDS, as for example in February 2006 in a series of letters to the editor of a major paper, prompted by a recent ban on miniskirts and tight trousers in Tanzania (*Weekend Post*, 2006). Young women are aware of the sexual implications of miniskirts, and they reckon with them in situational terms. In fact women, both young and adult, claim that men have a much easier time dressing because they have far fewer issues to be concerned with in terms of body shape, covering specific parts of the body, and coordinating garments and accessories. When young women from middle-income and *apamwamba* backgrounds move about in public settings away from home, they are very much aware of male society's problematic attitude to their dressed bodies. Some of them seek to avert the male gaze through their dress whereas others hope to catch it.

Interacting with young people of both sexes of middle- to upper-income background in 2002 and 2003, an assistant and I sought to learn where they spend their free time, with whom, and how they dress on such occasions. Here, I focus on the women we interviewed. Such women constitute a very small segment of Lusaka's huge youth population. Pursuing further education at a variety of colleges, training institutions, and universities, including some abroad in Australia and the United States, most of these young women have the means, usually because of well-placed parents, to hang out with friends at Lusaka's new shopping malls, other shopping venues, popular pool halls, bars, and parks. There is a nightclub scene which some of them also frequent. In their daytime interaction, aside from sharing news about friends and talking about relationships, sex, the entertainment scene, and their futures, these young women spend considerable time discussing "looks," exchanging information about the availability of particularly desired garments, and who has been seen wearing what and where. Most of them love clothes. Unlike some parts of the world, their interest in dress is valued in positive terms by the friends with whom they move about. They all spend considerable time and effort discussing the latest. "It is the combination of clothing," said a twenty-two-year-old psychology student," that demonstrates your sense of style."

"Clothes," said a twenty-four-year-old marketing student, "place me in my class." Like many others, she did not like baggy jeans, "no boring loose slacks," as one expressed it, "because they are tomboyish, and gangsta," a comparison that we also heard some young men make. During the daytime interactions when we interviewed the young women, they dressed decently but casually, meaning—controlling for body size—in tight jeans, or knee-length jeans skirts resting on the hips with waistlines accentuated by cropped short tops. Young women who were heavy-set wore long, fitted skirts with slits. A twenty-two-year-old university student explained that her outfit, combining jeans, matching top, and smart shoes, "makes me look mature and outlines my model body." Altogether, by Zambian norms, there was nothing too revealing in the way these young women dressed their bodies when moving about in public space. Their hair was either elaborately braided or cut short, the most popular women's hairstyles at the time. Their overall look was accessorized by cell phones, handbags, shoes, and jewelry.

These young women sourced most of their clothing from stores and boutiques, including from abroad. They also, as I indicated earlier, shop from *salaula*, but as a pastime, not a need. Some had never been to a tailor. They were not keen to wear *chitenge* dresses, and they did not all own one. Young

Figure 7.4 Women dressed up for a party occasion, three in *chitenge* suits, and one (on the left) in a tailor-made office outfit, 1997. Photograph by Karen Tranberg Hansen.

women's attitude to wearing *chitenge* outfits revolves around body size and age. Looking best on "traditionally built women," these elaborately styled dresses evoke a level of maturity which some young women consider to be old, something that they associate with what their mothers and grandmothers wear (Hansen 2000a: 265). With such an outlook, no wonder that "casual" is the thing to wear (Figure 7.4).

"Everything I wear," said a twenty-one-year-old woman, "should make people look and say 'wow, she is nice . . . '." In their concern to create their own fashion statements and demonstrate an individual sense of style, these young women from middle- to upper-income backgrounds make sure that they show off their *apamwamba* status. While their self-styling has something in common with the hip, cutting-edge, middle-class lifestyles that Sarah Nuttall has described for the Y generation of Rosebank in Johannesburg (2004), it does not come close to the sartorial, visual, and sonic dimensions of youth culture of Rosebank. The reasons may have to do with Zambia's status as one of the world's least-developed countries. In their self-styling through dress, *apamwamba* women in Lusaka seek to avoid "sliding down" in local socioeconomic terms. While they wear world or global fashions, the presentation of their dressed bodies becomes meaningful on Zambian terms; that is, in the local context of economic decline, urban poverty, and other processes set into motion by Zambia's unequal place in the global economy.

Conclusion: moving with the times and keeping up with fashion on Zambian terms

Cities like Lusaka are the prime stages for globalization's translation into local understandings and experiences. Monitoring the way they dress in public, clothing-conscious Zambians pay considerable attention to the possibilities of their garments when dressing in world or global styles, seeking to anticipate their desired effects. Across class, the dress of young Zambians invokes aspirations, desires, and imaginaries. Young men eager to become adults desire suits because they convey notions of authority and independence which their everyday life in school and at home denies them. Young male street vendors dress in oversize jeans not only because they are durable and easy to care for but also because such garments are part of a global dress style turned fashionable by international performers. Young *apamwamba* women reckon with their body size and shape, making careful choices to present their dressed bodies in public, decently, in what is "in fashion now" but with their local sense of class distinction.

Will they pull off wearing it? The meaning and value of Zambian preoccupations with clothing do not inhere in garments themselves and therefore do not have much to do with whether clothes are secondhand or new. Clothes are not worn passively but require people's active collaboration. Experiences of dress, the evaluations viewers make of it, are not given or fixed but created anew in each context. In their daily rehearsal for dressing and dressing up, young people try to anticipate the situations and contexts in which they will be finding themselves. Seeking to negotiate the specific moment of such situations, they may experience the thrill of enjoyment or disapproval. In this affecting experience of dress, the distinction between used clothing and fashion becomes irrelevant, as does the problematic differentiation between Western and non-Western dress styles. The attraction of secondhand clothing to consumers in Zambia about which I inquired at the outset is now evident. Masked in accounts of global inequities, imported secondhand clothes are not incidental accessories but active participants in transforming the lives of their new wearers. In spite of the aggressive forces that structure the global circuit of garment production and, along with it, the international secondhand clothing trade, there do exist spaces within which locally authored dress distinctions may take over.

Acknowledgments

This chapter is based on research into secondhand clothing undertaken during the 1990s (Hansen 2000b). It also contains observations from research in progress that I have conducted in Zambia since 2001 on youth and urban social reproduction. The discussion of young men's dress is taken from a recent publication (Hansen 2005). Oscar Hamangaba assisted me in 1997 with interviews of street vendors, and Tamara Nkhoma assisted me in 2002 and 2003 with interviews about *apamwamba* lifestyle and dress.

Notes

1. Eileen Moyer offers comparable insights in her research on young men working and living on the streets of Dar es Salaam, Tanzania. While influenced by American hip-hop culture and Jamaican Rastafari ideals, they dress to achieve a look that is suitable to their living environment and reflective of their own desires (2003).
2. I have seen the names of hairdressers acknowledged on Zambian television.
3. Keeping up with fashion, Ms. Dora Siliya has indeed moved with the times. In 2006 she was elected member of parliament representing Petauke district and appointed deputy minister of commerce and industry.

References

Eicher, J. B. (1995) "Introduction: Dress as Expression of Ethnic Identity," in J. B. Eicher (ed.), *Dress and Ethnicity*, Oxford: Berg.

Eicher, J. B. and Sumberg, B. (1995) "World Fashion, Ethnic, and National Dress," in J. B. Eicher (ed.), *Dress and Ethnicity*, Oxford: Berg.

Entwistle, J. (2000) *The Fashioned Body: Fashion, Dress, and Modern Social Theory*, Cambridge: Polity Press.

Finkelstein, J. (1998) *Fashion: An Introduction*, New York: New York University Press.

Gereffi, G. and Korzeniewicz, M. (eds.) (1994) *Commodity Chains and Global Capitalism*, New York: Praeger.

Haggblade, S. (1990) "The Flip Side of Fashion: Used Clothing Exports to the Third World," *Journal of Development Studies*, 26(3): 505–521.

Hansen, K. T. (2000a) "Other People's Clothes? The International Second-hand Clothing Trade Dress Practices in Zambia," *Fashion Theory*, 4(3): 245–274.

—— (2000b) Salaula: *The World of Secondhand Clothing and Zambia*, Chicago: University of Chicago Press.

—— (2003) "Fashioning: Zambian Moments," *Journal of Material Culture*, 8(3): 301–309.

—— (2004a) "Dressing Dangerously: Miniskirts, Gender Relations, and Sexuality in Zambia," in J. Allman (ed.), *Fashioning Africa: Power and the Politics of Dress*, Bloomington: Indiana University Press.

—— (2004b) "Helping or Hindering? Controversies around the International Second-hand Clothing Trade," *Anthropology Today*, 20(4): 3–9.

—— (2004c) "The World in Dress: Anthropological Perspectives on Clothing, Fashion, and Culture," *Annual Reviews of Anthropology*, 33: 369–392.

—— (2005) "From Thrift to Fashion: Materiality and Aesthetics in Dress Practices in Zambia," in D. Miller and S. Kuechler (eds.), *Clothing as Material Culture*, Oxford: Berg.

Kopytoff, I. (1986) "The Cultural Biography of Things: Commoditization as Process," in A. Appadurai (ed.), *The Social Life of Things: Commodities in Cultural Perspective*, Cambridge: Cambridge University Press.

Lipovetsky, G. (1994) *The Empire of Fashion: Dressing Modern Democracy*, Princeton: Princeton University Press.

Mauss, M. (1973) "Techniques of the Body," *Economy and Society*, 2(1): 70–89.

Maynard, M. (2004) *Dress and Globalisation*, Manchester: Manchester University Press.

Mitchell, J. C. (1956) "The Kalela Dance," *Rhodes–Livingstone Papers* no. 27.

Mitchell, J. C. and Epstein, A. L. (1959) "Occupational Prestige and Social Status among Urban Africans in Northern Rhodesia," *Africa*, 29: 22–39.

Moyer, E. (2003) "Keeping up Appearances: Fashion and Function among Dar es Salaam Street Youth," *Etnofoor*, 16(2): 88–105.

Mukota, Augustine and Phiri, Colin (photographer) (2005) "Lookout for 'Fresh' Designs . . . as Two Young Designers Churn Out Their First Dresses," *Weekend Post*, December 2: 4.

Ngoma, Samuel (1995) "Wanted: Quality Clothing in Zambia," *Times of Zambia*, August 26: 4.

Nuttall, S. (2004) "Stylizing the Self: The Y Generation in Rosebank, Johannesburg," *Public Culture*, 16(3): 430–452.

Post (1997a) "Dora Siliya's Minis Annoy ZNBC Bosses," May 22: 1, 5.

—— (1997b) "Dora Siliya's Miniskirt Defended" (letter to the editor), May 26.

—— (2005) "Trendsetters," December 2.

Powdermaker, H. (1962) *Copper Town: Changing Africa. The Human Condition on the Rhodesian Copperbelt*, New York: Harper and Row.

Rivoli, P. (2005) *The Travels of a T-shirt in the Global Economy: An Economist Examines the Markets, Power, and Politics of World Trade*, Hoboken: John Wiley & Sons.

Susser, I. and Schneider, J. (2003) "Wounded Cities: Destruction and Reconstruction in a Globalized World," in J. Schneider and I. Susser (eds.), *Wounded Cities: Destruction and Reconstruction in a Globalized World*, Oxford: Berg.

UNDP (United Nations Development Programme) (2001) *Zambia Human Development Report 1999/2000. Employment and Sustainable Livelihoods*, Ndola: Mission Press.

Weekend Post (2006) "Miniskirts Debate," 19 February, available at http://www.postzambia.com/post-print_article.php?articleId=6740 (accessed on March 7, 2006).

Wilson, G. (1941–1942) "An Essay on the Economics of Detribalization" vols. 1 and 2, *Rhodes–Livingstone Papers* nos. 5 and 6.

Chapter 8

Fashion design and technologies in a global context

Michiel Scheffer

Introduction[1]

Apparel is part of an economy of signs. It embodies cultural capital, as the result of design and marketing activities. It is also the fruit of technology and labor. Goods are linked to material culture changing over time and space and to the mobilization of technology changing over time and space. Or, to be more precise, the conditions of production and consumption are a reflection of a specific capital formation at a given time. In this chapter the change from a Fordist/modernist mode of production and consumption to a post-Fordist/postmodern mode will be examined, using the analysis of David Harvey in his seminal work *The Condition of Postmodernity*, first published in 1989. Goods are traded in a globalized economy, both as commodities and as brands. There is a clear spatial dimension to the diffusion of changes in product configuration and meaning. There is also a spatial dimension to the localization of production. The two levels are not linked as international division of labor may differ between design and marketing on the one hand and production on the other. Evolution in the organization of production can be analyzed in the framework of the global value chain model (Gereffi 2001). In addition to examining the quantitative aspect of globalization, this chapter will also assess more qualitative changes in production in developing countries, which may enable processes that are not economically possible in developed countries.

This research is based on the analysis of a garment archetype that has established a position over the last 100 years. Jeans are truly the palimpsest of cultural and technical capital formation. A product made of denim fabric, jeans were developed in the fifteenth century from "Toile de Nîmes," an indigo-dyed twill fabric made of hemp fiber. The blue color was referred to as "bleu de Gènes" from the Italian city of Genoa. In the industrial age jeans became the standard workwear under the impetus of Levi Strauss & Co. Between 1890 and 1970, jeans, and more specifically the vintage Levi's 501 model, became as it were the "model-T Ford" of apparel. Made with a rotor-spun yarn, woven on high-speed looms and produced in a Taylorist production organization, jeans became a modern and Fordist product: accessible to all but existing in only one model. In the 1960s and 1970s, they were the symbol of modernity and informality and at the same time they become a globalized product. In the 1980s jeans entered a state of crisis and lost their attractiveness to other styles of pants, such as chinos. They were revived in the second half of the 1990s through the mobilization of a range of techniques and artifacts creating a new grammar of style. As a result, jeans today are a mass-customized product, mobilized as a fashion luxury item that is affordable to many.

Cycles of capital

Since 1920, modern industrialization has been driven substantially by product standardization and large-scale manufacturing. Homogenization of taste, codification of products, and standardization of design and industrialization methods are key to organizing economies of scale from a marketing perspective. Manufacturing itself is standardized and organized in an extreme segmentation of processes. It is also increasingly oriented to productivity: volume production drives economies of scale further in the supply chain; low costs create lower prices and thus give the largest number of consumers access to mass consumption. The volume and growth in volume create a model of accumulation linking increased productivity to increased wages (Aglietta 1979). The modern, or Taylorist, production mode is linked to modernism in design, where products were mainly designed and optimized in terms of function rather than form.

The Fordist regime entered into crisis in the 1970s and was replaced by a model of flexible accumulation. The latter no longer assumes an extension of mass markets but, instead, tries to accommodate a more mature and differentiated demand. Production must become leaner and more adaptable (Piore and Sabel 1984). As far as fashion is concerned, Harvey describes the following:

> Acceleration in turnover time [is] a strong feature in the recent period of flexible accumulation . . . Heightened competition certainly provokes individual firms to speed up their turnover time. Those firms with the fastest turnover time tend to gain excess profits thereby and so survive more easily.
>
> (Harvey 1989: 182)

Fashion itself thus becomes an important dynamic of competition.

> The mobilization of fashion in mass markets provided a means to accelerate the pace of consumption . . . The first major consequence has been to accelerate volatility and ephemerality of fashion. This volatility makes it extremely difficult to engage in long-term planning. Indeed

learning to play the volatility is as important as accelerating turnover time. This means either by being highly adaptable and fast-moving in response to market shifts, or by masterminding volatility . . . through being a fashion leader or by so saturating the market with images as to shape the volatility to particular ends.

(Harvey 1989: 285–287)

Harvey points to two different strategies. The first one involves a speeding up of product turnover and the shortening of product life cycle. Fashion is therefore a permanent run of incremental innovation, i.e. a constant recombination of techniques mobilizing a wide style lexicon. The second is a strategy of masterminding that aims at maximizing gross margin and requiring the development of a strong brand identity associated with a clear and unique style, preferably protected by strong intellectual property rights on brands, design features, and technologies.

In other words, the first strategy is to build on fast adaptive routines partly based on copying successful trends; the second strategy is to develop a highly structured company iconography. Both strategies require excellent market intelligence, best acquired through rapid collection of sales data. Information technology, both for trend analysis and for analysis of information from the cash register, is crucial for launching new designs and assuring store replenishment. Beyond that, the next step for many brands is to control brand identity at the store level and to gain direct intelligence from the shop floor. This has led many brands to set up their own retail chains, a strategy often referred to as verticalization. Benetton and Gap were the first brands with retail chains. Abercrombie & Fitch and G-Star are more recent examples of this strategy.

Three consequences of these strategies are useful to highlight. The first one is the emergence of brands and retail forms focusing on fast turnover in fashion. Such turnover is best measured through the accounting concept of the rotation of current assets, which is calculated as a ratio by dividing annual sales by the current assets used over the year. When current assets are not known, the working capital or stocks can be used as a proxy. This ratio is the translation in accounting terms of Harvey's concept of the turnover time of capital, and is a key ratio used by retailers to calculate profitability. The other important ratio is gross profit expressed as the difference between wholesale price and retail price, or in accounting terms between annual sales and the value of goods bought.

For most of the twentieth century, fashion retailing had a rotation of current assets with a factor between two and three (turnover divided by current assets or sales/stock). This reflects a traditional bi-seasonal pattern with two buying periods, a season start and end-of-season sales. However, nowadays retailers such as Zara, H&M, Vero Moda, and Abercrombie & Fitch reach ratios over five. This ratio implies that the firms can operate on a lower level of working capital in relation to sales. They achieve this by more frequent season changes and fashion updates, and the replenishment of successful lines. In order to speed up turnover time control over retail is crucial, including information linkages with point of sales.

The second consequence is that the supply chain must follow. Manufacturers usually have a longer pipeline than retailers as they use more exclusive materials. They then buy materials and finance stock in stores. Retailers, however, rarely engage in manufacturing and prefer subcontracting to specialized manufacturers, demanding shorter lead times of them. Speeding up turnover time requires a reorientation of product development toward an endless recombination of incremental innovations in technologies at the end of the manufacturing cycle such as dyeing and finishing, washing, flat-screen printing and embroidery. This is an industrial and logistical principle of differentiating products as late as possible in the supply chain (van Hoek 1998).

The third consequence is, as Harvey suggests, that the strategy of the speeding up of assets requires a disinvestment from manufacturing and a focus on design, marketing, and retail activities that create more important margins and control over the supply chain. Brand manufacturers in France and Italy have been the first to move toward subcontracting in order to be more flexible (Scheffer 1992; 1994). Scheffer (1992) also suggests that brand development ought to be compatible with global branding as the relative marketing costs decline if a larger market is being served. Brands must then have the potential to reach out to consumers in different cultural settings, either by adjusting the message to the local culture, by conveying a universal message, or by catering for a niche market. It is mainly food brands that have adapted to the local context. In contrast, Levi's is an example of a brand with a universal message, while Burberry caters for a niche market with a characteristic "British" brand identity.

The increase in the rotation of capital has consequences for the production and consumption of taste. As far as fashion is concerned, the impact of the increase of capital rotation on technical and design choices has not yet been studied. It may be assumed that the speeding up of fashion cycles leads to a focus on techniques of differentiation at the end of the production cycle, for instance: embroidery (childrenswear), digital printing and flat-bed screen printing (sportswear), washing (jeans), and patchwork. These techniques give a high degree of differentiation to basic fabrics and make. Yet because they are highly labor-intensive, they are also only affordable by tapping into low labor-cost production in developing countries. In a context of globalized production the availability of low labor costs and labor-intensive techniques may guide the choices of designers. This supply-driven innovation somehow limits the assumption of a sovereign consumer since the relative price of labor-intensive fashion made of simple materials has declined considerably compared to sober garments made of expensive materials. This shift also applies to jeans, a case that is analyzed in more depth below.

The technical grammar of jeans

Jeans have a number of basic features that characterize the product as an archetype. This comes first from a range of technical features in the denim fabric. The starting point is the use of a coarse uncombed pure cotton yarn. The warp is dyed in a blue indigo dye, nowadays always a synthetic dyestuff, but up to 1870 a natural dye.[2] The warp is heavily sized with a natural or artificial starch in order to give sufficient strength and enable high speeds in weaving. The weft is a white yarn, giving a bicolor appearance where the right side of the fabric is blue and the wrong side is white. The usual weaving pattern is twill, giving a diagonal look to the fabric. Unlike most other fabrics, it is not treated before making up, so that the fabric remains starched, which makes it easy to handle and to assemble.

Jeans have a number of standard features in the model, which combines fit, make, and details.[3] The fit is often close to the body, with a flat front. Most stitches are apparent and double seams are prevalent. Reinforcement of intersections with rivets is a regular feature, as are stitched-up back pockets and belting loops. Jeans have two slant side front pockets and three small stitched-up pockets, making five pockets in total. An important feature in the manufacturing process is that the product is washed after making up, in order to remove the starch and soften the product to make it wearable. Traditionally, most jeans have a leather tag on the back in order to identify the brand.

While these are the characteristics of traditional jeans, e.g. the Levi's 501, many points of differentiation have emerged in other brands by modifying the basic yarns and fabrics, applying finishes and washings, or adding or omitting features to the model. The first differentiation is in the fiber choice. Levi's first made a pair of jeans from imported hemp denim, which was a dominant fiber for functional fabrics until 1850 (Blackburn et al. 2004). It then took cotton as a standard in the 1870s, using denim from a mill in Massachusetts (Downey 2005). Since 1970, cotton has been blended with other fibers in order to change form or functionality. Blends with synthetic fibers lower the price and ease the care, but at the cost of comfort. Elasthane gives stretch, a closer fit and more comfort. Kevlar is appreciated by motorcyclists because of higher strength and lower abrasion. Blends with linen, nettle, or hemp are being tested as an environmental experiment.[4] Finally, organic cotton is increasingly used, mostly for motives of sustainability.

Differentiation has appeared in fabric technologies. Originally, the denim was made with a ring-spun yarn, the classic yarn spinning technology using a mechanical twist and stretch to a fiber bundle. In the 1960s, denim yarns were increasingly made on an open-end spinning frame using rotation and mingling fibers through air flow (Elsasser 1997). Ring-spun yarns have more strength and a closer and smoother look and feel than open-end yarn but demand more production steps and are therefore more expensive. In the

1990s there was a comeback of ring-spun yarns because of their strength, look, and layered fibers. This, in combination with innovations in washing, enabled a wide range of finishing effects. While the warp is often dyed on the beam, manufacturers adopted a succession of baths in order to create layers of dyes that create specific effects in washing and post-treatments. One of many methods was to apply first acid dyes for lighter colors and then basic dyes with darker colors. When the fabric is later washed or brushed the upper layer is removed and a lighter layer appears. Polyurethane resins are also used to achieve a "batik effect" with patches not being affected by washing. Weaving can be a modified twill (e.g. a herringbone), but 95 percent of jeans are made of standard twill.

Changes in the model are manifold: lower or higher waists, looser or slimmer fit, boot legged or with a tapered leg. They reflect different approaches to the relationship between the pants and the body. The number and position of the pockets may change; additional pads on the knee may reinforce a workwear look. The front opening may be a zipper or buttons. Pockets may be decorated with studs, stitches, or strasses (diamond-shaped glass pieces). Embroidery may be chosen, or other forms of application (printed, painted, etc.). Washing has become a crucial area of differentiation that depends on the length of the wash and the addition of specific chemical compounds, stones, oil, and grass, creating forms of dirty washes. In addition, special processes have been introduced such as laser marking that creates white areas, scrubbing with permanganate in order to create lighter patches (called flares or flames), creating lighter zones on the hip areas or the back of the jeans. The use of abrasion and grinders destroys specific areas or seams (Figure 8.1).[5]

This set of technologies creates a full grammar of types, which combined create a fashion style and/or a brand style. The fashion style is created from the combination of elements that identify a fashion season, while a brand style is a combination of elements identifying the brand. The vast majority of identifying features are achieved by low or medium technology tools. All are to be considered as incremental innovations (Lester and Piore 2004). Most aspects in the model such as fit and detail do not depend on the fabric construction. There is a linkage between yarn features and fabric finishing, and washing, since some washing effects are only obtained if they are baked into the fabric.

Conceptually, jeans can be considered as a product developed in four layers that together form the style or design. The first layer is a fabric system with a fiber composition, a yarn construction and a fabric pattern. It is relatively generic and not highly differentiated across brands. The second layer refers to the model and the fit, which may be generic or specific to a brand. Some brands have a wide range of fits (traditional brands such as Levi's); other brands have a fit targeted to a specific consumer group (most often young women). The third layer is a range of washings and special treatments

Figure 8.1 Back-pocket selection. Clockwise from top left: Diesel (seam coloring); Levi's (V-pocket and leather tag); Calvin Klein (loop on pocket); G-Star (G-shape seam, label and rivet); 7 For All Mankind (transversal seam and label); Factory Demo (W-shape seam and zipper on pocket).

that may contribute to a product/brand identity, but are rarely exclusive to one brand. Finally, the fourth layer consists of a range of visual features very specific to the brand that are often concentrated on and around the back pocket.

The grammar of jeans and brand identity

The mobilization of all these elements in the grammar of jeans has created a turnaround in their design and commercialization, referred to as a revolution in jeans.[6] This is reflected in a rise in the sales of jeans from the second half of the 1990s onwards, fed by increased product and brand differentiation. The washing process plays an important role. Until the 1990s, washing was essentially a technical process aimed at taking the starch out of the end product. Normally, such a process takes place after weaving, but Levi's discovered that productivity in sewing improves dramatically when using still-sized fabrics. Indeed, doing so eases fabric handling and allows a further automation of jeans manufacturing. Levi's Fordist factories in Europe, which closed in 1998, were highly efficient as they were able to make jeans in fourteen standard minutes. High productivity went at the expense of product differentiation and created large quantities of intermediate and final stocks, and thus a slower turnover of capital. By the mid-1990s the sales of Levi's 501s had declined. References in company advertising and publicity to the mythical cowboy, James Dean, or the American way of life did not seem to help.

Meanwhile, a new approach to the design of jeans was being developed in southern France and northeast Italy. Key players were a group of designers, and some small factories, that specialized in washing jeans. They were experimenting with resins, enzymes, and additives of all kinds to work on different aspects of fabrics and to mobilize washing as a technology of differentiation (Who's Next 2005). The work entailed enhancing a destroyed look (François and Marithé Girbaud) or maintaining a raw look (Pierre Morisset). Girbaud developed their own brands of jeans, Closed and MFG. Morisset was the designer behind French brands such as Liberto and C17, and since 1996 he has been the designer for the Dutch G-Star. The Italians worked more on the interaction between fabric construction and washing (Wilbert Das with Renzo Rossi at Diesel, and Claudio Buziol as the founder of Replay).[7] They mobilized a wider range of features by working on studs, seams, shapes, embroidery, and localized patches. All these effects involved working on standard denim and mobilizing a vast array of washing and sewing technologies.

Some designers pushed manufacturers to move techniques further, especially the Jewish-Californian cluster (Elbaz, Guez, Dahan, Ohayon),[8] which actually emerged from the southern French pioneers around Girbaud and Morisset, using destroyed effects, localized scrubbing with permanganate, and laser marking. Another style started with the Japanese company Evisu in Osaka who developed vintage denim woven on 1950s looms using ring-spun yarns (Japanese denim is often woven on vintage looms). Italian weavers Tessitura di Robechietto Candiani, Montebello, and Italdenim applied layered dyeing on ring-spun yarns in order to influence the washing and scrubbing effects in a subsequent stage of production. These weavers developed techniques together with specialty chemical suppliers such as Lamberti and textile machinery builders in the Lombardia industrial district (Museo dell Tessuto 2005).

The dominant trend in differentiation since 1995 has been in washing. This has been the route taken by most brands, but with different choices of process and effect. Many Italian brands have developed a highly distressed style with aggressive washing, localized scouring with permanganate of potassium, and grinding of seams, and with the use of laser marks, resin, and stain effects (Tagliabue 2006). This makes for a very rough and casual look, with a high degree of differentiation between each product. American brands, especially branded jeans from California, have chosen a quieter look with use of localized scouring with permanganate and some laser marks. Italian and Californian brands have been massively copied for different target groups, the former being younger and more urban, and the latter older and suburban.

Both design trends are achieved mainly by differentiation in washing. There has been little change in the basic fabric used. Differentiation in fabrics has been mainly achieved by creating a vintage look by using 1950s-type denim woven with traditional looms and a traditional ring-spun yarn. This avenue has mainly been developed in Japan and is epitomized by Evisu using Japanese denim. However, other brands have followed this approach (Nudie Jeans, Earnest Sewn). G-Star was the pioneer of raw denim: non-washed or slightly washed denim that keeps a stiff and somehow metallic look. Within this trend, different positions also exist between the very urban industrial look of G-Star and the more artisan look of La Durance.

Differentiation through fit is a classic strategy of Levi's that enables the company to cater for a much broader audience than the new brands of jeans and to maintain its market leadership in the over-forty age group. Specific fits have been developed, such as the low hip line pioneered by the Italian brand Indian Rose, the slim line developed by Citizens of Humanity, the butt-lifting jeans of 7 For All Mankind and the grunge baggy look of FUBU. The fit is mainly a tool to narrow or broaden an audience in age and size, and to create customer loyalty as fit is still considered an important factor in the choice of consumers in the over-thirty age group (*Journal du textile* 2007). Differentiation through features is, however, the main strategy among luxury brands and retailers, who follow main trends in the first three layers of the product and only bring a brand signature in buttons, leather labels, and minor details.

Personalization of jeans can also be at the hands of the consumer. There are four major forms of personalization. Firstly, place washing and finishing technologies may create minute differences between similar products. Observation by the author of over a hundred pairs of similarly-styled premium jeans at Bloomingdales, New York, in March 2006 enabled an identification of each pair through a minor difference in wash. This was achieved by a purposely vague instruction to the production workers to scrub or grind.[9] Secondly, some brands (e.g. Evisu) advise their clients not to wash their jeans so that use creates a network of stains and marks—wear creates personalization. Thirdly, consumers are invited to personalize their jeans by making their own special treatments, for instance through websites that explain how to chemically personalize a pair of jeans.[10] Fourthly, the versatility of jeans today means that they have become a basic that can be accommodated in a streetwise style with sneakers as well as for "casual Friday" style with a jacket and brogues. Therefore jeans have become a highly differentiated and individualized product. The wide range of style elements and the possibility of wearing jeans in a broad array of combinations from streetwear to casual chic have made jeans a staple element in the eclecticism of postmodern dress (Lannelongue 2004).

The rise of new jeans

The range of techniques has created a premium-jeans sector, with leading brands Diesel and G-Star noting prices between 40 percent and 100 percent higher (at around seventy to ninety US dollars) than the standard Levi's. The premium-jeans segment developed in the first half of the 1990s but made its breakthrough in the second half. The rise of luxury jeans, either as Californian brands worn and promoted by Hollywood stars, or as brands such as Louis Vuitton and Dolce & Gabbana, is a feature of the twenty-first century. For these brands, jeans have become a means to make luxury brands available to a larger public (Lipovetsky and Roux 2003) and to demonstrate how marketing has democratized luxury (Agins 1999). Since 2000, large retailers such as Zara, H&M, and Abercrombie & Fitch have discovered the impact of jeans as fast-rotating items in stores, targeted with a price range comparable to or below Levi's 501s.

The dynamism in jeans innovation is best researched in France, where the *Journal du textile* has been tracking their sales for over twenty years (e.g. *Journal du textile* 2007). In France, growth in the sales of jeans was more than 10 percent a year between 2000 and 2005. The share of denim in total sales of trousers in specialty stores has grown from around 50 percent in 1996 to around 80 percent in 2005. Sales growth is mainly deriving from product differentiation in washing. Fabrics from twisted cotton yarns represent 85 percent of products; woven twills in classic blue denim are dominant. Also, differentiated washings represent over 70 percent of sales, thus reinforcing the conclusion that differentiation occurs mainly in the later stages. Moreover, jeans have yielded increased profits for retailers. Their gross margin has grown from 53 percent in 1995 to 57 percent in 2006. Other brands have moved from a gross margin below 35 percent (Levi's) to over 40 percent (Diesel). Increased gross margin results from commanding higher prices, achieved by design and branding and control over retailing, and from cost control achieved by economies of scale and subcontracting.

Globalization/localization

The change in the design and branding of jeans has had an impact on market structure. Although jeans are probably the most concentrated segment in apparel, the absolute size of companies is small and their absorption limited, compared to the automotive or food industry, for instance. Levi's is still the clear global market leader, even if its turnover has halved over the last ten years, to US$ 5.6 billion and a market share of around 12 percent. However, its leading products are no longer at a premium, but represent the mid-market. Levi's competes on service and fit and appeal to an over-forty audience, and has been followed by a number of medium-size brands, often established in a strong local market. In the 1970s and 1980s these were often targeted to "national" differences in taste, like the preference for stripped jeans in Italy (e.g. Fiorucci). Nowadays, they more often use the lexicon of product differentiation and branding for specific target groups and product identity. Examples of these firms are Tommy Hilfiger (US, preppy jeans), G-Star (Netherlands, raw jeans), Diesel (Italy, lifestyle jeans) and Nudie (Sweden, vintage jeans). These brands have a turnover of US$300–800 million but can still be counted in the largest 100 fashion brands in the world. Smaller brands cover niches with a much narrower product and audience definition. Evisu (Japan), 7 For All Mankind (USA), Indian Rose (Italy), Cheap Mondays (Sweden), and Girbaud (France) are typical examples. They have a turnover below US$300 million but often a targeted approach to a global niche audience. Designer jeans can be characterized as lines within a broader brand and collection. Many designers and couture houses have explored jeans as an affordable luxury, but some brands have clearly developed a specific brand identity (Calvin Klein, Ralph Lauren) or design identity (Dolce & Gabbana, Armani). Finally, many retailers, like H&M, have a range of jeans at basic prices or with a design component, while some, especially Zara, apply the strategy of following dominant trends and brands with a price discount.

Despite the presence of global brands, the design of jeans is concentrated in a few regions that are also interlinked. The dominant clusters, and their linkages, are not only shaped by economics, but also by migration. The jeans revolution actually started at the end of the 1970s in the Veneto and in southern France. The origins of Diesel and Replay are closely linked (Tagliabue 2006) and related through personal connections to the French cluster that started in the same period. The French jeans designers and entrepreneurs Guez, Elbaz, and Dahan developed the California brands in the 1990s. Hence the French and Americans cluster are linked (Who's Next 2005). The Dutch cluster was also a spin-off of the French cluster and of the American brands as it was born from the association of Pierre Morisset and G-Star and the establishment of the European headquarters of Dockers and Tommy Hilfiger in Amsterdam. The USA (California), France (Provence), Japan (Osaka), Italy (Veneto), and the Netherlands (Amsterdam) each represent more than US$2 billion in brand volume.

In 2006, the production of jeans was concentrated in a small number of countries, with Mexico, Turkey, Tunisia, China, and Bangladesh representing over 70 percent of global jeans production. Denim manufacturing was also concentrated amongst a few countries and companies; the USA, Italy,

Turkey, Mexico, Brazil, India, and China are the main players. Larger firms have followed a strategy of global alliances. Cone Mills and Swift-Galey (USA) have factories in all the major countries and regional alliances in Mexico and Turkey. Tavex (Spain) and Santista (Brazil) merged operations in 2006. UCO (Belgium) and Raymond (India) created a global joint venture in 2005. Each of these groups produces volumes above 100 million meters (roughly a market share of 5 percent for each). Italian and Japanese weavers have chosen a specialization strategy catering for niche markets. Kaihara (Japan) is an example of a vintage denim weaver, TRC (Italy) is master of baked-in effects in yarn dyeing. The making-up sector is the most fragmented with some large subcontractors having more than 2,000 workers (e.g. Sartex in Tunisia, Lajat in Mexico) but also many small and medium-size subcontractors. A clustered pattern is also prevalent with concentrations in the Torreon area (Mexico) and in Sousse (Tunisia). Washing jeans has also a dual pattern of companies operating in several countries (Martelli in Italy, Romania, and Tunisia) but with regional clusters in each of the countries, often close to garment-making. In terms of innovation leadership, the Veneto (Italy) stands out as the center for washing. This cluster is closely related to Italian manufacturers of laundry technology (e.g. Tonello) and suppliers of specialty chemistry such as resins (e.g. Lamberti). Hence a true industrial district has developed (Crestanello and Della Libera 2003).

The jeans industry is thus characterized at all levels by a pattern of global alliances or global brands, but combined with national and regional concentrations. This pattern is determined by regional economics as innovation is fostered by close distances to suppliers and the presence of specialized local labor markets or networks, for both productive (e.g. laundry workers') and nonproductive (e.g. designers') activities. It is also determined by business methods enabling a global outlook and presence. The clustering is accompanied by vertical integration as making up and washing are amalgamated, and denim production shifts to important regions of making up. Speed of response, desirable to accommodate the same in the market, is also shaping the global geography of jeans production (Figure 8.2).

The global trade pattern is guided by three factors: product differentiation, logistics, and trade policy. Product differentiation responds to differences in fit, fabric preferences, make, and finishing, which are gradual but substantial enough to justify specific sourcing. The differentiation argument is closely linked to the logistical argument. The jeans market is predominantly driven by replenishment techniques: stores are supplied according to reported sales. Various markets will report differences in sales in terms of fit, model, fabric, and washing; for example, Swedes need different sizes from Greeks. Sourcing nearby will enable more flexible response and contribute to lower levels of work-in-progress and of capital. This is in line with Harvey's argument stated above. The third factor is that the trade policies of both the European Union (EU) and the USA are shaped by free-trade

Figure 8.2 The jeans wall: the main retail presentation concept combined with constant replenishment and quick response production.

agreements with nearby countries. Local sourcing with regional fabric gives a tariff rebate of at least 10 percent. There is, for example, no benefit for the USA to source in Tunisia or for the EU to source in Mexico. As far as basic products in Asia are concerned, there is no specific difference in tariffs toward the EU or the USA.

The global jeans market is estimated to have a size of US$40 billion (*Journal du textile* 2006). However, the trade in jeans is at a much lower level and should be estimated at around US$15 billion.[11] One of the most striking features is the imbalance in trade between developed and developing countries. The USA and the EU each import more than US$4 billion worth of jeans. Trade between the USA and the EU, however, is below US$150 million. Trade between Japan and the EU and the USA is below US$35 million for all relative trade flows. In terms of trade with developing countries, the EU and the USA source around half their jeans in their regional trade zone and the other half in Asia. Mexico, the Dominican Republic, Turkey, and Tunisia are leaders in close sourcing, and Bangladesh and China are leaders in distant sourcing.

There is hardly any interregional trade. Mexico is a marginal supplier to the EU while Turkey is only a minor supplier to the USA. The jeans market is dominated by global brands, but trade is mainly regional. Levi's supplies the USA market with regional production and regional fabrics in the North

American Free Trade Area yet services the EU market with production and fabrics from the Mediterranean countries. Tommy Hilfiger USA is made in Mexico and Sri Lanka; Tommy Hilfiger Europe is made in Tunisia.

Trade between developed countries operates at substantially different price levels than between developed and developing countries. Jeans exported from the USA to the EU have a trade value of US$100 per item. Jeans exported from the EU to the USA trade at seventy-five US dollars per item. These are clearly premium-priced branded goods. Trade values between Japan and other developed countries are comparable. Exports from the USA are concentrated on women's jeans (typically Californian brands), while European trade to the USA is mainly in men's jeans (Italian designer brands). Products from developing countries are traded at much lower values. The average import value of Chinese and Indian jeans to the EU is thirteen US dollars per piece. It is even lower for Bangladesh. Products from nearby countries derive a much higher price, at around thirty-two US dollars. This reflects higher-value fabrics, more sophisticated products, smaller volumes, and shorter lead times.

Trade in materials is also regional in character. The EU exports US$490 million in denim fabrics, of which 70 percent is oriented toward the Mediterranean countries, 17 percent toward Asia, and 13 percent toward other developed countries. The EU exports US$70 million to the USA, but imports from the USA are small. USA exports are chiefly oriented toward Mexico and other Central American countries. Imports of denim into developed countries are also small. The EU imports US$300 million worth of denim fabrics, 45 percent of it from Turkey and 15 percent from other Mediterranean countries. India and China are self-supporting in fabrics. Mexico and Turkey have developed an integrated supply chain for nearby supply (Gereffi and Martinez 1999; Tokatli 2007). Sri Lanka and Tunisia have integrated textile finishing, making up, and washing, but use imported grey fabrics.

Conclusion

In this chapter, jeans have served as a case illustrating the transition from Fordism to post-Fordism in industrial terms, and from modernism to post-modernism in fashion culture. This transition has happened by mobilizing a combination of incremental innovations to create a wide lexicon of stylistic details with the objective of speeding up fashion cycles, increasing profit margins, and broadening the appeal of jeans by achieving both customization and luxury appeal. In fashion terms, jeans have been transformed from a classic item with archetypical features to a bearer of a wide range of style elements, entailing a complex grammar in which features can be endlessly recombined. Jeans have therefore supported and epitomized a more eclectic dress style typical of postmodern times, including vintage elements, blending of styles, and the emulation of movie stars. Jeans can be considered as the palimpsest of the transition from modernity to postmodernity, not only in fashion terms but also as a consequence of deeper trends in capital formation, such as speeding up the turnover time of capital and the shift of production to developing countries.

However, this transition happened long after Harvey predicted it in 1989. While the technical modification of jeans started in the 1980s, it only achieved commercial impact in the second half of the 1990s. This required the loosening of the grip of the dominant brand—Levi's—on the jeans market and the emergence of brands with alternative signatures. These brands were developed in very specific regional clusters, in particular the Veneto, southern France, western Japan, and California. Their breakthrough was fed by new methods of washing in combination with traditional spinning and weaving techniques. These innovations were not motivated by post-Fordist accumulation of capital, but were recuperated by a post-Fordist logic in accumulation of capital. Industrially, the transition required low-cost manual labor as most special treatments are highly labor-intensive. Commercially, the transition was enabled by verticalization and the use of information technology to feed back sales data into design and manufacturing.

The innovation pattern for postmodern jeans is truly global in its adoption by consumers, albeit with regional differences. Most surprising is the diffusion of styles of jeans from localized nodes of creativity on the one hand to strong creative linkages between these regional clusters on the other. This geography of jeans innovation in developed countries is fed by strong clusters in manufacturing. Even more surprising is the predominant regional character of production. While there are design influences between the USA, Europe, and Japan, trade flows are minimal. This pattern, however, does not conflict with a market structure with dominant global brands and a small number of global production alliances. Hence postmodern jeans also reflect very intricate arrangements in terms of global capital and production.

Notes

1. This chapter is based on a research project carried out at Saxion Universities by the author and Kishan Jalimsing, George Kara, and Larissa Westendorp in 2005–2006 based on object analysis, systematic analysis of the fashion and textile trade press, financial analysis of companies, and around twenty interviews with jeans manufacturers and fabric manufacturers in the Netherlands, Belgium, France, Italy, Turkey, Tunisia, and Sri Lanka.
2. Natural indigo was derived from the root of the woad plant or the indigofera leaf. Natural dyes were reintroduced in Europe in 2000.
3. See at: http://www.leecooper.com/the-denim-a-to-z.php for a full dictionary of jeans techniques.
4. See Grado Zero Espace for nettle, Hecking-Deotexis for hemp, Berti for linen.
5. See: http://www.1888articles.com/author-fibre2fashion-1093.html for a description of chemical processes.

6. See http://www.fashionfreak.de/vol06/editorials/editorial_03en.html.
7. See http://www.jeans.com/Brands/.
8. See http://www.jeans.com/Brands/.
9. Evidence from work process observation at Brandix (Sri Lanka) and Sartex (Tunisia).
10. See http://scienceonstage.nl/modules/websitepercent20EN/03-P-Customise-your-own-jeans-2007.pdf for advice on how to chemically personalize jeans by using potassium permanganate.
11. All trade statistics derive from EU Market Access Database and US Department of Trade and Commerce. Year of reference is 2006.

References

Agins, Teri (1999) *The End of Fashion: How Marketing Changed the Clothing Business Forever*, New York: HarperCollins.

Aglietta, M. (1979) *A Theory of Capitalist Regulation: The US Experience*, London: Verso.

Blackburn, K., Brighton, J., James, I., Riddlestone, S., and Stott, E. (2004) *Feasibility of Hemp Textile Production in the UK*, Report for BioRegional, Wallington (UK).

Crestanello P. and della Libera, P. (2003) "International Delocalisation of Production: The Case of the Fashion Industry of Vicenza," paper presented at the conference on "Clusters, Industrial Districts and Firms: The Challenge of Globalisation" in honor of Professor Sebastiano Brusco, Modena, September 12–13.

Dicken, P. (2004) *Global Shift: The Internationalisation of Economic Activity*, London: Sage Publications.

Downey, Lynn (2005) "A Short History of Denim (by Lynn Downey, Levi Strauss & Co. Historian)," available at http://www.levistrauss.com/Heritage/ForStudents AndTeachers.aspx (accessed June 25, 2008).

Elsasser, V. (1997) *Textiles: Concepts and Principles*, New York: Delmar.

Gereffi, G. (2001) "Beyond the Producer-Driven/Buyer-Driven Dichotomy: The Evolution of Global Value Chains in the Internet Era," *IDS Bulletin*, 32(3) (July): 30–40.

Gereffi, G. and Martinez, M. (2000) "Torreón's Blue Jeans Boom: Exploring La Laguna's Full Package Solution." *Bobbin* 41, 8 (April): 44–54.

Harvey, D. (1989) *The Condition of Postmodernity: An Enquiry into the Origins of Cultural Change*, Oxford: Blackwell.

IFM et al. (2007) "Study on the Competitiveness of the Textile, Clothing, Furniture. Leather and Textile Industry," Study for the European Commission (forthcoming).

Journal du textile (2005) Jeans Special in no. 1829, April 18, 2005.

—— (2006) Jeans Special in no. 1871, April 17, 2006.

—— (2007) Jeans Specials in no. 1912, April 10, 2007.

Lannelongue, M. P. (2004) *La Mode racontée à ceux qui la portent*, Paris: Hachette.

Lash, S. and Urry, J. (1994) *Economies of Signs and Space*, London: Sage Publications.

Lester, Richard K. and Piore, Michael J. (2004) *Innovation: The Missing Dimension*, Cambridge, MA: Harvard University Press.

Lipovetsky, G. and Roux, E. (2003) *Le Luxe éternel: Dès l'Âge du sacré au temps des marques*, Paris: Collection Le Débat, Gallimard.

Museo del Tessuto Prato, Italy (2005) "Jeans!: Le origini, il mito Americano, il made in Italy," Catalogue of exhibition (illustrated).

Piore, Michael J. and Sabel, Charles F. (1984) *The Second Industrial Divide*, New York: Basic Books.

Scheffer, M. (1992) *Trading Places: Fashion, Retailers, and the Changing Geography of Clothing Production*, Nederlandse Geografische Studies 150, Utrecht: KNAG.

Scheffer, M. and Duineveld, M. (2004) "Final Demise or Regeneration, 'The Dutch Case'," *Journal of Fashion Marketing and Management*, 8(3): 340–349.

Scheffer, Y. M. (1994) *The Changing Map of European Textiles: Production and Sourcing. Strategies of Textile and Clothing Firms*, Brussels, OETH (research funded by a grant from the European Commission, DG Industry).

Scott, A. (2000) *The Cultural Economy of Cities: Essays on the Geography of Image-Producing Industries*, London: Sage Publications.

Tagliabue, John (2006) "State of the Art Denim: A Cut Above the Rest," *International Herald Tribune* (online edition), July 12.

Tokatli, N. (2007) "Networks, Firms and Upgrading within the Blue-Jeans Industry: Evidence from Turkey," *Global Networks*, 7(1): 51–68.

Van Hoek, R. (1998) "Reconfiguring the Supply Chain to Implement Postponed Manufacturing," *International Journal of Logistics Management*, 9(1): 95–110.

Who's Next trade fair (2005) *La Révolution française du jeans*, fair catalogue.

Chapter 9

Fabricating Greekness
From fustanella to the glossy page

Michael Skafidas

A hundred years ago Virginia Woolf visited Greece for the first time. She strolled around Athens, where "all people seem poor" and sit "about on classic marble, chatting and knitting" (Woolf 1993: 212). Her Greek travel diary depicts a time and era when Greek culture was still trying to overcome the trauma of Turkish rule. Four centuries under Ottoman rule, which ended in the 1820s, was enough time to derail the illusion of racial purity for the descendants of Aristotle and Pericles. Most likely Woolf had read Percy Shelley's *Hellas*, whose preface claimed that "the modern Greek is the descendant of those glorious beings whom the imagination almost refuses to figure to itself as belonging to our kind." What Woolf saw in Athens, instead, was a new fused Greek being born in the ruins of history. "Like a shifting layer of sand these loosely composed tribes of many different peoples lie across Greece," she notes in her diary,

> calling themselves Greek indeed . . . but the language they talk is divided from the language that some of them can write as widely as that again is divided from the speech of Plato . . . You must look upon Modern Greece as the impure nation of peasants, just as you must look upon the modern Greeks as a nation of mongrel element and a rustic beside the classic speech of pure bred races.
>
> (Woolf 1993: 210)

Woolf was not alone in her disappointment with the mismatch of the reality of post-Ottoman Greece vis-à-vis its classical legacy. "The imagination does assert again and again," she admits as she walks by the "tremendous stones" which "are not to be ignored" (Woolf 1993: 205). Curiously she never notices the absence of the Elgin marbles. Nineteenth-century English painter Edward Lear, in his Greek diary, also regrets "the mongrel appearance of every person and thing (in Greece)." As a critic observes,

> although few people had actually visited Greece, English literature was cluttered with conventions and clichés about Greece and about the

modern Greeks. Visitors to the country inevitably saw it in terms of their education, which was heavily slanted towards the classics, and when they wrote down their impressions their books helped to pre-set the opinions of their successors. It was very easy . . . for visitors to Greece to be sentimental and patronizing . . . Most travelers in Byron's day simply assumed that the Modern Greeks were the descendants of the Ancient Greeks without bothering too much with the implications. They looked at their faces to see if they could find Grecian profiles familiar from ancient sculptures and vases.

(St. Clair 1983: 158)

It was language and dress coding that provided Woolf with some clues about an iconic civilization demystified by the forces of history and immigration. "The people of Athens are, of course, no more Athenians than I am," she observes.

They do not understand the Greek of the age of Pericles—when I speak it. Nor are their features more classic than their speech: the Turk and the Albanian and French—it seems—have produced a common type enough. It is dark and dusky, small of stature and not well grown. It is true that the streets are dignified by the presence of many rustics, in their Albanian dress; the men wear thick white coats, kilts, much pleated and long gaiters . . . I have seen no native women who could be distinguished from an Italian woman; and indeed you see very few women.

(Woolf 1993: 213)

It has been asserted that "the history of Greece is the story of endless movements of people: invasions, migrations, resettlement" (Winnifrith 1983: 43). Arguably, the Greek of the age of Pericles had ceased to exist long before the Ottoman centuries. Ethnic groups such as Albanians, Vlachs, Sarakatsani, Turks, and Serbs, among others, started immigrating to the land of Pericles as far back as the fourteenth century. It took centuries for all the different ethnic groups identified with the Greek world to reach the point where today they "consider themselves Greeks first and members of an ethnic group second" (Welters 1995: 56). Historians remind the modern reader that despite the pejorative and historically inaccurate association of a Vlach with a rootless bumpkin, the Vlachs, as well as most of the above-mentioned ethnic groups, have a long and strong presence in Greek history.[1] In the second millennium the Vlachs were known as nomads who spread from Dacia, the area that stands north of the Danube in Romania.[2]

The Albanians, on the other hand, were brought to Greece by the Byzantines at a time when there was not sufficient population to cultivate the land.[3] They also brought their own customs, languages, and dress codes. Even though they resisted Hellenization and they avoided intermarriage, eventually they assimilated through a cultural exchange with the Greek world that perhaps corroborated the ancient notion that Greekness is more about one's survival than about one's identity. No wonder, as Welters observes,

> nineteenth-century travelers in search of the descendants of the ancient Greeks were disappointed to find so little of what they considered pure Greek blood in the towns and villages surrounding the famous ancient sites, yet exhilarated at the colorful human landscape created by this ethnic mix.
>
> (Welters 1995: 55–56)

Despite modernization, the illusion of racial purity permeated the modern Greek notion of identity. "Haunted by the glory that was ancient Greece," Welters maintains, "modern Greeks have resisted acknowledging their country's mixed ethnic heritage. The dress of the country's various ethnic groups has been downplayed, as have other aspects of ethnicity such as customs, folklore, and language. Instead, Greek writers have emphasized the uniquely 'Greek' characteristics of clothing" (Welters 1995: 55).

As a visual manifestation, Greek dress mirrors the complexity of a mixed ethnic legacy; it is part of the experience of the ethnic, cultural, and national identity of an era. It has been said that "patterns of behavior and expressive emotional style include styles of dress and the meanings associated with them" (Eicher and Sumberg 1995: 296). Once upon a time, a visitor in Greece could draw some conclusions about the ethnic or national qualities of the locals through their dress code. But, as Welters asks, is "Greek dress really 'national'?" (Welters 1995: 54). The distinction between ethnic and national dress is the fine line between cultural identity and national image-making. As it has been defined, "ethnic dress indicates common or shared ways of dress that identify a group of people who share a common background and heritage. National dress, linked to the socio-political concept of nation-state and political boundaries, identifies citizens with their country" (Eicher and Sumberg 1995: 302). In Greece in particular, Greek national dress originated as the dress of certain ethnic groups within a newly independent nation-state composed of a people determined to preserve its Greek heritage and the will of the ethnic groups to be part of it. As a Greek scholar maintains, "Vlachs and Albanians who found their way into Greece became Greek through the centuries as much as Englishmen who emigrated to America became Americans. Their history is intertwined with Greek history. Their dress is also intertwined with Greek culture" (Papantoniou 2007).

Nowhere in modern Greek dress history is this merge of ethnic and national elements more epitomized than in the fustanella, the costume of Albanian origins which was declared Greek in the nineteenth century, at a time when "the creation of 'national dress' in Greece was part of an international trend in the Western world, which idealized rural life and its down-to-earth values in the aftermath of social changes brought on by the Industrial Revolution" (Welters 1995: 54). But long before it came to symbolize Greek independence from the Ottoman Turks, the Albanian kilt, or fustanella, was common dress for men in the thirteenth century when it was worn by the Dalmatians, one of the Illyrian progenitors of the Albanians. The historical and etymological roots of the fustanella, however, date back to the days of Rome, when the Albanian or Illyrian kilt became the original pattern for Roman military dress. The word "fustanella" originates in the Italian *fustagno*, "from which the word fustana is derived, with the diminutive form fustanella" (Papantoniou 2000: 206). The Hungarian sociologist and paleontologist Baron Nopcsa has theorized that the Celtic kilt emerged after the Albanian kilt was introduced to the Celts through the Roman legions in Britain. The historic link to the fustanella involves an ancient statue found in the area around the Acropolis in Athens dated from the third century BC. Nevertheless, no ancient Greek garments have survived to confirm that the origins of the fustanella are indeed in the pleated garments or chitons that were worn by men in Pericles' Athens.

The modern fustanella appears in Greece worn by the Albanians, and especially the Arvanites, as Greeks of Albanian ancestry were called, most of whom fought alongside the Greeks against the Turks in the long war of independence (Figure 9.1). In the early years of the Greek revolution the fustanella remained generally a military outfit at a time that most men in occupied Greece actively resisted the Ottomans. A notorious group of rebels against the Ottomans, the Suliotes, glorified by Byron as well as by Greek historians, were entirely Albanian (Winnifrith 1983: 45). As Welters notes, "identifying the Greek-Albanian man by his clothing was more difficult after the War of Independence, for the so-called 'Albanian costume' became what has been identified as a 'true' national dress of the mainland of Greece" (1995: 61). According to Papantoniou,

> it is difficult to naturalize the fustanella as one hundred percent Albanian. We lack ethnographic testimony to base this postulation except for impressions of travelers recorded according to each author's motive. We know that most likely the fustanella emerged from Rome, when the Roman legions started going north where they saw the Celts who were wearing the kilt.
>
> (Papantoniou 2007)

From the time of the Greek revolution until the present, there are constant references to the garment by visitors. The most famous English philhellene of his time, Lord Byron, fancied wearing the fustanella himself when he went to Greece to fight alongside the Greeks. (He eventually died in Mesologgi wearing one.) But neither Greeks nor visitors seemed to be preoccu-

Figure 9.1
Young Greek fighter
with long fusta-
nella. L. Dupre, 1819.
Courtesy of the
Peloponnesian Folk-
lore Foundation.

pied with the origins of the garment. The speculation by the revered Greek contemporary artist Yannis Tsarouxis that the origins of the fustanella lay in India is not entirely disconnected from the idealization of the golden age of the Macedonian empire. Is it possible that the pleated Greek dress code eventually integrated with the Persian dress style after Alexander's conquest of Asia? As Papantoniou explains,

> it is difficult to believe that the costume with a fustanella worn by the klephts (Greek freedom-fighters in the nineteenth-century) has any con-nection with a similar dress worn by the Moghuls of India. There is a basic difference in the way the triangles are cut. In Greece, as we have seen, they are right-angled triangles, with the hypotenuse of one triangle stitched to the vertical side of the next, to prevent the hem from bagging.
> (Papantoniou 2000: 208)

The fustanella is made from long strips of linen sewn together to make a pleated skirt. The whiteness of the fustanella for many modern Greeks mis-leadingly echoes the vision of a classical past where marble sculptures and temples were white. As a scholar reminds, "in reality the fustanella was utterly dirty and soiled with pork fat in order to resist water . . . The lads used the pleats of the fustanella as a towel to wipe off their hands or to clean their knives" (Petropoulos 1987: 16). Following the defeat of the Ottomans by the Greeks, King Otto, the Bavarian prince imported by the Greeks to be their first king in 1833, declared the fustanella the official court dress. Otto even posed wearing one. Ever since then, the fustanella has been acquiring its reputation as a dress of Greek pride. But as Petropoulos maintains,

> when the fustanella entered [Otto's] court a dress-designing Babylon emerged. We still don't know who inspired the hermaphrodite uniform worn to this day by the officers of the Greek presidential guard . . . The fustanella was already established as a typical uniform since 1813 for the Greek volunteers of the two regiments of the Greek Light Infantry of the English army . . . The fustanella is a product of theft. The Greek state snatched the national dress of the Arvanites and established it as a military uniform copying the English.
>
> (Petropoulos 1987: 13–14)

The assumption that the Hellenized version of the fustanella acquired 400 pleats, supposedly one for each year that Greece was under Ottoman rule, is also in dispute. Papantoniou claims that "the pleats, or *lagiolia*, of the fustanella are not always 400. This is an inaccuracy" (Papantoniou 2007).

It was during the Bavarian regency that the fustanella was shortened to create a billowy garment that hangs above the knee and is worn with hose and decorative clogs. In Otto's time making the fustanella was the craft of specialized tailors, the first of whom appeared in Nafplion, the first capital of liberated Greece, in the Peloponnese. By the turn of the century the *hellinoraptes* (tailors specialized in making the fustanella) were gradually displaced by the *frangoraptes* (the suit tailors). The waning of the fustanella coincided with the advent of the Western two-piece suit, "One of the major contributing factors to a sense of sameness in the modern world" (Maynard 2004: 43). It has been noted that "the dramatic division between male and female appearances, which began with the emergence of the bourgeoisie, is often accounted for by industrialism, capitalism, and the segregation of private from public domains" (Finkelstein 1998: 55). In Greece the tradition of men in skirts came to an end as trousers "signified the transition of the world from the Greco-Roman civilization to the next" (Petropoulos 1987: 73).

The very short fustanella, or *fustanellitsa*, worn today by the *tsoliades*, the picturesque presidential guard, for some appears to be a misinterpretation of the original (Figure 9.2). "The short *fustanellitsa* makes the tsoliades appear as ballerinas," banters Petropoulos. "Those in charge should remodel the length of the fustanella to the knee because that's what history is instructing us" (Petropoulos 1987: 28). Regardless of its length, the fustanella, as a heroic relic, remains a constant ironic reminder of the two heterogeneous groups which are part of modern Greek history and which most modern Greeks openly distrust: Albanians and kings. No wonder that in today's Greece the fustanella is often mocked as a folk costume that used to be worn by Greek schoolboys at Halloween parties.

At a time when the global supersedes the local, the fustanella represents

Figure 9.2
The short version of the fustanella—or *fustanellitsa*—as worn by the Presidential Guard. Courtesy of the Peloponnesian Folklore Foundation.

a bygone era of tradition that most young Greeks, especially the Internet generation, do not identify with. In view of Appadurai's stipulations, Maynard observes that "objects circulate in different regimes of space and time, acquiring meaning and new value in the process of exchange, or in the local context of wearing" (Appadurai 1996, cited in Maynard 2004: 19). A characteristic example is the response of young Athenians to the modern interpretation of the fustanella as shown at the Benaki Museum exhibition "Ptychoseis = Folds and Pleats: Drapery from Ancient Greek Dress to 21st

Figure 9.3 Reinterpreting the fustanella on the glossy page. Concept and styling: Tassos Sofroniou. Photograph: Konstantinos Rigos. *Free* magazine, October 2007.

Century Fashion," which was presented in 2004 on the occasion of the Athens Olympics. The fustanella had long been considered unfashionable in Greece until it was reinterpreted by modern international designers for this exhibition. As the fashion editor of the Greek edition of *Marie Claire* notes,

> it was interesting to observe the faces of all the young Greeks at the show. Most of them considered the fustanella as an outdated piece of folk. It appeared to be something foreign in their Westernized eyes. The fact that the Greek folk might have inspired designers such as Alexander McQueen and Vivienne Westwood puzzled them. They looked at the fustanella with awe and wonder as though it was a resurrected mummy.
> (Papa 2007)

In a recent endeavor, Greek fashion editor Tassos Sofroniou, in a spread entitled "It's All Greek to Me," appearing in the Greek men's magazine *Free* in October 2007, mixes Greek traditional ethnic dresses with contemporary clothes from fashion's current hot list. Thus a young Greek man poses wearing a leather jacket by D-squared and a wool cardigan by John Richmond on top, with a traditional fustanella instead of trousers (Figure 9.3); a young woman's body is almost entirely covered by a long fustanella dress matched with a short metal jacket by Pinko and stiletto heels by Cesare Paciotti

Figure 9.4
Reinterpreting the fustanella on the glossy page. Concept and styling: Tassos Sofroniou. Photograph: Konstantinos Rigos. *Free* magazine, October 2007.

(Figure 9.4). In this rare postmodern magazine editorial approach the past integrates with the present in a synthesis of surreal proportions: folk dress might be considered unwearable and even unbuyable in practical terms, yet it serves as the symbolic foundation of Greek modern appearance, a decorative relic floating like a teardrop on the surface of a glossy page. It has been argued that, as opposed to modern fashion,

> national or popular costumes are in most cases adjusted by competent critics to be more becoming, more artistic, than the fluctuating styles of modern civilized apparel . . . They have been worked out by peoples or classes which are poorer than we, and especially they belong to countries and localities and times where the population, or at least the class to which the costume in question belongs, is relatively homogeneous, stable, and immobile. That is to say, stable costumes which will bear the test of time and perspective are worked under circumstances where the norm of conspicuous waste asserts itself less imperatively than it does in the modern civilized cities, whose relatively mobile, wealthy population to-day sets the pace in matters of fashion.
>
> (Veblen 1994: 175)

One may view the failure of the fustanella to bear the test of time as an outcome of its mixed origins, which challenge the conventions of Greek homogeneity, especially at a time when modern Greek society has joined the affluent world. Papantoniou notes that

> unlike the Japanese who did not forget for a minute the tradition of their own dress, which has been successfully reinterpreted and adapted to modernity, the modern Greeks never successfully turned the tradition of their dress into an inspiration for something new. They would either mimic and reproduce it in a servile manner or they would turn to foreign trends for inspiration.
>
> (Papantoniou 2007)

Some critics have asserted that "ethnic dress is the opposite of world fashion" (Eicher and Sumberg 1995: 300). If ethnic dress is about distinguishing one group from the other, world fashion, especially in our global style-conscious time, is about reducing ethnic homogeneity and eliminating national singularity. Unlike ethnic dress, fashion "abhors fixity, of form or meaning, of knowledge or feeling, of the past itself" (Hollander 1994: 17). In countries like modern Greece, in particular, fashioning the self means reinventing one's historical self; the imported aesthetics of Western fashion do not simply abhor but defy the past along with the authenticity it represents. No wonder that the resurfaced fustanella at the Benaki Museum left young Greek viewers, most of them unquestionably readers of fashion and lifestyle magazines, with an aftertaste of funereal respect. Not only because "never *again* will the real have to be produced" (Baudrillard 2001: 1733, emphasis added), but also because the comparison between the old and the new takes place in an ideological vacuum of compressed memories and hyper-real images.

It is in this vacuum that the old and the new are yet to be reconciled in the land of Homer. The radical transformation of Greece into another Starbucks nation has not entirely silenced the voices of the phantoms. It is Odysseus's son Telemakhos who ponders, in the presence of the goddess Athena, "Who has known his own engendering?" To this day, no riddle has triggered more controversy or introspection in the annals of the modern Greek state than the irresolvable question of the origins of its constituents: are modern Greeks the direct descendants of Aristotle or the "mongrels" of the Balkans? Is Greece the home of a homogenized society linked culturally and historically to its ancient glory, or is it an invented modern nation of Balkan nomads, in which East and West, past and present, ethnicity and nationality constitute the structure of a reformed identity? If time is a maniac scattering dust, the primordial landscape of Homer is the place where the ruins of history and the exuberance of modernity perform an odd duet. Under the shade of the Acropolis, a modernized Greek capital vibrates with all the consuming intensity of a city that desires to be part of the global market. Major European and American fashion houses, along with local editions of international fashion magazines, established their operations in Greece in the dawn of the new millennium. Unlike other southern European markets like Italy, Greece (an EU member since 1981) joined the arena of the culture of global enticement relatively late. Economic disparity, a military dictatorship (1967–1973) which reversed the path of the country's socioeconomic growth and suppressed its cultural input, and a subtle resistance from the older generations to abandoning their tradition in order to embrace the Faustian rules of an intrusive market kept the country close enough to the West, yet ages away from what it is today: a jingling verse in the unfolding narrative of globalization.

Paradoxically, in this postmodern narrative Greeks appear as uniformed and as undistinguished as they never were in any of their own ancient epics. As we have seen, among other visible particularities of Greek culture that evaporated in the maelstrom of progress is Greek dress. Gone are the days when a proud Greek would express his patriotism by showing up wearing his fustanella on Greece's Independence Day. Older Greeks still go by the notion that "it's not the dress that makes one a priest," a notion which ironically coincides with the spirit of an age when the artistry or the tradition of the local dress have been swept away by the legions of the industry of global style and the fluctuating styles of modern clothes. Nowadays, a Zara skirt or a Gucci suit might indicate the class of the wearer but certainly they do not signify much of the wearer's ethnic or national background.

The assertion that history ended after the fall of communism verbalized the exaggerated urgency of the post-Cold War world to break free from "the extreme pessimism" of the twentieth century (Fukuyama 1992: 12). The short-lived euphoria of the millennium was the corollary of the shift of the post-Cold War world order from a fractured to a homogenized capitalist system of heterogeneous societies at the crossroads of globalization. As we will see, the shift allowed Western fashion magazines to expand to new markets and establish new partnerships. As the purveyors of Western chic, fashion magazines cashed in on the post-Cold War euphoria as they addressed effectively the needs of previously unexplored markets, such as Greece, at a crucial moment of change and transition which followed the century of pessimism.

The launching of the local edition of an internationally acclaimed fashion magazine such as *Vogue*, which is often recognized as "the highest representative of the empire of seduction" (Bartlett 2006: 176), allegedly connects a market previously detached from the sphere of the Western fantasia with the realm of fashionableness. Fashion magazines were originally conceived and structured in countries where fashion was looked upon as "eminently a 'higher' or spiritual need," as no other expression of consumption revealed a "more apt illustration than expenditure on dress" (Veblen

1994: 167). *Vogue* was originally conceived in nineteenth-century America at the time when the phrase "when good Americans die, they go to Paris," expressed what Paris symbolized in the nineteenth century for the American elite: the epicenter of elegance and consumerism. When *Vogue* was first published in New York in 1892 as a social gazette for the Eurocentric elite, Greece belonged to a part of the world that that Eurocentric elite considered "a kind of lost paradise, a great golden past in which souls too timid or trivial for anything else could find relief from horrors and afflictions of contemporary megalopolitan life" (Sherrard 1964, cited in Eisner 1991: 30). While late nineteenth-century New York thrived as the epicenter of the American Gilded Age, or across the Atlantic, in Baron Haussmann's Paris, the creation of the department store preceded the modern form of the magazine and the advertising industries (Appadurai 1996: 73), Greece remained an unfashionable antique land entirely unexposed to the emerging culture of enticement.

Umberto Eco once bantered that "it is impossible to build a perfect society if people are ill dressed" (1986, cited in Finkelstein 1998: 70). Echoing Veblen's early observations on the role of fashion as a maker of one's social image, Eco's sarcasm accentuates the unabashed impatience about fashion that marked the twentieth century. As both visual and verbal communication, the aesthetics of modern fashion emerged from the modernized West to express Western civilization's wish for refinement. Through film and photography, magazines and advertisements, Western fashion intrigued the imagination of the middle classes no end and affected both sexes equally and most civilizations generally. Hollander observes that "nobody with eyes escapes [fashion]" (Hollander 1994: 11). As a powerful tool in the process of projecting and spreading fashion's rules, fashion magazines consistently propagate a specific idea of a Western lifestyle that goes beyond dress coding; it is an idea of homogenization that serves the needs of the global market, while it transforms the desires of the local market. Fashion is a substantial part of today's gigantic machine of consumerism not simply because people can afford to buy clothes more than ever, but also because fashion, as the power generator of fashion magazines and other media, constantly dictates its rules to a receptive audience accustomed to being tutored on the aesthetics of living. This process of "fashionization" shapes the dialectics of public and private realms, of social space and the individual. Fashion, in a nutshell, not simply shapes but *inhabits* space. It normalizes people's fantasies, regulates their appearances and propels their aesthetic choices on both a local and a global level.

On another level, fashion has drawn inspiration from art as much as it has served as a muse of style to many artists. To a modern audience, a skirt by Yves Saint Laurent or a dress by Balmain indicate the style of their era as much as a modern painting carries the signs of its own time. Furthermore, the evaluation of fashion as a form of modern art has been encouraged and affirmed by institutions such as the Metropolitan Museum of Art in New York, which often presents internationally acclaimed fashion exhibitions in its Costume Institute. Thus the consideration of fashion as an extended form of modern art reinforces its power as an industry that requires not simply the pecuniary participation of the consumer but also his or her knowledge. It has been asserted that "a work of art has meaning and interest only for someone who possesses the cultural competence, that is, the code, into which [it] is encoded" (Bourdieu 2001: 1810). The fashion magazine culture presumes that the reader's judgment of taste is already shaped and predetermined by the "universal significance" principle of Western aesthetics as projected by the Western expression. As Bartlett points out, for instance, the success of the Russian edition of *Vogue*, launched in 1998, "depended on how fast the new rich Russians could be *taught* the subtleties, half shades, and fine distinctions of *Vogue*'s style" (2006: 180, emphasis mine). The standard of fashionableness proposed by the fashion magazine milieu reflects, recycles, and perpetuates a Western aesthetic ideology as conceived and embedded in the Western consciousness. Long before German *Vogue* was published it was Kant who, living and writing in the remoteness of eighteenth-century Königsberg, envisioned the world as "peoples of our part of the world" and the "savages" (Kant 2003: 111).

One may argue that in postmodernity the fashion industry's grand ambition, aside from immense profit, became to dress the gap between the Westerners and the "savages," turning fashionization into a global phenomenon. The aesthetic gentrification that derives from the fashionization of modern lifestyle leads to a bifurcation. On a local level, as in the case of Greece, it creates the *fashionable* and the *unfashionable* citizen; in a global perspective it divides the new world map in the light of a softer post-Cold War prejudice: the *fashionable* and the *unfashionable* world. It is a prejudice reminiscent of the division that Edward Said described between an emergent West and its abject Other, according to which the Other that was excluded and negated gives birth to a positive identity for the Western colonizer (Sharma and Sharma 2003: 303). The competition between the *fashionable* and the *unfashionable* citizen in Greece followed the tension between the ethnic Greek and the natural-born Greek. In the new landscape of affluence and consumption, ethnicity and nationality became of minor importance as long as one was *fashionable*, in other words, someone adequately educated in the subtleties of the fashion and the media culture.

Modern Greece remained part of the *unfashionable* world long after it acquired the benefits of its European membership in 1981. When international fashion magazines started establishing their Greek editions before the Internet revolution the Greek market was still a virgin and ambivalent territory full of potential younger consumers somehow eager to embrace the Western aesthetic due to the lack of a serious local alternative. In today's Greece, a country of ten million with poor reading habits, more than twenty mainstream international fashion magazines are successfully published monthly with a total circulation of more than 300,000, not counting fashion magazine supplements in major dailies. That is more than countries which produce fashion, like Italy or France, have to offer. Top-selling titles such as *Marie Claire* (launched in December 1988), *Elle* (October 1988), *Cosmopolitan* (launched in 1965; relaunched in 2001) and *Vogue* (2000), among others, gradually topped the once-strong local Greek fashion magazines. Eventually they succeeded in obliterating the local competition in a culture which traditionally imported rather than exported fashion. The oldest and most respected local Greek fashion magazine *Gynaika* (Woman), which could be described as a cross between *Vogue* and *Vanity Fair*, discontinued publication in September 2007, fifty-seven years after its first issue hit the stands. In its heyday in the 1970s and 1980s *Gynaika*'s circulation exceeded 100,000, which is roughly the cumulative circulation of the three top-selling fashion magazines in today's Greek market. A marketing practice that was unknown in *Gynaika*'s time is the packaging of today's Greek fashion magazines with gadgets such as accessories or cosmetics that lure the consumer. In the satiated Greek publishing market, without such a gadget a fashion magazine's monthly circulation may plummet as much as 50 percent. Turning the reader into a greedy and unreliable consumer who acquires a magazine for its gadget irrespective of its contents is the epitome of today's crisis in fashion magazine publishing, not only in Greece but also in most European markets including the British and the Italian.

As in other former *unfashionable* European markets, like Spain or Portugal, foreign fashion magazine titles arrived in Greece at a crucial time of change. It has been argued that countries that had "earlier been seen as the black sheep of Europe . . . by the 1980's had made a successful transition to functioning and stable democracy, so stable in fact that (with the possible exception of Turkey) the people living in them could hardly imagine the situation being otherwise" (Fukuyama 1992: 13). In tune with the new political optimism of the expanded Western world, the international editions of fashion magazines promoted the idea of fashion and consumption as a democratizing duet able to switch the aesthetic direction of societies in transition. In Athens or in Moscow, the "new" woman and the "new" man became the new guests in the unfolding spectacle. As a critic asserts, "the society which carries the spectacle does not dominate the underdeveloped regions only by its economic hegemony. It dominates them as the society of the spectacle" (Debord 1995, cited in Bartlett 2006: 177). As in the case of Russia, the success of the international fashion magazines in Greece depended on how fast the Greeks could be taught their subtleties. Prior to their arrival, the great majority of Greek readers were unfamiliar with the brand of the international magazines; however, like in Russia, their quick response guaranteed their eventual success. The first issue of the Greek *Vogue* hit the stands in March 2000 with the single blurb "At Last, Greek!"

Figure 9.5
The cover of the first issue of Greek *Vogue*: "At Last Greek!" ("Επιτέλους Ελληνίδα!"). March 2000.

(Figure 9.5), echoing the similar exclamation of the Russian edition whose premiere edition had already declared "In Russia, at last!" The transition from pre-*Vogue* to *Vogue* gives a fashion market a new potential *marketability*. As Veblen had anticipated, "the method of advertisement undergoes a refinement when a sufficiently large wealthy class has developed, who have the leisure for acquiring skill in interpreting the subtler signs of expenditure" (Veblen 1994: 187).

As the founding pillar of the fashion magazine industry, advertising dynamically invaded the territory of the reformed Greek consumer. As in previous cases, it reinforced in the Greek market "the entrenchment of the new selling practices (that) decisively changed the network of social relationships, changed the outlook for democracy, changed what it meant to be a person" (Ohmann 1996: 115). In the years that followed the magazine and television boom, as a scholar observes, "advertising is no longer built around the idea of informing or promoting in the ordinary sense, but is increasingly geared to manipulating desires and tastes through images that may or may not have anything to do with the product to be sold . . . the acquisition of an image (by the purchase of a sign system such as designer clothes . . .) becomes a singularly important element in the presentation of self in labour markets . . . it becomes integral to the quest for individual identity, self realization, and meaning" (Harvey: 288). Hence Greek fashion magazines offered their audience, among other things, accessibility to a system of signs previously and largely unavailable.

Unable to embody the new Western chic at once, the former *unfashionable* citizen first looks upon it with desire and admiration. As a new *flâneur* the reader is enthralled by the allure of the projected Western fantasia. In the beginning, Greek editions of international fashion magazines as a rule avoided featuring Greek models or local brands on their covers and in editorials. "It was not an option," clarifies a former editor of the Greek *Marie Claire*. "The French (publishers) would object to it on the grounds that the Greek market was not ripe to impose its own modern Western symbols and brands. It took a while to infuse the Greek society with the mentality of the international fashion culture" (from discussion with the author, 2001).

Furthermore, Greek fashion magazine readers gradually conformed to the temporal aspect of fashion. Part of the everlasting mystique of modern fashion is its ability to turn death into life. According to Baudelaire the final voyage of the *flâneur* is death, its destination the new (Benjamin 1999: 22). The capsule of Western style transcends real time and space. Despite Veblen's observation that "no explanation at all satisfactory has hitherto been offered of the phenomenon of changing fashions" (Veblen 1994: 173), the main generator of Western fashion, newness, emerged in modernity as "a quality independent of the use value of the commodity. [Newness] is the source of that illusion of which fashion is the tireless purveyor" (Baudelaire, cited in Benjamin 1999: 22). Thus the familiarization of the fashionable Greek with the principle of novelty took place in a landscape of modern consumption that replaces the aesthetics of duration with the aesthetics of ephemerality (Appadurai 1996: 85). Nowadays, fashion magazines serve fashion's own calendar of ephemerality on a global scale. Featuring bathing suits in March issues, or presenting the winter collections in July, are standard editorial practices. Natural phenomena, such as global warming, do not affect fashion's calendar. Ladies might appear in fur jackets on a balmy October evening in Athens simply because it's in *Vogue* and, as the magazine's slogan suggests, "before it's in fashion it's in *Vogue.*"

It goes without saying that the "impure nation of peasants" that haunted Virginia Woolf a century ago has today been transformed into another *Vogue* country. Most Athenians still do not understand the Greek of the age of Pericles but they *do* understand Woolf's language better than ever. An image of American actress Julianne Moore, in a recent advertisement which appeared in most Greek fashion magazines, promotes a foreign luxury brand to Greek readers in plain English: "Time is precious. Use it wisely." Employing the patterns of the advertising industry, it is common practice for most Greek fashion magazine editors to incorporate English catchphrases

Figure 9.6
"Fashion Onwards":
the cover of the
Greek *Marie Claire*,
November 2007.

on their covers, such as "Fall in Love," "Fashion Onwards," or "Date Is Dead" (Figure 9.6). As the publisher of the Greek editions of *Marie Claire* and *Cosmopolitan* explains,

> it's not that we snub the Greek language; it's that young consumers, when it comes to consuming or digesting fashion messages need to feel part of the global tribe, and English language is a tool for the modern Greeks to connect with the world. On the other hand, this trend has its drawbacks, as it disconnects the young generation of Greeks from their own language. Sometimes, I believe, the English language is incorporated in the Greek magazine culture more than it should be.
>
> (Andrianou 2007)

It is hard to imagine that modern Greece ever existed without its Western profile, especially at a time when the Ottoman experience has long faded deep into the pit of oblivion. Nowadays most modern Greeks tend to evaluate the fustanella in similar terms to Veblen's assessment of national costume as something that was worn by people who were "poorer than we."

The "we-ness," which "includes a common heritage with shared language, similar dress, manners, and lifestyle" (Eicher and Sumberg 1995: 301), is no longer what Greeks have in mind when they speak of ethnicity or nationality in the days of the euro. The "we-ness" of postmodern Greeks, marked by the evasive traits of their ethnic origins, rather seems to be a concentrated effort to make up for their disadvantaged centuries by appearing confident, craving for affluence and thinking fashionably in the global age. After all, the unabashed confidence of the fashionable world, which modern Greece has finally joined, goes by the wonderful illusion that "fashion . . . is a witness, but a witness to the history of the great world only" (Benjamin 1999: 71).

Notes

1. "Olympias and Philip and their son Alexander the Great are perhaps the most suitable starting point for a discussion of the Vlachs," Winnifrith maintains. "Not surprisingly, as Macedonia is a bone of contention between various nationalities, the racial origins of the ancient Macedonians are a matter of dispute. It has been claimed that Aristotle was a Bulgarian, and almost as far-fetched are the theories which seek to prove that Macedonians were somehow Greeker than the Greeks. A more moderate approach would suggest that by the end of the Classical period the influence of Greek from the coastal cities of both Epirus and Macedonia had spread to the aristocracy of most of the semi-barbarian tribes of northern Greece" (Winnifrith 1983: 71).
2. Some of the greatest benefactors of modern Greece, such as Zapas and Tositsas, came from the Vlach tribes.
3. Historical records indicate that a group of 10,000 Albanians with their families and flocks turned up at the Isthmus of Corinth in around 1338; they were offered land and were admitted to the Peloponnese by Theodore (Hammond 1983: 44).

References

Publications

Appadurai, Arjun (1996) *Modernity at Large*, Minneapolis: University of Minnesota Press.

Bartlett, Djurdja (2006) "In Russia, At Last and Forever: The First Seven Years of Russian *Vogue*," *Fashion Theory*, 10: 175–203

Baudrillard, Jean (2001) "The Precession of Simulacra," in *The Norton Anthology of Theory and Criticism*, New York and London: W. W. Norton & Company, Inc.

Benjamin, Walter (1999) *The Arcades Project*, Cambridge, MA: The Belknap Press of Harvard University Press.

Bourdieu, Pierre (2001) "Distinction," in *The Norton Anthology of Theory and Criticism*, New York and London: W. W. Norton & Company, Inc.

Eicher, Joanne B. and Sumberg, Barbara (1995) "World Fashion, Ethnic, and National Dress," in Joanne B. Eicher (ed.), *Dress and Ethnicity*, Oxford and New York: Berg.

Eisner, Robert (1991) *Travelers to an Antique Land*, Michigan: The University of Michigan Press.

Finkelstein, Joanne (1998). *Fashion: An Introduction*. New York: New York University Press.

Flaubert, Gustave (1989) *Travels in Greece*, Athens: Olkos.

Fukuyama, Francis (1992) *The End of History and the Last Man*, New York: Avon Books.

Hammond, Nicholas (1983) "Migration and Assimilation in Greece," in Tom Winnifrith and Penelope Murray (eds.), *Greece Old and New*, New York: St. Martin's Press.

Harvey, David (1990) *The Condition of Postmodernity*, London: Blackwell.

Hollander, Anne (1994) *Sex and Suits*, New York: Alfred Knopf.

Kant, Immanuel (2003) *Observations on the Feeling of the Beautiful and Sublime*, Berkeley and Los Angeles: University of California Press.

Lear, Edward (1965) *Journal of a Landscape Painter in Greece*, London: William Kimber.

Maynard, M. (2004) *Dress and Globalization*, Manchester: Manchester University Press.

Ohmann, Richard (1996) *Selling Culture*, New York: Verso.

Papantoniou, Ioanna (2000) *Greek Dress*, Athens: Commercial Bank of Greece.

Petropoulos, Elias (1987) *The Fustanella*, Athens: Nefeli.

Sharma, Sanjay and Sharma, Ashwani (2003) "White Paranoia: Orientalism in the Age of Empire," *Fashion Theory*, 7(3/4): 301–317

St. Clair, William (1983) "Byron and Greece," in Tom Winnifrith and Penelope Murray (eds.), *Greece Old and New*, New York: St. Martin's Press.

Veblen, Thorstein (1994) *The Theory of the Leisure Class*, New York: Penguin Books

Welters, Linda (1995) "Ethnicity in Greek Dress," in Joanne B. Eicher (ed.), *Dress and Ethnicity*, Oxford and New York: Berg.

Winnifrith, Tom (1983) "Greeks and Romans," in Tom Winnifrith and Penelope Murray (eds.), *Greece Old and New*, New York: St. Martin's Press.

Woolf, Virginia (1993) *Travels with Virginia Woolf*, London: Pimlico.

Interviews

Andrianou, Molly (2007) interview with the author, Athens, Greece, July.

Papa, Matilda (2007) interview with the author, Athens, Greece, August.

Papantoniou, Ioanna (2007) interview with the author, Nafplion, Greece, August.

Chapter 10

Fashion Brazil

South American style, culture, and industry

Valéria Brandini

Behind Latin hype

> This cultural mixing process, already a characteristic of Brazil, demands the creation of fashions that are sensitive to this reality, ones that do not dishonor the Brazilian mentality, but rather honor it, not merely as democratically interracial, but as meta-racial.
>
> (Freyre 1986: 116)

The symbolic appeal that stimulates consumer interest in fashion is usually based on aspects of the "new," the singular, the different. In an attempt to confer meanings, cutting-edge fashion designers have made aesthetic references to the clothing of "exotic" countries, as a stimulus to new fashion cycles and trends. Nowadays, as European fashion designers search for greater and more diverse design inspiration, they are also paying attention to the new styles that are emerging in countries formerly marginal to the global systems of haute couture and ready-to-wear. "Latin style" has emerged as a fashion focus, centered in particular on Brazil. From Havaianas sandals and Rosa Chá bikinis, to Alexandre Herchcovitch's more conceptual designs, Brazilian fashion, with its strong ethnic appeal, and sometimes almost theatrical tendencies, is becoming a new fashion tendency. Brazilian fashion designers are referencing the exotic, the urban, and the marginal, as sources of design innovation, and in turn they are providing a stimulus to a once-dwindling clothing industry.

The search for the new in fashion, as in other areas of creative practice such as music and the arts, has drawn attention to "Latin style." Fashion entrepreneurs in the northern hemisphere are acknowledging *latinidad* as a new fashion reference. This is not the stereotyped Carmen Miranda style of the 1950s, but based rather on the culture of the streets, on gang behavior, and on Brazilian beach life. So as Brazilian fashion professionals begin to gain recognition, Brazil's ethnic and creative identity is becoming a new focus of attention in European and North American fashion circuits. The pale and anorexic stereotypes of Europe have given way to Latin curves, bright colors, and natural materials, such as canvas, raw cotton, and "vegetarian" leather substitutes associated with Brazil. These have been seen in the collections of Brazilian brands such as Osklen (using canvas and raw cotton) and the sports gear brand Rainha (using vegan leather for footwear), which are challenging the synthetic fabrics generated by new technologies.

Operating under a fashion system that expresses the cultural differences between the "Old World" (Europe) and the "New World" (America), Brazilian fashion highlights the differences between the values of tradition and modernity. In South America this system does not function according to the cultural capital accumulated by a fashion house or designer, referred to by Bourdieu (1975). Latin America's very recent history in the fashion business has given designers carte blanche to experiment and take risks with their creations, and in the process to build a legitimate Brazilian fashion industry.

Unlike France or England, Brazil's fashion has been founded on young fashion brands, established mainly in the 1990s. The respect acquired by some Brazilian fashion designers like Dener (in the 1970s), and more recently by Ocimar Versollato (in the 1990s), was built on their following the fundamental rules of European fashion: the principles of style and elegance, signified by haute couture. But these examples, which made no reference to Brazilian culture, no longer represent a growing majority of Brazilian designers. In Brazil, young fashion designers do not need the experience of working in a famous house (acquiring what Bourdieu calls symbolic capital) to enhance their careers. They need the economic capital to produce a collection and "work it" in the fashion market as well, of course, as the necessary talent as a designer, which will attract the attention of the right journalists and put their name in the fashion media. The new Brazilian fashion is not established in the couture tradition, with its references to high art, but derives its aesthetic from local culture and ethnicity.

Now that street fashion has become acknowledged as an influence amongst designers at the top of the fashion hierarchy, Brazilian fashion entrepreneurs have gained confidence in the "street style" favored by new and talented young couturiers, potential "names" to enhance the local fashion market. Toward this goal, the 1990s brought events like Morumbi Fashion, a sequence of shows of new Brazilian designers (which later became São Paulo Fashion Week), and Phytoervas Fashion, a contest for new talent. These seasonal events were created to draw the attention of fashion consumers and the media to new designers and fashion brands, thus giving them the opportunity of showing their work, while providing the market with potential new names for the Brazilian fashion circuit.

The Brazilian fashion industry

The Brazilian "clothing industry" (focused on production and manufacturing) joined the "fashion industry" (global clothing production oriented to fashion's seasonal tendencies) only in the last decades of the twentieth century. Until the early 1980s Brazil had only clothing production, not a fashion industry. Ready-to-wear was copied directly from European styles, without the intervention of any Brazilian fashion designer, generating what Brazilians called "little fashion."

Many of the first clothing factories in Brazil were established by immigrant families in the second half of the nineteenth century, in the Bom Retiro district of São Paulo. By 1882 the industry had developed so much that a lodging house had to be created for the workers. The first were Italians who set up factories to weave cotton. They were followed, at the beginning of the twentieth century, by Jews from Central and Eastern Europe, who manufactured clothes and produced handcrafted items, which they peddled from house to house. They created their own clientele, called "clientelchicks," who purchased from them clothing, towels, fabrics, and neckties. The Jews remained a predominant force in clothing in the Bom Retiro until the Korean immigrants began to move there in the 1970s (Garcia and Castilho 2001).

The factories were all family-run businesses, passed from father to son. The fact that they were managed by inexperienced family members could be a professional disaster, and resulted in many family businesses eventually going bankrupt. Today, by comparison, most companies are operated by skilled professionals, rather than according to bloodline. In the last two decades the companies that remained began to operate not just as clothing producers but as fashion brands, hiring talented designers and skilled managers, in order to finally enter the fashion circuit. They began creating collections based on cultural concepts that also highlighted Brazilian culture. Most successful today are Compania Maritima and Rosa Chá, a brand created in Bom Retiro that still operates there but has become a worldwide fashion phenomenon. Rosa Chá bikinis, using fabric prints that reference Brazilian folklore entities such as Sasci-Pererê, Mula Sem-Cabeça, and Curupira have become objects of desire for many Hollywood stars and top models like Naomi Campbell. The growing professionalism of Brazilian fashion led to the emergence of talented young designers at the end of the 1980s. The establishment of fashion graduate schools, and big fashion events such as São Paulo Fashion Week, have widened new horizons for the Brazilian fashion scene and created a real fashion circuit in the country.

Some well-known brands, once they were consolidated economically, began to experiment with more conceptual fashion as diffusion lines within their companies. One of the best known is the M. Officer brand of jeans, owned by designer Carlos Miele, who has since developed a more sophisticated brand under his own name. Miele produces clothes that evoke Brazilian folklore and culture. He has a store in New York's fashionable Meatpacking District, and has shown at New York and London fashion weeks. He is part of a group of people who are searching for authentic Brazilian cultural and aesthetic references, one which has opened new perspectives for the discussion of a "real Brazilian fashion." They have increased the space for new aesthetic experiments and business ventures for many Brazilian brands, and attracted international media attention.

In Brazil, as in many other countries, there is a question of whether fashion expropriates cultural meanings for commercial ends, or whether it elevates them, turning their aesthetic content into clothes that exalt cultural richness. Despite the questions arising from the legitimacy of fashion's use of aesthetic and cultural aspects, this cooption can be viewed positively as a means of bringing the cosmology of Brazilian life and history to the central stage, nationally and internationally. In fact many Brazilian fashion designers are not just communicating Brazilian cosmology (the beauty, the sensuality, as well as the poverty and the political corruption) through their design concepts, but are also working directly with individuals and collectives.

Marcelo Sommer, a well-known Brazilian designer, is now the creative director of Coopa-Roca, a women's craft and fashion cooperative located in Rocinha, one of the biggest and most dangerous *favelas* (slums) in Rio de Janeiro. The main goal of the cooperative is to provide its participants, who are living in poverty, with the possibility of work and a family income without having to leave Rocinha. It employs over eighty female artisans to create handcrafted work from remains of fabric and recycled materials for brands including M. Officer, Osklen, and the swim-suit label Lenny. Other brands have been generated by the "hype" around luxury goods and fashion in Brazil (Figure 10.1).

One example is the Daslu, the biggest store for high-end consumption in Latin America, named after the association of two women named "Lu" and the preposition "*das*" (meaning "of"). It is a 17,000-square-meter (183,000-square-feet), four-story neoclassical Italian-style palazzo that houses 120 designer boutiques. Here shoppers can buy just about anything from a pair of Dolce & Gabbana jeans for US$1,750 to a Maserati convertible for US$306,000, all while sipping free champagne and Scotch whisky (Benson 2005). The store has a helipad on the roof allowing its clientele to bypass the city's notorious traffic jams, street crime, and prostitutes (or *putas*, an abbreviation of the word *prostitutas*). Ironically, the helicopters that bring socialites and celebrities to Daslu fly over where Daspu prostitutes work. The latter have organized under the name DaVida,[1] a non-government organization created by prostitutes from Rio de Janeiro. The brand name Daspu, based on the ironic combination of Daslu and *putas*, features clothes designed and made by prostitutes, based on their lifestyle. The clothes are sold to raise funds to help aging prostitutes who have been abandoned by the government without retirement pensions or health care. Daspu is now supported by many celebrities, fashion designers, brands, and social activists, and they show at big fashion events and have their collections designed by successful Brazilian designers who have joined the cause.

Daspu and Coopa-Roca are examples of the way that Brazilian fashion

Figure 10.1 Rosa Chá bikinis. Photograph by Jacques Faing.

has drawn attention to the street, to create a symbiotic relationship between the life of the outcast, the excluded, and the world of celebrities. Brazilian fashion can bring about these new projects that engage with the image and the reality of society's rejects, in ways similar to international brands such as Benetton or Diesel. If the mainstream discourse of fashion nowadays is "difference" as differentiation (following Baudrillard's logic of differentiation), to denote superiority in the social hierarchy, the discourse of brands like Daspu and Coopa-Roca evolved from difference based on the socially rejected, whose clothes reflect their life at the margins of society. This new type of fashion based in a peripheral country generates ideological and aesthetic roots that are now being pursued by the new generation of Brazilian designers, most of them just out of fashion schools. While sometimes criticized for their radical, almost theatrical, creations, these recent graduates are quite quickly building successful careers supported by national and international investment.

The cultural territory of Brazilian fashion

Contemporary Brazilian fashion aggregates the meanings of cultural identity, which serve to differentiate it from the country's clothing industry. The street, as a category of cultural analysis, was theorized by Brazilian anthropologist Roberto Da Matta based on concepts created by the renowned Brazilian novelist Jorge Amado, author of *Gabriela Cravo e Canela (*Gabriela

Figure 10.2 André Lima fashion show. Photograph by Jacques Faing.

Clove and Cinnamon). Da Matta writes about the emotional and physical territory inhabited by typical Brazilian social groups (conmen and heroes), which represent Brazil's quotidian culture. The Brazilian street is defined by Da Matta (1997: 55), as the place of individualization, of fighting and *malandragem* (the actions of conmen). It is a space where power relationships are established, and social groups dispute physical and symbolic territories; a space located beyond geography, occupied by multiple identities that pass through real, virtual, and imaginary spaces. The experience of the street has been reflected in Brazilian art and music and made available on the Internet. New technology in particular is facilitating new forms of communication between groups and individuals in Brazil, as elsewhere, and is disseminating new experiences of the street (Figure 10.2).

Da Matta (1997) conceived the street as an anthropological category that signifies an outside world—unforeseen, accidental, passionate, and new. It forms a stark contrast to the category of the "house" as a controlled universe, where things are in their right places, where there is harmony and calm. The familial hierarchies that govern the traditional house and home form a stark contrast to the street, a place of conflict, dispute, birth, and death. For Da Matta the domain of the house includes more intimate relationships and less social distance, whereas the street references lack of seclusion or control. The public space is ruled by impersonal forces; it is the location of vagabonds, conmen, and society's outlaws, the transgressors and the uncontrollable; all of whom have come to signify contemporary urban living in Brazil.

Based on Da Matta, it can be said that Brazilian fashion "dresses the street." Fashion has incorporated in its aesthetic the diverse and contradictory entities that constitute the cultural and emotional space of the chaotic urban environment. The styles of fashionable clothing can be seen as reflecting the hierarchies, power relationships, and assumed positions shared in the real, virtual, and imaginary territories of the street. The multiple and successive hierarchies taking place in the street, and perpetually rearticulating position and meaning, are reflected in Brazilian fashion. Fashion derived from the street is more than mere clothing or style; it has become a significant form of communication.

The aesthetic and culture of Brazilian fashion incorporates values, meanings, and, most important, the everyday realities of Brazilian quotidian life. Created by new younger Brazilian designers such as Ronaldo Fraga (Figure 10.3), André Lima, Alexandre Herchcovitch, and Maria Bonita, this fashion "dresses itself" with elements of Brazilian culture and social life that date back five hundred years. The designers seek the attention of contemporary urban individuals by drawing on the symbolic universe of Brazilian street culture, whose fluidity and mosaic of values and perspectives are translated into a clothing aesthetic analogous to art. For example, in summer 2003 São Paulo Fashion Week, the biggest fashion event in the country, took as its theme "Brazilian culture" in an attempt to establish a Brazilian fashion identity (in the same year the theme of the São Paulo Art Biennale was "The City"). One of the most distinctive events of the week was the Brazilian Color Chart, created by Mauricio Ianês, Alexandre Herchcovitch's fashion stylist. Like a fashion fabric color chart, it presented images of the different skin tones of individual Brazilians, exposing imperfections, scars, and body hair. The idea was to associate the theme of color in fashion with the ethnic diversity of the Brazilian population.

Even though the fashion industry manipulates and rearticulates authentic cultural roots, Brazilian fashion can be seen as a totemic manifestation of Brazilian culture. Traditional signs and icons are combined with aspects of modern urban life to represent a cultural universe where individuals, collectivities, and quotidian life together create a new aesthetic that is communicated through clothes. According to Ted Polhemus (1995: 7), high culture gives place to popular culture and in this context the street is legitimated as a space of authenticity. The seduction of the street is that it becomes an end in itself; metropolitan culture produces fluid styles that acquire legitimacy and dictate clothing patterns. It is its particular representation of the street that is providing Brazilian fashion with a unique identity, which attempts to express the essence of Brazilian culture, where the street serves as a stage full of "Brasility"; quotidian life is dramatized in fashion design. These compositions are the essence of the work of a new generation of Brazilian fashion designers.

This cultural universe can be seen in São Paulo Fashion Week. Occurring

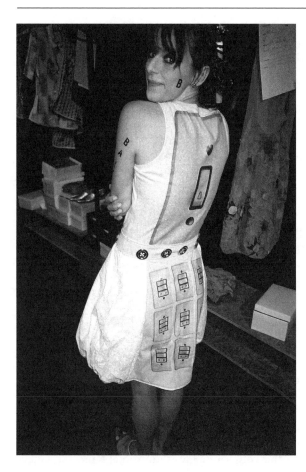

Figure 10.3
Design by Ronaldo
Fraga. Photograph by
Jacques Faing.

twice a year to promote Brazilian designers, the event has become a display
of how fashion is absorbing and integrating Brazilian culture. Dozens of
sponsors, from cosmetic companies to cable television networks, provide
financial support to make the week possible. The investment in fashion is
not just as a business, but as a cultural event, which includes parallel exhibitions of photographs and artwork, some by the fashion designers themselves. The work of photographer Mary Stockler, for instance, showed
girls from the *favelas* having fun at funk parties in Rio de Janeiro, wearing
tight spandex clothes in green, pink, and white. No top models, no beauty
queens, but simple girls from the slums, with their fat legs and stomachs,
celebrating life and creating their own fashion oblivious to fashion as elegance and glamour—just real people from the street.[2]

Not just clothes and glamour make São Paulo Fashion Week; the event
has been attempting, year by year, to help search for an identity for Brazilian
fashion. Curiously, one of its events in 2002 was themed "the city, the street,"

similar to Da Matta's concept. São Paulo Fashion Week has attempted therefore to show the consistency, the content, and the depth of the fashion system, to generate a fashion calendar able to tell Brazilian history and build Brazilian fashion history. Fashion has become a "language" through which Brazil has gained international exposure. An attempt to create a Brazilian fashion identity reflects a broader desire within the country to establish a Brazilian identity beyond the stereotyped outsider's view of a tropical paradise eternalized by Carmen Miranda. Brazil wants its identity to reflect the cultural diversity of a country of continental dimensions. Brazilian fashion has played a key role in "discovering" the Brazil of the street—its culture, its colors, its aesthetic forms, its history, its everyday life.

A case study of Brazilian fashion

Bourdieu's theory (1975) that an apprenticeship at a famous fashion house (Saint Laurent at Dior, for example) serves as a reference for the quality of one's work does not apply to the young Brazilian designers. Alexandre Herchcovitch, the *enfant terrible* of Brazilian fashion, started creating clothes for his transvestite friends when he was only twenty-two, following his graduate fashion show in 1994. His work attracted the attention of international fashion journalists because it was bizarre and daring when compared to any other contemporary fashion design. His brand acquired legitimacy for breaking rather than abiding by the commercial rules of Brazilian fashion, where designers and brands copied and edited European and North American styles for consumption in South America. The rupture generated by Herchcovitch and the young Brazilian designers of the 1990s opened a new market niche, by enlarging consumer horizons to noncommercial styles. Curiously, both the young rebellious consumers and the Gucci and Chanel-loving Brazilian socialites became Herchcovitch supporters.

The son of Polish parents, Herchcovitch received a restrictive formal education at an Orthodox Jewish school. As a pastime he used to play with threads and collar studs in the lingerie factory owned by his mother. There he learned to sew doll's clothes for imaginary characters. The underwear fabrics and moldings fascinated him, and influenced the gothic sensuality of his later fashion designs with their binding and erotic zippers. The designer claims the urban reality of the city of São Paulo as one of his strongest inspirations (Herchcovitch 1994). The aesthetic of the ghettos, the style groups, the gangs, gays, and prostitutes were a main reference for his earliest collections. The street, with its undefined characters and their ambiguous sexuality, inverted roles, and unstable gender relationships, continues to be evident in several aspects of his work, such as men's shirts with surplus fabric at the breasts, and women's pants with extra fabric at the crotch. According to Herchcovitch (1994), his clothes need to have a life history in order to express the individuality of the characters that have inspired him. This was

Figure 10.4 Design by Alexandre Herchcovitch. Photograph by Jacques Faing.

evident in his early collections, where pants had stonewashed fabric only at the knees and some shirts and dresses had excess fabric at the elbows, knees, back, and backside, as if resembling the shape of a body.

Besides his individual talent, the importance of Herchcovitch's work for Brazilian fashion was in drawing upon references to Brazilian society and culture. When most brands were copying European styles and principles of beauty and sensuality, Herchcovitch went out of the way to create bizarre and unusual clothes that exposed ugliness, age, physical handicap, and pain. He is considered important as one of the first Brazilian designers to generate an awareness of fashion in the Latin world based on Brazilian culture. The Brazilian press accused him of immaturity as a very young designer just out of fashion school, but almost fifteen years later he has consolidated his image as a talented and competent fashion businessman, skilled in tailoring, favoring a gothic style mixed with Brazilian cultural influences. The fetishist and sadomasochistic themes that characterized his early work are still strong, but he now searches for new inspirations in Africa and in Brazilian folklore (Figure 10.4).

Now aged thirty-five, Herchcovitch appeared on the Brazilian clothing scene creating clothes for some of the most famous São Paulo transvestites like Marcia Pantera, a legendary character in gay and alternative society. Since then Herchcovitch has become one of the most successful Latin designers, showing his clothes in European fashion weeks and opening stores in the USA, Europe, and Asia. "I have a special concern about zippers, everything that seems to tie, to bind, to chain . . . I create clothes for characters that do not exist . . . with tortuous arms, humpbacks, flaccid asses" (Hercovitch 1994).

A Brazilian perspective

The research for this chapter was based on a comparative analysis of European and South American fashion design and industry. Brazilian fashion was found to compare favorably with the more established British fashion system, as fashion companies, brands, and the fabric industry have subsidized the development of a new Brazilian fashion circuit. Not only have they given support to new designers but they have also provided sponsorship to big fashion events that have helped to consolidate "real Brazilian fashion."

Many established Brazilian fashion brands were dedicated to what Zandra Rhodes (2001) has called pure fashion edition, rather than real fashion creation. That is, they did not create anything new, but just "edited" styles and patterns developed in Europe and the United States. The European fashion industry generates the patterns and trends that will be top fashion in future months or years. These patterns are related to the availability of raw material, color palettes, developments in textile engineering, industrial machinery, and an optimized system of marketing and sales. They are led by the world's largest fashion houses, and by fashion magazine editors, who chart a relatively safe commercial course for fashion designers. But some designers detour from these patterns to create marginal fashion, drawing on art and ideology that is different from, but has emerged in parallel with, the developments in big companies.

Over the last decade, the advent of fashion schools in Brazil, allied with investment in the talent of young designers and the production of huge fashion events, has opened new horizons for the fashion industry in Brazil. Some new designers now follow the path of British designers, but with one difference. In London the alternative fashion circuit developed because of financial difficulties in the 1980s, when talented young designers graduated from schools like St Martin's without the money or investors to create solid brands and join the mainstream. In Brazil, by comparison, nationwide, many companies that for many years produced clothes—not fashion—are now trying to join the international fashion circuit. Clothing factories are hiring fashion graduates fresh out of university to upgrade their business plans and production in order to reposition their companies in the emerging fashion scene. At the same time, new companies are starting and searching for talent, sometimes hiring students still in fashion school.

Brazil has gone from being a country that just produced "edited styles" based on European big-brand collections to becoming an emerging global focus of fashion design and style, with an established clothing industry that nowadays comprises 5 percent of the national economy. Acclaimed by the English specialist press as a new center of fashion (Cartner-Morley 2001), many Brazilian designers such as Alexandre Herchcovitch, Rosa Chá, Fause Hatten, and Carlos Miele have had their catwalk collections covered by international journalists. Brazil continues to move toward the development of its own distinct fashion circuit, under its own management. At the same time as fashion consolidates industrially and commercially, the most important national designers turn their interests to cultural questions in the search for an authentic identity to underpin Brazilian fashion. The more market interest grows, the more the cultural element shows up as a Brazilian fashion pattern. In the process the new fashion designers become less interested in editing European tendencies and more interested in the creation of conceptual and aesthetic elements that "speak" to their Brazilian origins.

Brazilian fashion benefits from a good industrial and technological structure, but it still lacks trained professionals for the technical and business side. The partnership between fashion designers and huge companies is a quantum leap for national fashion. Many of these young designers are sponsored by fabric companies that not only provide financial resources to their collections and fashion shows, but can also create high-technology fabrics, accessories, and other elements. Unlike, say, in Britain, Brazilian couturiers can count on a developing internal fashion system.

Some scholars and media critics have suggested that all this "hype" about the creation of Brazilian fashion is no more than a self-fulfilling prophecy.[3] Be that as it may, what really matters is that opportunities exist for thousands of young talented designers that would not have had a place in the fashion market fifteen years ago—there are real jobs for the hundreds of students who graduate annually from fashion schools in Brazil. A new generation of fashion journalists has also emerged, eager to create a critical environment to analyze South American fashion. Also, for the consumer, events like São Paulo Fashion Week have provided more democratic access to fashion. The search for a Brazilian fashion identity continues to be a process of the discovery of inner cultural knowledge—a search for a fashion imbued with the colors and flavors of Brazil.

Acknowledgments

I would like to thank Eugenia Paulicelli for her comments on this chapter, and Hazel Clark for her comments and revisions.

Notes

1. "DaVida" (or "from life," where "life" is slang meaning a prostitute's life).
2. This photographic essay was turned into the book *Meninas do Brasil* (Girls from Brazil) (Stockler 2002).

3.   "Imprensa internacional massacra desfile com Gisele Bündchen no Fashion Rio"—International press massacres fashion show with Gisele Bündchen in Fashion Rio. http://ego.globo.com/ January 11, 2008

References

Publications

A folha de São Paulo newspaper (1998) September 20.

Amado, Jorge (1978) *Gabriela Cravo e Canela*, Rio de Janeiro: Editora Record.

Baudrillard, Jean (1983) *Para uma economia política do signo*, São Paulo: Editora Martins Fontes.

—— (1995) *A Sociedade de Consumo*, Artur Mourão (trad.), Rio de Janeiro: Editora Elfos.

—— (1997) *O Sistema dos Objetos*, São Paulo: Editora Perspectiva.

Benson, Todd (2005) "Brazil's 'Temple of Luxury' becomes Symbol of Excess," *International Herald Tribune* online July 16, available from http://www.iht.com/articles/2005/07/15/business/daslu.php.

Bourdieu, Pierre (1975) "'Le Couturier et sa Griffe': Contribution à une théorie de la magie," in *Actes de la recherche en sciences sociales*, 1: 7–36.

Brandini, Valéria (2003) "Dressing the Street: Fashion, Culture, and the City," unpublished doctoral thesis developed at the University of São Paulo.

Canevacci, Massimo (1999) *Cultura eXtrema, Mutazione Giovanili tra i corpi delle metropoli*, Rome: Meltemi Editore.

Cartner-Morley, Jess (2001) "Spiral of the Grotesque Winds Up Fashion Stakes" *The Guardian*, February 10.

Da Matta, Roberto (1987) *Relativizando: Uma introdução à antropologia social*, Rio de Janeiro: Editora Rocco.

—— (1987) *Carnavais, Malandros e Heróis*, Rio de Janeiro: Editora Rocco.

—— (1997) *A Casa e a Rua: Espaço, Cidadania, Mulher e Morte no Brasil*, Rio de Janeiro: Editora Rocco.

Freyre, Gilberto (1986) *Modos de Homem e Modas de Mulher*, Rio de Janeiro: Editora Record.

Garcia, Carol and Castilho, Kátia (2001) *Moda Brasil—Fragmentos de um Vestir Tropical*, São Paulo: Editora Anhembi Morumbi.

Geertz, Clifford (1978) *A interpretação das culturas*, Rio de Janeiro: Editora Zahar.

Polhemus, Ted (1995) *Streetstyle: From Catwalk to Sidewalk*, London: Thames and Hudson.

Stockler, Mari (2002) *Meninas do Brasil*, São Paulo: Editora Cosac & Naif.

Interviews

Herchcovitch, Alexandre (1994) interview with the author, May 20.

Rhodes, Zandra (2001) interview with the author, October 23.

Chapter 11

Fashioning "China style" in the twenty-first century

Hazel Clark

Introduction

For the last 400 years, Western fashion has flirted with Orientalism as a source of reference and "inspiration" for a diversity of designs. This was never more apparent than in the 1990s when the international fashion system, from Paris haute couture to the diffused mass market, employed exotic tropes taken from Asia as stylistic references. "Oriental" dress became the subject of major exhibitions and associated publications, such as Orientalism: Visions of the East in Western Dress, held at the Metropolitan Museum of Art, New York, 1994/5, and China Chic, held at the Museum of the Fashion Institute of Technology, New York, in spring 1999. The reasons for this turn to the Orient were not unrelated to the general "opening up" of China after 1981, and to more specific events. The return of Hong Kong's sovereignty from Britain to the People's Republic of China in 1997, in particular, accelerated a sense of Chinese identity, and began to develop a confidence in that identity in the colony and beyond.

Today, China presents many facets in its emerging global identity, not least as an economic force fueled by cheap labor central to the production of the world's fashionable clothing.[1] The country is also moving rapidly from being a low-cost factory for Western brands to purchasing those big names,[2] and also creating its own brands. Shanghai is setting its sights on becoming a global fashion city by 2010, producing merchandise that will enable it to compete in quality, style, and prestige with Paris, Milan, or New York, as well as appealing to the growing middle class in China. Yet it remains the case that Orientalist images continue to shape outsiders' ideas about China, as an exotic and mysterious place, despite knowledge of contemporary China being widely available (Louie 2004: 19). These impressions have proved a strong undercurrent in recent fashion, and at the same time, perhaps curiously, Orientalism is providing the design focus for some emerging Chinese fashion brands.

This chapter will question why a mythic notion of China and Chineseness continues to pervade global fashion design visually, materially, spatially, and textually, and how it has impacted emerging Chinese brands. Is this "China style" simply another fashion trend, a new version of chinoiserie, nostalgia, or an indication of a more substantial shift in the global fashion system? To address these questions the chapter discusses two brands which were established in Hong Kong just before the 1997 handover of the former British colony to China: Shanghai Tang and Blanc de Chine, who have subsequently opened stores in mainland China, Asia, and New York City.

Fashion and Orientalism—the 1990s

The impact of Orientalism on global fashion in the 1990s has been well documented.[3] One of the most memorable and successful markers of that trend (certainly in terms of media coverage) was John Galliano's first prêt-à-porter collection for Christian Dior for autumn/winter 1997/8. Based on the fashions worn in Shanghai in the 1930s, Galliano echoed an Orientalist theme that had appeared regularly on the Paris catwalks since about 1993 (Steele and Major 1999: 69). While other fashion designers, such as Christian Lacroix, Valentino, Dries van Noten, and Donna Karan had also drawn widely on Chinese history, Galliano featured in particular the cheongsam or *qipao*, an iconic Orientalist signifier of the exoticism and eroticism of Chinese women.[4] Accessorized with stiletto heels and dangling jewelry, the garments hugged the bodies of the models as they paraded the runway, their cheeks rouged red, like exoticized "China dolls."

The collection was characteristic of Galliano's design strategy, which has been described as having

> pretty much invented the mix-and-match style that continues to rule the runways. For the past twenty-odd years he has grabbed at references from the world over, throwing them together with an irreverent abandon that remains unparalleled despite having spawned a million imitations.
>
> (Frankel 2005: 25)

While it would be true to call Galliano a master of the mix-and-match his approach characterized much fashion design in the late twentieth century (although no other designer undertook Galliano's amount of detailed research). Placed in a broader historical context this design strategy is characteristic of the "cultural economy of distance" that Appadurai observes as being the "driving force of merchants, trade, and commodities, especially of the luxury variety," since the sixteenth century (Appadurai 1996: 71). In this process "distance" connotes the cultural and economic capital of the consumer, who has both the taste and the money to know of and be able to purchase goods from faraway places. Such treasures are designed to signify their "exotic" origins while being modified to suit the Western Orientalist gaze. Given that experience of the reality of China has been limited for most Westerners, it was perhaps inevitable that the "imagining of China was always more fanciful than real"(Martin and Koda 1994: 18). Despite trade with the West from coastal cities such as Shanghai, and also from the Pearl River Delta, China remained remote. Even the British colony of Hong Kong was more myth than reality in the West.

Hong Kong

The 1984 signing of the Sino-British Joint Agreement between Britain and the People's Republic of China gave Hong Kong people notice of a political change, one that was feared as potentially undermining the economic stability that had been built during a century of British rule. It also signaled for many Hong Kong people the need to establish an identity independent of Britain, but also at a slight distance from China, especially politically. A century of colonialism made this a difficult task. Colonization, by definition, makes it difficult for colonized groups to recognize the value of their own cultural, historical, and natural resources. As Ackbar Abbas has written, after a century of colonial rule "Hong Kong did not realize it could have a culture" (Abbas 1997: 6). In response to this problem, from the early 1990s creative practitioners, including writers, actors, filmmakers, and designers, sought to establish a Hong Kong cultural identity through their work.[5]

In fashion, the idea of creating a cultural identity came comparatively late. Some Hong Kong fashion labels had tried to establish global brand identities, but without acknowledging their geographic and cultural origins, and often consciously obscuring them with Italian-sounding names such as Giordano or Bossini. However, in the 1990s a few designers and brands began to see commercial as well as cultural value in manifesting their Chinese identity, initially through self-exoticization. One of the most commercially successful and internationally well known is Vivienne Tam. Originally from Guangdong Province, Tam was raised and educated in Hong Kong and established her business in New York (Tam 2000). She has preserved strong connections with Hong Kong and China in her production and in her design by drawing liberally on Chinese cultural references. Her spring 1998 collection, for example, was inspired by Chinese cosmology. Tam's design strategy corresponded to an expectation, which developed in the 1990s, that Asian designers would "stage themselves as its exotic other" (Skov 2003: 216) at a time when they had begun to gain some self-confidence to enter the international fashion system. Almost in parallel with Tam, Shanghai Tang and Blanc de Chine were also developing brand identities based on "Chineseness," with the shared aims of being the first luxury Chinese brand to capture the global market.

Both companies interpreted Chineseness on four key levels: visually, materially, spatially, and textually. Visually, brand identities depend in particular on the shapes, colors, and motifs used on products and in advertising.

From their beginnings the two brands had distinct visual design strategies: Shanghai Tang relied on bold, colorful text and images, including Chinese-themed advertising campaigns, while Blanc de Chine took a more restrained approach, as will be explained below. Materially, a brand is represented by its merchandise, in these two instances especially fashion womenswear, menswear, and soft furnishings. Spatially, the design of the retail interiors is crucial in creating a setting conducive to the brand image and its merchandise, and also to the location of the particular shop. Textually, the written word is key in establishing and developing a brand image, in what the brand writes about itself in its advertising and promotional materials, and also in what is written about it, especially in the media. These levels are addressed below in more detail and reveal the similarities and differences of their respective interpretations, which reflect the extent and the diversity of China's culture, plus Hong Kong's relationship with that culture and history during a century of colonialism. Where they differ is how they read Chineseness today as at once a cultural and a commercial factor for their brand identities. Blanc de Chine's emphasis is more subtle and material based, whereas Shanghai Tang has a bolder image.

Shanghai Tang

Shanghai Tang was established in 1994 by Hong Kong-born and British-educated entrepreneur and international socialite David Tang. It employed a nostalgic and self-Orientalizing approach in its brand image, merchandise, and retail environment. The design played off an imaginary of Shanghai in the 1930s at the height of the city's internationalism and modernism, as a parallel to Hong Kong in the 1990s. The label promoted merchandise "Made by Chinese," identifying Chinese people as makers, rather than the more negative, nation-based, "Made in China," with its connotations of factory mass-production and cheap goods.[6] Part of the impetus for the brand was to attempt to revive the skills of the original Shanghai tailors, who came to Hong Kong as refugees in the 1940s and 1950s. The sense of craft and tradition was reinforced in the bespoke tailoring service, "The Imperial Tailor," offered as an exclusive feature of the brand.

The Imperial Tailor specialized in made-to-measure cheongsam or *qipao*, the women's garment originating in Shanghai in the 1930s that had become particularly associated with Hong Kong in the 1950s and 1960s. Revived again in the global fashion system in the 1990s by Galliano, Vivienne Tam, and others, the cheongsam was itself a hybridized garment, based on the Manchu gown combined with the Western dress (Clark 1999; 2000). Cheongsam and also *mien lap* (padded men's) jackets were standard features of the brand's ready-to-wear collections (Figure 11.1).

They were sold in the original Hong Kong flagship store, in a retail environment that was designed to complement the nostalgic Orientalist theme of

Figure 11.1
Shanghai Tang short
cheongsam, shown at
a benefit in Hawaii,
2006. Reproduced
with the permission of
Shanghai Tang.

the garments. The Hong Kong store was, and still is, located in the Pedder Building, an original 1930s edifice, in the Central shopping area alongside expensive retailers. The store was designed to complement the styles of the clothing, soft furnishings, accessories, gifts, and novelties on sale. It acted as a quasi-theatrical backdrop. From the moment consumers walked through the front door they entered an Orientalist performance of Chinese identity. Dark wooden shop fittings and period furnishings served as a backdrop for the bright color palette of the merchandise. Here, a design identity based on ersatz nostalgia transformed history into spectacle. The design strategy was not unique; it can be compared to upscale global fashion brands such as Ralph Lauren and Paul Smith.[7] A sense of authenticity is implied by referencing the names of the individual originators. David Tang played on his own name, linked with Shanghai at its high point, commercially, culturally, and internationally, as a direct comparison with contemporary Hong Kong. Just as Donna Karan cleverly and unambiguously associated herself with

New York in her DKNY brand, David Tang linked himself with Shanghai, past and future.

Shanghai Tang did not intend to accurately represent Shanghai of the 1930s, or furthermore, China of the 1990s. The decor and the merchandise playfully parodied historical and contemporary Chinese cultural icons, such as Mao Zedong or Deng Xiaoping, whose images were displayed on the faces of watches, which became popular souvenirs. The walls were originally hung with paintings by contemporary mainland Chinese artists, such as the laughing self-portraits of Yue Minjun.[8] But Hong Kong Chinese people were not the target consumers; the majority of the customers were local expatriates and foreign tourists, who were not seeking authenticity but recognizable and acceptable signs of Chineseness. At the time Shanghai Tang opened, Orientalism and nostalgia were both features of global fashion and contemporary merchandising (Appadurai 1996: 76). The implied longing was not for a China that had existed and it was certainly not for the China that actually did exist just across the border. What was being retailed was a playful, even a theme-park, vision of China not dissimilar to that provided by the Folk Culture Village, which could be visited in a day in the Special Economic Zone of Shenzhen, to the north of Hong Kong.

Blanc de Chine

Two floors above Shanghai Tang, also in the Pedder Building, Blanc de Chine had opened a shop in 1993. Both companies were established by local businesspeople, but Blanc de Chine's brand image was subtly different from Shanghai Tang's. The distinction is clear in the brand name, taken from the prized eighteenth-century white Chinese porcelain. The connotation was of quality and of the Chinese and European blending which inspired the original *blanc de chine*. Its brand logo was the Chinese character "yuen," meaning the source of the river—suggesting returning to one's roots—reproduced in monochrome color combinations, pale and ambiguous, completely different from Shanghai Tang's original brightly colored logo. Blanc de Chine did not advertise; they built a reputation on cultural capital to create a customer profile of high-income local people who got to know the brand through their friends and contacts (Louie 2004: 21).

Blanc de Chine's clothes can be distinguished from Shanghai Tang's by their materiality—that is, by the particular way of using cloth—and by their relationship to the body. The owner, Kin Yeung, established the brand from a background in the family jewelry business, with a desire to produce the perfect *mien lap*, the traditional Chinese man's jacket. Yeung sought a garment that felt comfortable to wear and had an aesthetic appeal that promoted Chinese culture at a quality level. The impression of "Made in China" as equating with cheap fabric and shoddy construction was dispelled by high-quality workmanship and the use of fabrics imported from Italy and

Switzerland, which had visual and tactile appeal. The colors were subtle and muted, and thus avoided identification with a seasonal fashion palette and suggested a longer lifespan for the garments. Blanc de Chine aimed to create what fashion jargon would term "classics"—that is, pieces that would be appreciated for their quality as well as their aesthetic and were designed to be worn for longer than a passing fashion season.

Blanc de Chine's particular interpretation of Chineseness is distinct from Shanghai Tang's, as is evident in their comparative designs of the cheongsam or *qipao*. It has been a staple for both brands since their origins, but subject to distinctly different design approaches. Shanghai Tang typically styles the cheongsam along the lines of the form-fitting garment worn by the fictional Wanchai bar hostess in the 1960 movie *The World of Suzie Wong* (Figure 11.2). Blanc de Chine originally styled it looser, referencing the origins of the female garment in the full-length male *changpao*. In fact their creative director, Lydia Reeve, has been quoted as describing the "tight Suzie Wong style cheongsam as 'an insult to Chinese women'."[9] This statement highlights the subtle distinctions in the two brands' interpretations of Chineseness. Blanc de Chine is more traditional and more classical in its references to Chinese history and culture; there are never signs of Shanghai Tang's visual puns or its "retro Communist kitsch."[10] This distinction was drawn more clearly in 2008 when Blanc de Chine launched a new range named Bleu de Chine, which featured more relaxed shapes (Figure 11.3).

The different design strategies of the brands are reflected in the spatial design of their retail interiors. Although they share the same building, use the same dark wood shop fittings, include a ready-to-wear and a tailoring section, and each employ patina as a symbolic property to create a sense of age and authenticity (McCracken 1990; 32; Appadurai 1996: 75), there are distinct differences in their approach to Chineseness. Their use of color in the stores, as well as for the merchandise, distinguishes their visual identities, as Shanghai Tang's bright orange, green, red, yellow, pink, and blue logo, contrasts with the visual neutrality of Blanc de Chine's logo, which, like their garments, invites the touch, not just the eye. The overall sensibility of Blanc de Chine's interior and merchandise is more subtle and more rarefied than Shanghai Tang's. Their space in Hong Kong is smaller and more enclosed, away from passing trade and much quieter than that of their larger neighbor downstairs. Comparatively, the total impact of the interior and the merchandise of Blanc de Chine could be described as conveying a sense of "old money," whereas Shanghai Tang signifies new wealth.

Beyond Hong Kong

In the ten years since the companies began, their design strategies have developed to keep abreast of fashion trends and to accommodate new global markets. As part of this ambition both brands opened their second

Figure 11.2
Shanghai Tang black embroidered cheong-sam, 2007. Reproduced with the permission of Shanghai Tang.

major stores in New York City. Shanghai Tang did so soon after the opening of their Hong Kong store, as part of a vigorous, although not uniformly successful, campaign to develop its global market, whereas Blanc de Chine took its global development more slowly, having opened a very small shop in Beijing before its much larger New York store.[11]

It is not coincidental that in developing their global retail presence both brands looked to New York City. In doing so they were establishing themselves in a world economic, creative, tourist, commercial, and fashion city, but also one with substantial cultural diversity. Hong Kong, by contrast, retains a majority local Chinese population, plus a small community of international residents and foreign tourists. In moving to New York the brand merchandise no longer retained a resonance with the majority culture, neither could Shanghai Tang provide souvenirs reflecting the host culture. How the two brands dealt with their development reveals something of the limits and possibilities of cultural identity as a commercial strategy.

Figure 11.3
Blanc de Chine, denim cheongsam, pants, and shirt from the Bleu de Chine line, launched in 2008. Reproduced with the permission of Blanc de Chine.

Shanghai Tang—New York

Shanghai Tang launched its New York store on Madison Avenue, Manhattan's wealthy Upper East Side shopping area, in November 1997 with considerable publicity. An auspicious hour was chosen by a feng shui master for the opening ceremony, which involved lion dancers, a roasted suckling pig, the burning of incense, and other Chinese ceremonial gestures to bring good luck and press attention. *The New York Times* referred to the style as "Chinese maximalism at its most exuberant" (Louie 1997: F1). David Tang planned the timing of the new store for what he saw to be a burgeoning market, and he was not alone in that view. *Money Magazine* noted, "New York's Shanghai Tang will do for all things Chinese what Ralph Lauren's clothing and accessories did for Americans."[12] In reality however, some of Shanghai Tang's merchandise was hard to distinguish from objects and garments available in New York's Chinatown.

Only eighteen months later, the 11,000-square-foot store closed and relocated to smaller premises on Madison Avenue, where it now remains. Part of its lack of success was due to the Asian economic downturn, which began in July 1997. But another factor was the difficulty of selling styles, colors, and products more associated with Chinatown in the exclusive and expensive retail market uptown. In 1999, Hong Kong's handover had passed and the interest in Orientalism was no longer at fashion's cutting edge. Also, Shanghai Tang did not have a plan to provide a strong enough design identity and direction. Its product lines were bought in by merchandisers, not designed specifically for the brand. What worked in the Hong Kong store was not enough to sustain commercial success—the company needed a concerted design and marketing strategy.

In 1998 David Tang sold his majority share to Richemont, the Swiss luxury goods company that owns brands such as Mont Blanc, Chloé, Cartier, and Dunhill. The new owners embarked on an ambitious expansion plan, which included a design strategy that retained the image and the "feel" of the brand, but attuned it to international fashion trends. An executive chairman was appointed, Raphael Le Masne de Chermont, who had formerly worked at Piaget. Joanne Ooi was hired from a commercial fashion background in Hong Kong, as creative director. Together they set about revamping the brand identity, introducing themed seasonal collections, expanding the number of stores, and developing an international design team.[13]

Since 1999 Shanghai Tang has established twenty-five stores in major world cities in Asia, Europe, the Middle East, and the United States, including London, Paris, Shanghai, and Dubai, with a projection of thirty-five stores being open by 2010. It is significant that five of the Asian stores are in airports, with two in the Hong Kong International Airport. These Asian "non-places" (Augé 1995) are in many ways ideal for the brand, which can loosely resonate with the dominant culture without having to deal too closely with issues of authenticity.

Shanghai Tang has also diversified its product lines for the global market. In the process the brand has "loosened the Chineseness"[14] and become more focused on the seasonal dictates of the fashion system. Their design team is charged with creating a Chinese style to suit a global market, including well-off consumers in mainland China. The commercial success of the brand has been due largely to the strength of the Asian market, which is responsible for 80 percent of sales (Jana 2005). Their public-relations company describes the brand as having "changed from the early beginning when David Tang had a vision of dressing Westerners in Chinese nostalgia." The "Made by Chinese" epithet disappeared from the logo, and the garment styles were segmented into two types. The "authentics" were based more on traditional Chinese clothing, as distinct from the more fashion-oriented styles, which are described as being "relevant for the modern individual."[15]

The change to a more "modern" image is evident also in the company's recent spatial design strategy, applied to new stores and to the redesign of existing stores (with the exception of the Hong Kong flagship store). Their London shop on Sloane Street reopened in April 2006 with a fresh interior. The New York store was scheduled to be relocated to newly designed premises at the end of 2007.[16] The changes are intended to present Shanghai Tang in the twenty-first century as "a modern and relevant lifestyle brand with a Chinese twist."[17] This reflects the synergy that has been observed between high fashion and architecture in global cities in the twenty-first century, particularly in New York (Gilbert 2006: 28).

Strategies to achieve a more modern Chineseness in fashion design have included the casual Kung Fu Collection launched in June 2005 at the IFC Mall in Hong Kong. In the same year the womenswear collection for spring/summer 2006, named Chuang Yi, featured printed fabrics based on paintings by student-artists studying at the Central Academy of Fine Arts in Beijing. Thus the skills of the international design team were complemented by the work of "authentic" mainland Chinese students. The garments reflected Shanghai Tang's ongoing reiteration of the Suzie Wong-style cheongsam, but also sanctioned its appearance in mainland China, where it had been outlawed since the middle of the twentieth century. The changes in mainland China as a growing economy, a developing consumer market, and a more open society increasingly impact how "China style" is designed and consumed in the twenty-first century.[18]

Blanc de Chine—New York

For Blanc de Chine, more informed global attitudes to Chinese culture and history are potentially very positive in supporting the distinct design strategy they are developing in the millennium. In February 2006 the brand opened its first store in New York, which has a very different retail interior from the Hong Kong store. It is located on the corner of Fifth Avenue and Fifty-third Street, a prime and high-end fashion retail location, just down the block from the Museum of Modern Art. The interior decor is pale, with clean lines to create a more anonymous and modern style (Figure 11.4). With womenswear on the ground floor and menswear and soft furnishings on the floor above, the conceptual and design identity had taken into consideration its new location adjacent to retailers like the luxury leather goods brand Fendi. Blanc de Chine takes a longer-term approach to Chineseness. A new design concept was based on eight elements advocated as necessary to a balanced life—simplicity, serenity, functionality, comfort, sensuality, subtlety, harmony, purity.

A book of photographs, published to celebrate their tenth anniversary, described the brand as promoting a new "body language appropriate to modern urban life." The text is used to enhance this impression, describing

Figure 11.4 Interior of the Blanc de Chine New York store, 2006. Reproduced with the permission of Blanc de Chine.

their garment designs as valuing the "inside" and the "outside" of the wearer, "allowing an individual's unique character to shine through" while feeling "wonderful—even sensual next to the body" (Richards 2004). Phrases such as "embedding a sense of history and tradition" or "a certain timeless quality" were applied to the garments. Some were photographed on figures in movement, where the body language has particular cultural reference, such as a tai chi position (Figure 11.5). The book features, not professional models, but "the kinds of people that normally buy and wear Blanc de Chine," which includes artists, athletes, bankers, dancers, doctors, housewives, lawyers, professors, and actors.[19] Amongst them are the actors and Hong Kong celebrities Jackie Chan and Michelle Yeoh, reinforcing the implied sense of cultural capital associated with wearing the brand.

The opening of the shop provided the launch for the spring/summer 2006 womenswear collection named Dao, based on "the way" and on the *du dao* or simple bodice traditionally worn in China by women, men, and children as an undergarment. The designs were based on the ultimate simplicity in dressing—the piece of cloth which is draped or wrapped around the body. The design strategy recalls that of the Japanese designers who have come to prominence in international fashion since the 1980s. Jennifer Craik, amongst others, has noted how the Japanese designers helped to redraw "the boundaries of fashion away from 'western' ideals of the body, body–space relations, and conventions of clothing" (Craik 1994: 41). Such approaches favored the materiality as well as the visuality of the clothes,

Figure 11.5 Tan Yuan Yuan, principal dancer with the San Francisco Ballet, practicing tai chi in a silk tunic and pants by Blanc de Chine, 2006. Reproduced with the permission of Blanc de Chine.

and reinforced the wearer, and particularly the female wearer, as subject rather than as object of the (male-gendered) gaze.

In aiming to develop new global ways of dressing, inspired by Chinese tradition and culture, Blanc de Chine has created garments which are worn loosely, rather than being fitted to the form of the body, and which reference quality and longevity, rather than cheapness and speed. They characterize a new attitude toward clothing that transcends six centuries of Western-dominated fashion. Like Japanese designer Issey Miyake, who wanted to create "a new genre of clothing, neither Western nor Japanese but beyond nationality" (Miyake, quoted in Kondo 1997: 60), Blanc de Chine's designs seek to address Chineseness as more than a mere stylistic device.

Conclusion

The development of these two luxury fashion brands, visually, materially, spatially, and textually, indicates an evolution of "China style" from self-Orientalization to providing potential new ways of thinking about fashion and dressing globally in the twenty-first century. We can look at this development in four successive stages, following the 1984 signing of the Sino-British Joint Declaration, which was described by Ackbar Abbas as the end of Hong Kong as Britain's "last emporium" (Abbas 1997: 3). While Hong Kong had at that stage established a reputation as a global city, known for business, trade, and the production of fashionable clothes, it remained very much a colony—a tangent of a Western country with a distinctly different cultural heritage from its own. As a result Hong Kong's designers created Western-style fashion anonymously for global brands.

In the mid-1990s, in the pre-handover period, "China style" began to develop internationally. Design tropes of Chineseness were used largely for their decorative features, and were often the products of self-exoticization, as in the work of Vivienne Tam. Retro and pop imagery characterized the second stage that marked the handover period and the emergence of Hong Kong designers and brands, notably Shanghai Tang with its design strategies based on Chinese nostalgia.[20] The approach of Blanc de Chine, and then the revamped, globally savvy Shanghai Tang, signals a third stage, of design transformation that equates with the late 1990s (see also Steiner and Haas 1995: 2). A fourth stage was the emergence, in the twenty-first century, of China style in China itself.

In 2001 there was evidence that Shanghai had begun to embrace China style as being appropriate for Chinese people. According to a press report, a marketing executive with the Mega Department Store said, "Chinese-style clothes have staged a comeback. The traditional cotton-padded coat, vest, and *qipao*—with some modification to suit modern-day tastes—are selling well" (Eastday.com 2001). This popularity links China to global fashion trends and signifies how its major cities, especially Hong Kong, Shanghai, and Beijing, were developing and consuming fashion. What Hong Kong and mainland China's greater involvement in global fashion reveals is the potential for "China style" to offer more than a passing fashion reference. As one scholar has noted, "In a sense, the idea of Chineseness has always been a fiction uniting the very diverse and often antagonistic subgroups within the (sometimes flexible borders of the) territory of China" (Louie 2004: 214 n. 2). In the twenty-first century, China style, as we have seen it emerging with Shanghai Tang and Blanc de Chine, offers the potential for new visual tropes, but also, and more significantly, the possibility of alternative ways of dressing that could challenge centuries of the Western dominance of fashion.

Notes

1. The lifting of global production quotas on clothing and textiles on January 1, 2005, under a World Trade Organization agreement, resulted, for example, in a reported 99 percent growth of Chinese-made apparel imports at US ports during the first half of 2005. See http://seattlepi.nwsource.com/business/237006_china imports18.html (accessed November 28, 2007).
2. The Chinese computer group Lenovo, for example, acquired IBM's personal computing division in 2005.
3. For example, in the exhibition China Chic in 1999 (Steele and Major 1999: 84–87).
4. As epitomized originally in the popular imagination for Westerners by the 1960

Hollywood movie *The World of Suzie Wong*, starring Eurasian actress Nancy Kwan, and based on the novel of the same name.

5. Included amongst them would be filmmaker Wong Kar Wai; graphic designers Henry Steiner, Alan Chan, and Kan Tai Keung; and members of the performance collective Zuni Icosahedron.

6. Exacerbated recently with articles in the international press drawing attention to the lack of safety codes in products as diverse as children's toys and toothpaste produced in factories in China.

7. Paul Smith has been a particularly popular brand in Japan, where retail interiors have been created from old shop fittings shipped from Britain (Goodrum 2005: 120).

8. Many local Hong Kong residents disapproved of the brand's Chinese image, considering that it "made fun of" Chinese people, to quote a comment made to me by fashion design students at Hong Kong Polytechnic's Swire School of Design, *c*.1995.

9. See http://www.variety.com/ September 9, 2001 (accessed October 1, 2001).

10. As described by a journalist in the context of a boom in Communist memorabilia in Russian fashion: Natasha Singer (2007).

11. Blanc de Chine did aspire to open its New York store much earlier than it did, and had acquired a prime property on Fifth Avenue, but the combination of the Asian economic crisis, September 11, 2001, and health issues in this family-owned and -run business delayed the opening.

12. http://www.goodnewsbroadcast.com/ShanghaiTang.html (accessed November 22, 2002).

13. At the time of writing, Shanghai Tang's chief menswear designer is Armele Barbier, French in origin and a former designer for Issey Miyake in Tokyo.

14. According to Shanghai Tang's creative director Joanne Ooi, interview with the author, Hong Kong, June 25, 2007.

15. E-mail to the author from Oberon of My Young Auntie, Shanghai Tang's public relations company, February 14, 2006.

16. At the time of writing Shanghai Tang New York was preparing to relocate once more, further down Madison Avenue at Fifty-eighth Street, close to the prestigious fashion department store Barneys.

17. Oberon, e-mail to the author, February 14, 2006.

18. Ernst & Young estimated that the consumption of luxury goods in China will grow 20 percent annually from 2005 to 2008 and by 2015 China will have overtaken the USA as the world's second-highest consumer of luxury goods after Japan (Jana 2005).

19. The strategy of using "real people" as models has already been used in the fashion system, not least by Japanese designers, such as Issey Miyake.

20. A comparative example would be the work of designer Alan Chan, who used iconic images such as the women portrayed on posters produced in Shanghai in the 1930s.

References

Abbas, M. A. (1997) *Hong Kong: Culture and the Politics of Disappearance*, Minneapolis: University of Minnesota Press.

Augé, M. (1995) *Non-places: Introduction to an Anthropology of Supermodernity*, London and New York: Verso.

Appadurai, A. (1996) *Modernity at Large: Cultural Dimensions of Globalization*, Minneapolis: University of Minnesota Press.

Clark, H. (1999) "The Cheung Sam: Issues of Fashion and Cultural Identity," in V. Steele and J. Major (eds.), *China Chic: East Meets West*, New Haven and London: Yale University Press.

Clark, H. (2000) *The Cheongsam*, Hong Kong: Oxford University Press (Images of Asia).

Craik, J. (1994) *The Face of Fashion: Cultural Studies in Fashion*, London and New York: Routledge.

Eastday.com (2001) January 26, available at http://www.chan.org.cn/english/2001/Jan6882.htm (accessed October 1, 2001).

Frankel, S. (2005) "Anything Goes," in J. Brand and J. Teunissen (eds.), *Global Fashion Local Tradition*, Belgium: Terra.

Gilbert, D. (2006) "From Paris to Shanghai: Changing Geographies of Fashion's World Cities," in C. Breward and D. Gilbert (eds.), *Fashion's World Cities*, Oxford and New York: Berg.

Goodrum, A. (2005) *The National Fabric: Fashion, Britishness, Globalization*, Oxford and New York: Berg.

Jana, R. (2005) "Shanghai Tang: A Taste of China," *Business Week Online*, available at http://www.businessweek.com/innovate/content/nov2005/id20051130_575911.htm_(accessed February 27, 2006).

Kondo, D. (1997) *About Face: Performing Race in Fashion and Theater*, New York and London: Routledge.

Louie, A. (2004) *Chineseness across Borders: Renegotiating Chinese Identities in China and the United States*, Durham and London: Duke University Press.

Louie, E. (1997) "The Great Mall of China," *New York Times*, House & Home, November 20, F1, F7.

McCracken, G. (1990) *Culture and Consumption*, Bloomington and Indianapolis: Indiana University Press.

Martin, R. and Koda, H. (1994) *Orientalism: Visions of the East in Western Dress*, New York: The Metropolitan Museum of Art.

Mitchell, K. (1996) "In Whose Interest?" in R. Wilson and W. Dissanayake (eds.), *Global/Local*, Durham and London: Duke University Press.

"New York's Shanghai Tang Will Do for All Things Chinese what Ralph Lauren's Clothing and Accessories Did for Americans," *Money Magazine Online*, available at http://www.goodnewsbroadcast.com/ShanghaiTang.html (accessed October 22, 2002)

Richards, L. Wayne (2004) "New Body Language," in K. Yeung (ed.), *Blanc de Chine*, Hong Kong: Blanc de Chine.

Singer, Natasha (2007) "The USSR is Coming Back (at Least on Clothing Racks)," *New York Times*, November 27, A29.

Skov, L. (2003) "Fashion-Nation: A Japanese Globalization Experience and a Hong

Kong Dilemma," in S. Niessen, A. Leshkowich, and C. Jones (eds.), *Re-Orienting Fashion*, Oxford and New York: Berg.

Steele, V, and Major J. S. (eds.) (1999) *China Chic: East Meets West*, New Haven and London: Yale University Press.

Steiner, H. and Haas., K. (1995) *Cross-cultural Design Communication in the Global Marketplace*, New York and London: Thames and Hudson.

Tam, V. (2000) *China Chic*, New York: Regan Books.

Tischler, L. (2006) "The Gucci Killers," *Fast Company*, January Online. http://www.fastcompany.com/magazine/102/shanghai.html (accessed February 27, 2006).

Chapter 12

From factories to fashion

An intern's experience of New York as a global fashion capital

Christina H. Moon

In the course of the neoliberalization of global trade that took place in the 1990s, two powerful forces in the New York garment district drastically transformed the social, economic, and cultural geography of the neighborhood. The first was the near complete destruction of the local garment production factories, which coincided with the second, the simultaneous expansion of design-culture industries in the New York fashion industry. Although the offshoring of garment production had devastating effects on the district, it was this very devastation that gave the industry incentive to adapt and transform into an industry of fashion design and not garment production. Amidst the destruction, visions of an imagined fashion capital emerged alongside new forms of design, cultural, and entrepreneurial labor that flowered in the New York fashion industry in the 1990s. By the end of the decade, the establishment of a permanent space for New York Fashion Week along with its new global positioning of fashion timing marked New York City as an emerging global fashion capital.

This chapter attempts to portray the cultural and economic changes that occurred in the garment district during the 1990s as changes in the landscape of workers emerged alongside those who imagined new cultural frontiers for fashion, and how these changes are reflected today. The contemporary study is based on ethnographic research conducted for my doctoral fieldwork research in anthropology as an intern at a New York City fashion design corporation on Seventh Avenue working toward the fall/winter 2006 runway shows. This provides context for the shifting scales of perspective of the everyday spaces an intern experiences while working in the district in the contemporary moment. In what is described as the emergence of a global era, where points in the apparel production process are described as economic, anonymous, and abstract, I seek to portray emergent global subjectivities found within the most tangible and intimate spaces of everyday life and work.

Influenced by Casanova's (2005) idea of a "world cultural space" I wanted to learn what world cultural space existed in New York fashion, why this might be important, and how one was to, as Tsing puts it ethnographically, "locate the global in order to study it" (Tsing 2005). Casanova's work is her effort to understand literature sociologically as an autonomous world cultural space—a kind of literary cultural system with its own internal logic, featuring its own economies, Greenwich Meridian of time, territories, and map, as well as mechanisms of legitimation and forms of violence. I aimed to find, as Casanova did, a world cultural space of struggle and possibility in fashion through the lens of my internship. Only, how to relate this world cultural space to the everyday spaces in which I was interning? While this cultural space occurs on many scales, this chapter attempts to reconcile these shifting registers with the anthropological—as a direct experience of the rapidly changing garment district. Upon arriving in New York City I learned that the garment district had undergone enormous cultural, social, political, and economic changes within the last two decades. In order to understand the contemporary spaces in which I maneuvered I needed to learn the social and cultural histories that existed within the district.

At the beginning of the internship the first two things to learn are the timing of the fashion cycle that ends and begins with New York Fashion Week, and the maneuvering through space within the garment district. Amongst the daily rounds, interns visit factories, sample rooms, showrooms, design studios, and the white tents of Bryant Park, running hundreds of errands in preparation for New York Fashion Week. The daily schedule involves "pick-ups" and "drop-offs" at the various factories; trips to source notions, trims, and fabric at garment district stores; and work within the warehouse opening up boxes of newly sewn clothing. Interns are found stuffing envelopes of invites for the PR team, drawing flats or hemming dresses for the designers, tracing patterns for the sample makers, or in the showroom pinning hang-tags onto dresses. Each fashion season brings hundreds of other interns like me who come to New York City, aspiring to work on internships at Seventh Avenue design companies.

The garment district was once a vibrant production center with store windows that displayed fabric, dress forms, or sewing machines. By the 1990s, however, buildings throughout the district began to house offices, condos, design studios, showrooms, and retail space. Newspapers consistently reported on the "decline" of the neighborhood, documenting the speed at which the district was "shrinking," predicting that the century-old garment industry would disappear with the end of the millennium (Kleinfield 1993; Bagli 1998; Sansoni 2000; Berger 2004). Although the district had experienced the gradual offshoring of mass garment production since the 1970s, it was not until the globalizing trade acts of the 1990s that the district was "doomed" for good.

By 1994 the North America Free Trade Agreement (NAFTA), the General Agreement on Tariffs and Trade (GATT), and the Agreement on Textiles and Clothing (ATC) had eliminated all trade protections of and tariffs on the US garment industry. The wardrobes of office clothing made for professional working women in the US were now being sewn by newly formed workforces of sewing women in other countries, with domestic garment assemblage and production offshored to Mexico and East Asia, then to the Caribbean, Central and South America, and finally to South and Southeast Asia. These regions contained lax laws poorly regulating the conditions of labor, child labor, and environmental protection, supported by the mass migrations of low-wage ethnicized and feminized workforces who worked in the informal sweatshops of urban cities and in state-run or privately funded factories found in free trade and export processing zones. A final moment of this transformation came on January 1, 2005 when the World Trade Organization (WTO) terminated the Multi-Fiber Agreement's quota system for apparels exactly at midnight, instituting an era of unregulated, quota-free markets of clothing made beyond the borders of the US (Bonacich 2004).

Economic policy reports of the 1990s hailed the emergence of a global era, describing the global phenomena of NAFTA and GATT in a universalizing language of economics using the composites, figures, and statistics of bureaucratic anonymity. Sociological texts of the era introduced the theoretical model of the global commodity chain as a powerful way to objectively understand the increasingly global spatiality of apparel firms beyond the ambiguous boundaries of nations (Light and Bhachu 1993; Scheffer 1998; Gereffi, Spencer, and Bair 2002; Bonacich 2004). Yet out on the streets of the garment district, the same laws created devastating conditions. The global consequences of NAFTA and GATT resulted in the closing of multigenerational family businesses by shopkeepers, factory owners, suppliers, and fabric retailers who blamed the legislators and politicians for loosening trade laws that allowed in the cheap imports that closed down the local factories. They cited the greedy manufacturers and design corporations that accelerated the move to produce garments overseas because of cheaper costs, or the new Korean and Chinese factory owners who undercut the price of labor with their nonunionized and illegal sewers. They blamed those who profited from the Internet boom, who artificially raised the price of Manhattan real estate making their rents virtually unaffordable. Tales of the 1990s from individuals working in the district's production sector are bleak, nostalgic, and dismal.

The meaning of "production" is changing within the district today, and no longer includes the mass garment production of former industrial days. Production in New York City now only includes the manufacturing of small batches of high-end clothing for local designers or boutiques and, more importantly, the making of samples for the runway collections of New York Fashion Week. With the rise of New York City as a global fashion capital along with the heightened visibility of New York Fashion Week within the last two decades, what remains of local production in the district remains because it involves highly skilled labor with close communication with designers in the making of fashion show collections. The majority of this work occurs in the small workshops that dot the district, many of which blur the definitions between sweatshop and craft atelier.

The largest, most financially powerful Seventh Avenue design companies produce multiple sample collections for the runway, for various showrooms, and for mass production abroad, and are able to afford the high cost of maintaining an in-house sample room of highly skilled patternmakers, cutters, sewers, and pressers. Yet it is the high cost of maintaining a sample room that has driven the majority of these design companies to subcontract sample-making to the remaining local factories in the district. In recent years however, in-house sample-makers and local sample-making factories within the district have been competing with "cut-and-sew" mass production factories in Asia that have begun to offer free sample-making, sourcing, and even design services to their US corporate design clients. As one of the last remaining vestiges of garment production in the district, in-house sample-makers feel much anxiety over the fact that their skilled work is increasingly outsourced to factories abroad.

The design company I intern for is a globally recognized brand pulling in annual sales of US$100 million and located in a Seventh Avenue industry building considered a neighborhood institution. In the company's front lobby, a side door leads interns past front offices into the back sample room. The sample room is filled with heat and steam from irons that raise the temperature in the room. There is bright fluorescent lighting, the constant sounds of whirring sewing machines, and the chatter of the sample-makers at work. All those who work in the sample room handle the clothes on an intimate and tactile level; they touch clothing constantly, are aware of its elements, construction, and fit. Their everyday work is to transmute and translate the designer's imagination, manifest in a sketch, into three-dimensional material reality.

The sample-makers have all worked for various design corporations in the district, each having a minimum of fifteen years' experience in corporate sample rooms. They are an ethnically diverse group, from the Dominican Republic, Columbian, Peruvian, Mexican, Vietnamese, Chinese, and Korean communities of New York, commuting in from Washington Heights, various parts of Queens, Sunset Park in Brooklyn, and areas of Long Island. James,[1] as usual, is leaning over his table, measuring out shapes and delicately cutting away. Arriving in New York City from Vietnam with his family, he began working in a Chinatown factory, sewing for five dollars an hour in the 1990s until he graduated with a patternmaking degree from the Fashion Institute of Technology. Rita is in the midst of creating a blouse, first making the pattern, then cutting and sewing the thin beige muslin that serves as the mock-up. Her mother, a seamstress from the Dominican Republic, never did teach her how to sew for fear she would end up sewing in the rag trade. Juan, the fabric cutter, started out working in a local factory, learned the business, and eventually partnered with his brother to start his own cutting factory in the district during the 1990s, only to shut it down after a decade and come work for this company.

The labor of these immigrants working in the corporate sample room is a reminder that in any global fashion capital or city, including Paris, Milan, and London, the rise of fashion industries, the expansion of fashion weeks, and the growing numbers of design collections shown during fashion weeks all depend upon the labor of low-waged ethnic immigrant and minority communities that cut, sew, and press the fashion collections.[2] The loosening of immigration laws and migration of immigrants to metropoles have been key to the transformation of garment industries into global fashion capitals. In the US, the 1965 Immigration and Nationality Act directly affected the ethnic composition of garment district workers from the 1970s onwards. While manufacturing gradually moved overseas, the demand for minimum-wage, unskilled, and part-time labor created jobs that were eventually filled by Latin American and Asian workers (Waldinger 1986; Lowe 1996). The presence of these garment workers from Asian and Latin American countries is testimony to a powerful juncture in US social history: as a new kind of "American" worker in garments, they are the cultural inheritors of a past fifty-year history involving US Cold War interventions in Korea, Vietnam, the Caribbean, and Central America. It is their labor, non-unionized and low-waged, as well as their non-citizenship status that allowed for the brief revitalization of the dwindling industry all throughout the 1970s, sustaining the domestic industry from its complete transfer offshore for at least the next two decades. The sample-makers of the described corporate design sample room, having arrived in New York City in the late 1970s and early 1980s, have made their way into the corporate sample rooms of Seventh Avenue by obtaining coursework and even degrees at local design schools. Having worked in the district for the past three decades, these sample-makers have the knowledge and experience as highly skilled workers to create the fashion week collections, and are simultaneously the witnesses to affirm postcolonial relationships, recent histories of neocolonialism, and imperialist projects of modernization and development.

With the overload of work for New York Fashion Week, the design company I intern for simultaneously uses local garment district sample-making factories. These factories are owned by Korean and Chinese entrepreneurs who surfaced within a small interstice of the local division of labor within garment production during the 1990s. Long-held family-owned leases expired among an aging generation of Jewish and Italian American factory owners unable to compete with the cheap cost of labor abroad or the rising cost of rent in the district. These Jewish and Italian factory owners felt it was time to make their way out of the business, selling their factories to former sewers and to newly arriving immigrant entrepreneurs. Dominican, Chinese, and Korean entrepreneurs became the next generation of factory owners within what was considered a waning industry (Trachtenberg 1986; Waldinger 1986; Chin 2005; Soyer 2005). Moreover, these factories have managed to survive by creating a particular niche in the industry—by making the samples of the runway collections they have "upgraded" the object's value and the "craft" of their work, creating yet another "fresh expression of value" or link in the value chain.

The interns are recruited to drop off patterns and pick up samples from one of these local sample-making factories, receiving instructions from the company's production manager, a man married to a Korean woman who owns a local factory. The factories line Thirty-ninth Street to Thirty-fourth Street and some are reminders of an old industrial era, complete with time clock, wage card, and lunch bell. Other factories are clean, with large windows and open spaces, with Department of Labor certificates of approval hanging up on the walls. The interns often visit Esther and John's Factory, a factory of twenty Korean and Chinese sewers with three Spanish-speaking cutters and pressers, run by a Korean husband-and-wife team. They are part of a generation of Korean factory owners that dominated the garment district's production sector, Koreans owning over 500 factories from 1980 to 2000 (Chin 2005; Soyer 2005). John had worked in garment factories since his teenage years in the South Korean countryside in the 1960s, when mass industrialization drives set by the military dictatorship had large populations of people working in enormous garment production factories. John tells me he worked for Korean factories that produced clothes for American sportswear labels like Nike and Reebok in the 1990s until the couple immigrated to New York City in 1999, chasing their "American dream," first working as sewers or floor managers before opening up their own factory (see Park 1997). They are part of a larger history of US military actions in Korea, of subsequent modernization and development, and of the introduction of foreign financial investment and capital that had American design corporations like Liz Claiborne and Donna Karan producing cheap exports in Korean garment factories for the American consumer of the 1980s.

Esther and John's entire factory is racing against the clock making multiple sample collections for twelve different design companies, all showcasing collections during New York Fashion Week. To be in the same space with competing designer collections and to recognize the value of the pieces has an incredibly lasting and memorable effect on all the interns entering the space—it is not unusual to see hanging side by side both a Marc Jacobs and a Zac Posen dress. In an industry where competitors guard their collections fiercely, shrouding the pieces in secrecy for fear of imitation or copy, it is ironic that a large number of New York designers and labels create their sample collections within the same few sample factories that exist within the district. The irony exposes a powerful contradiction: with all the mystique and value imbued in the object and its label, competing runway collections for New York Fashion Week are sewn by the same people, the same hands, in the same sample-making factories within the district.

The "de-garmenting" of the district took place over a thirty-year period and was part of the greater pattern of deindustrialization occurring across cities and industrial areas of the US. Manufacturing sites were transformed into new office complexes, hospitals, schools, science research laboratories, and pharmaceutical companies. In the garment district former manufacturing spaces gave way to showrooms, retail, media and advertising firms, and the headquarters of powerful design multinationals. American cities defined by large-scale production would have to restructure urban economic life by shifting industrial work into new forms of intellectual and cultural work, in the areas of research and information, finance, and software, and in the white-collar professions of culture, tourism, and entertainment industries (Carnoy et al. 1993). While the destruction of the New York garment district's garment production center continued to unfold given trade laws that changed the nature of work and industry within American cities, the transformation of the district's identity to one known for fashion would require an enormous amount of energy, financial investment, and promotion, and a powerful vision by fashion designers, industry leaders, real-estate developers, private investors, and city politicians of New York as a global fashion capital.

The city, however, was hardly a place where one could envision "fashion." The 1975 fiscal crisis of the New York City government created the vast economic and social problems that plagued the city for the next two decades. New York City had become a city of fear ravaged by crime, violence, and alarming increases in poverty rates. The garment district was a hotbed of organized crime, with the mob controlling trucking networks that managed the shipment and distribution of apparel within and outside the city. Amidst the crack epidemic and rising populations of the homeless, New York City was hardly a place to imagine an international fashion show.

In frustration, industry leaders pinpointed the problem as a lack of interest by city, state, and federal government in the importance of preserving, reanimating, or restructuring the industry both culturally and economically. These leaders pointed to Paris and Milan as their examples, as these cities had weathered their own de-garmenting of industry, and had grown into fashion centers with support from trade ministers who encouraged alliances between textile houses, mills, manufacturing, and design talent, and invested city and state funds. Furthermore, Paris and Milan were both known to culturally promote ceremonial rituals that showcased the city's design talent by advertising their fashion weeks on banners in their streets. Addressing these issues, American fashion designer Bill Blass believed the problem went beyond the isolating borders of a bankrupt city and imagined the issue as a national one, stating,

> "America has never been aggressive about exporting and becoming a global force," Blass said. "We can be frightfully isolationist. Too often, we don't think of ourselves as *international* designers, but as American designers ... Of course, the other problem is that American-made

clothes have a very high duty in Europe, which the European clothes don't have when they come here," Blass continued. "The government needs to do something, to rethink our export policies, to sell the U.S. around the world."

(*Women's Wear Daily* 1990)

Blass imagined American design as not a national but an international, global force—it was the *US* that needed to be sold around the world. By becoming a global force, the garment industry would need an export commodity, but not that of garments from the industrial manufacturing era, instead a cultural commodity in the form of American fashion design. By promoting American fashion to an international community, powerful international intermediaries, including buyers and retailers, editors, and the media, would bring not only cultural cachet to American fashion, but also foreign capital to the growing American fashion industry. Yet how to turn American fashion into a lucrative cultural export commodity known around the world as a global cultural force? Fashion designers, industry leaders, and city leaders alike would not only have to imagine the globality of American fashion, but root, brand, and define American fashion within the bounds of its most famous cultural city, New York City.

Fashion industry leaders banded together to make further appeals for city government to encourage and nurture the growing fashion industry. When asked what he envisioned for the changing garment district, Stan Herman, then president of the Council of Fashion Designers of America, stated to reporters,

The first thing I would like to see is a serious and helpful attitude from the city of New York and an awareness of the scope and size of our industry. Secondly, I would like to somehow find some funds to help us grow, such as sponsoring fashion shows, helping to find space within the parameters of the large real estate world for such shows, just like the governments do in Paris and Milan. Thirdly, I would like the city to find ways to encourage the new immigrants to stay here and grow within our industry and city through employment opportunities.

(*Women's Wear Daily* 1994)

Herman's speech pointed to the three elements needed to reanimate the New York garment industry. It would first include a study in the size and state of the district's garment production and fashion design sectors—a definition of what the industry had become; he then called for financial capital and real estate, a space for the showcasing of designer fashion shows; finally, he acknowledged the impossibility of the fashion industry existing without the labor of immigrants, who were needed for the making of fashion collections.

Herman's appeals would make their way to Rudolph Giuliani, the 1993 mayoral candidate, who campaigned around quality of life issues: stamping out crime, cleaning up the streets, and nurturing culture, business, and entertainment. Two decades earlier, the Association for a Better New York (ABNY) and the New York State Department of Commerce had set up the "I Love New York" and the "better New York" branding and marketing campaigns, making iconic the Twin Towers, the New York City skyline, and the Broadway theater district, all for state tourism (Collins 1995). Giuliani continued this branding of New York City, wanting to rebrand the garment district as well. In his inaugural address the new mayor promoted the New York fashion industry as a key business sector for the city and part of the city's "heart and soul," raising close to US$250,000 in a series of Seventh Avenue fund-raisers during his 1993 campaign. He helped to implement the "Made in New York" and "Designed in New York" campaigns for the next decade, encouraging links between manufacturing and design, just like Italy's successful "Made in Italy" campaigns (Chen 1997). He then proclaimed that New York fashion "defines New York as the capital of the world and the [world] capital of fashion" (*Women's Wear Daily* 1995). For Giuliani, the branding of New York City as the cultural capital of the world and the branding of New York City as the fashion capital of the world were one and the same project.

The appeals made by industry leaders to local businesses and government were successful, and resulted in major cosmetic changes to the neighborhood throughout the 1990s. In an effort to make the city "safe," Giuliani, industry leaders, and the newly formed Fashion Center Business Improvement District (FCBID) pushed for state laws to control, then oust, street vendors along the side streets of the district. A new "streetscape" program improved the aesthetics of the neighborhood with new curbs, sidewalks, decorative accoutrements added to industry building entrances, and lighting to improve security on the streets (Wilson 1998). Antique-looking lampposts were installed in an effort to preserve the historic feel of the district, while a bronzed statue of a Jewish tailor sitting at a sewing machine was placed on Seventh Avenue. Finally, a giant button with a needle, the modern Claes Oldenburg-inspired sculpture of the FCBID's association logo, was placed on the northeast corner of Seventh Avenue and Thirty-ninth Street next to the FCBID's new Fashion District information kiosk.

The same kind of "clean-up" program transformed the adjacent Times Square neighborhood from a former red-light district to a privatized "Disneyfied" theater district, the new site of New York's largest media, advertising, and marketing corporations who flashed advertisements to the growing number of tourists below (Chesluk 2007). Condé Nast Publications, headquarters to American fashion's most recognizable magazine, *Vogue*, moved into the heart of the theater district at 4 Times Square (Holusha 1996; Muschamp 1996; Pogrebin 1998). Capital from the Internet boom inflated the real estate market in Manhattan, attracting to the district real-estate agents hoping to buy and sell buildings with expiring leases. Garment industry buildings began housing a blend of advertising, marketing, media, and communications businesses, which had grown increasingly integral to fashion as a business. The territorialized takeover of garment industry buildings by advertising and media corporations was, to many, the ultimate symbolic act of "de-garmenting" the district. The old spaces of industrial manufacturing were transformed into the homogenous, private, and orderly compartments of office space, signaling the corporatization of fashion and space within New York City (Zukin 1995; Wilson 1998).

Design corporations on Seventh Avenue grew to enormous proportions as design, marketing, and merchandising empires. The building where I intern, which stands adjacent to Times Square, contains within it this 1980s and 1990s global corporate history, housing some of the most recognizable names in New York and international fashion: Oscar de la Renta, Donna Karan, Calvin Klein, and Ralph Lauren, among others. With the liberalization of international trade laws, these companies were among the first American manufacturers to produce overseas in a constellation of subcontracting networks—from the Asian NIC (newly industrializing country) "tiger economies" of Hong Kong, Taiwan, and South Korea; to the border industrialization programs of Mexico, Central and South America, and new export processing zones in the Caribbean; and finally to free trade and export processing zones in China, Southeast Asia, and South Asia (Bonacich 2004). These large American apparel companies began acquiring licensing agreements to capture wider segments of not just the national but an imagined and anonymous global mass market. American ready-to-wear companies expanded the variety of products, licensing out their branded logos to foreign companies that would pay a percentage of their profits for the use of the designer's powerful name on cosmetics, perfume, eyeglasses, and watches. Benefiting from the cultural capital of quality engendered by a company brand or logo, foreign companies used licensing agreements to organize new global spatial configurations in the production and retail of products. Working closely with media, advertising, and marketing companies in Times Square, fashion design and product development had become the focal point of work in the New York fashion industry. The now global demand for more products in greater variety created new tempos in fashion: shorter product life cycles, quick production turnover times, and greater merchandise availability were needed to satisfy the demands of a buyer-driven market (Smith 1997).

The emergence of giant American apparel manufacturing and retail conglomerates in New York fashion created the need for entire workforces of cultural workers who could design, develop, and market multiple lines and ranges of products (Appelbaum and Gereffi 2004). The complex division of labor in the district, which once centered on garment assemblage work, now includes numerous design and culture industries. From head designers to technical designers, tech-pack designers, design freelancers, and interns, an entire bureaucratic apparatus is needed to design, organize, and communicate a global process that begins with design and marketing in New York City; is organized in hub or port cities such as Los Angeles, Hong Kong, Guangzhou, Shanghai, and Seoul through trading, wholesale, and production-coordinating companies; is mass produced in specialized export zones in China, Mexico, Vietnam, and India by "cut-and-sew" factories; and is then packaged, marketed, distributed, and sold to consumers around the world.

On the floor of the company in which I intern, the elevator doors open to a white perfumed showroom. Sunlight exaggerates the white walls of the showroom space, which embodies cleanliness, thinness, and light. Garment racks line the walls, hanging delicate dresses, blouses, and jackets like rare pieces of art. The showroom space is more than just a waiting room for buyers and clients—it is a sensory holding area for first impressions of the company's image and ambience. Showroom spaces are worlds constructed with image, saturated with mood and aura to help along the imagination of buyers who need to be convinced of the clothing's potential desirability. Within the district today, the numbers of showroom spaces are growing, especially those of corporations that represent multiple design lines. There exist approximately 1,200 showrooms in former manufacturing spaces of the district (Berger 2004).

The composure of the showroom is pierced by the frenzy that exists behind double doors that lead into the front office space. The front office houses public-relations agents and marketers who actively construct, promote, and circulate the company's outer persona. Front-office workers in retail and sales construct the imaginary "market," sharing with their buyers their narratives and predictions on what sells. Those in the front-office design studio include designers, design assistants, textile and trim liaisons, involved in translating the company persona into actual design. Their space is full of inspiration and design boards, with company concepts matched with colors, fabrics, and trims to make the materiality of the story.

All those who work in the front office space and design studio are women who represent the face and persona of the company. They are highly educated with degrees in business, marketing, merchandising, and fashion design. Their work in fashion continues after work—up to date on the latest women's clothing trends, they constantly peruse fashion magazines and websites, receiving a company clothing allowance that updates their wardrobes, as their own bodies embody the design campaign's advertisements. The visual image of this white-collar worker seems far from the masculine imagery of an industrial era of American history or even the emergent global figure of the female garment worker sitting down at a sewing machine performing manual labor. Yet the work of this white-collar professional is physically and mentally challenging, requiring long hours at low pay, with low retention rates, working in a gradually degrading and casualized cultural workforce.

The interns in the front office attend prestigious colleges or design schools and are given countless numbers of responsibilities, from answering phones, double-checking inventory or sales lists, editing press releases, and organizing the clothes pulled for press and photo shoots. They dream of studying abroad to become designers like Alexander McQueen or Stella McCartney and learn to speak French or Italian in the hopes of landing fashion internships in Paris or Milan. Sample-room interns are students at local design schools like FIT and Parsons School of Design. They might spend the day stitching on clothing labels, making or tracing patterns, or sketching flats, working closely with patternmakers and designers. One of the interns told me she had dropped her resumé off on every single floor of the same building before being called to work New York Fashion Week. These interns hope their internships will help land them jobs in the corporate offices or design studios of New York name-brand clothing companies.

There are differences between the back and front room, based on agenda and class, on educational and cultural life paths, yet, despite these differences, interns share a common imagining—a complex of depictions and directives in an industry whose main commodity is image as much as clothing. Interns are all drawn to the fashion world for its complex of beauty, money, image, and glamour, gleaning information from magazines, websites, blogs, work, and observation in an effort to get on the inside of the industry to actively learn and read the system. From such varied backgrounds, completely different demographics, and entirely different countries, it is amazing to think that interns have such an astoundingly coherent and shareable knowledge of names, images, and ideas in fashion.

The emergence of the unpaid internship is a more recent phenomenon in the division of labor in the New York fashion industry. Interns, in particular, are recruited for the weeks leading up to New York Fashion Week when the entire industry is short of labor. The work of an intern is rarely monetarily compensated since payment is understood to come in the form of the cultural experience itself: to learn the work, make contacts, have the reference, and use the existing network to gain access into the insular fashion world. In today's postmodern culture industries, Andrew Ross describes the "cultural discount" as the rise of creative professionals who accept increasingly lower wages in return for performing more personally satisfying labor—free or discounted cultural labor that has become integral to a capitalist knowledge economy (Ross 2004). Ironically, the exploitative conditions of these cultural workers' work usually culturally glamorize them as "starving" artists or musicians. Since interns need other financial means to support their unpaid internships, stark class inequities exist between students who can financially cover an internship and access the industry's networks, and those who must work for pay, unable to afford the much-needed cultural capital to be hired in the fashion industry.

One week before New York Fashion Week, the interns head to Bryant

Park to get a glimpse of the white tents put up for the fashion shows. At the end of summer it is hard for the interns to imagine the park's green space transformed into fashion territory for the fall/winter 2006 "Seventh on Sixth" fashion shows. Located on Fortieth Street between Sixth and Fifth Avenues, Bryant Park is adjacent to the New York Public Library. New York Fashion Week had rooted itself into this permanent bounded space of the city in 1993. Modeled after the shows in Paris and Milan, the Council of Fashion Designers of America (CFDA)—a not-for-profit trade consortium of over 280 of American fashion and accessory designers, then headed by director Fern Mallis and president Stan Herman—were the first to pitch the tents for fashion shows. It is Bryant Park's symbolic location that makes it a powerfully marked site, sitting emblematically adjacent to the triad of industry that now defines New York fashion; the garment district's sample production factories west of Broadway, the Seventh Avenue design head-quarters immediately to the west, and the Times Square marketing and media nexus found north of the park. The physical rooting and symbolic location of New York Fashion Week in Bryant Park proclaimed to the global fashion world that New York fashion had its official center, territory, and week.

Ironically, Bryant Park was known for years as a space of crime and "perversion," a pick-up spot for men and a hangout for vagrants, prostitutes, and drug dealers (Berman 2006; Chauncy 1995). The park's neglect prompted the founding of the Bryant Park Restoration Corporation in 1980 by a group of prominent New York families that would privately fund the improvements to the park. While the association's main aim was to offer cultural events to the public, the association invested considerable funds in private security to keep "undesirables" out of the park (Zukin 1995). The park reopened to the public in 1992 as a formal French-styled garden, garnering accusations of Parisian mimicry and amnesia of its past history. Nearly a decade later, in 2001, IMG, the global entertainment, sports management, and mega-marketing agency, purchased New York Fashion Week, along with all of its trademarks and operations, from the CFDA, rebranding the name to that of its official corporate sponsor: Mercedes Benz/Olympus New York Fashion Week. The white tents of Bryant Park are big business for this global company, charging between US$25,000 and US$50,000 rental rates for a ten-minute fashion show. Yet state-of-the-art-lighting, staging, and production cannot fully cloak the late-capitalist quality of sameness, identical interchangeability, and commonality that the tents give off. For the young, up-and-coming, and startup designer, the uneven grounds of the New York fashion industry are already established with the unaffordable tent space of Bryant Park.

By 1993 American fashion had broken into the cultural arena of world fashion, its center the Parisian fashion scene. Curator Richard Martin opened the Versailles 1973: American Fashion on the World Stage exhibit at the Costume Institute of the Metropolitan Museum of Art to celebrate the 1973 Palace of Versailles fashion show where American designers Anne Klein, Stephen Burrows, Bill Blass, Oscar de la Renta, and Halston had presented the "wave of the future," American ready-to-wear collections, to the international fashion community against the waning French haute couture industry (Morris 1993). Then, in 1993, Oscar de la Renta gained acceptance into Paris's exclusive Chambre syndicale, becoming the first American designer to create and show a Paris haute couture collection (Luther 1993). Finally, toward the end of the decade in 1997 the darling of the global fashion world Helmut Lang moved his company's headquarters from Paris to New York City then boldly announced he would show his spring/summer 1999 collection in September, two months before its official timing in November after Milan, London, and Paris Fashion Weeks (Foley 1998). Lang's New York colleagues followed suit, permanently and radically changing design, production, and buying cycles across the entire global fashion industry. The recognition of American designers abroad and the changes in global fashion timing would culturally mark New York as an accepted fashion capital of the world.

The 1990s was a tumultuous decade in the New York garment district. Due to recession, bankruptcy, and the devastation of its production sector, the district had been doomed to decline. Yet the 1990s was also a decade that saw former immigrant sewers become factory owners and sample-makers who shaped and redefined new roles and meanings for workers in production. The decade also set forth new global visions for American fashion among industry leaders, who reacted to new spatial configurations in global garment production by physically, economically, socially, and culturally transforming the identity of the local garment industry into an exported cultural commodity of fashion design. American design as an imagined "global force," and New York City as a "fashion capital," would require enormous initiative and action—the vision of New York as part of the global fashion world; financial and political support from government and private funds; branding, advertisement, and promotion by local government and media; available real-estate space in an unaffordable city; and even an institutionalized cultural and ceremonial ritual, such as New York Fashion Week. As American design corporations both produced and marketed their products to an imagined global mass market, a globally connected anti-sweatshop movement emerged to uncover and protest exploitative factory conditions propped by American fashion worldwide. Today these New York-based design corporations continue to grow, attracting an international casualized workforce of predominantly female cultural workers to work in the expanding design, marketing, and production-coordinating sectors of the industry.

With the public's growing fascination with New York fashion—a result of fashion going mainstream—television reality shows, websites, blogs, and magazines seem to glamorize all aspects of work involved in New York Fashion Week. This glamorization produces the vast disparity between the image, the behind-the-scenes images on television, and the behind-the-scenes experiences of working in the district, influencing our understanding of what gets defined as labor in fashion production. One must remember the interns, models, front-office workers, design assistants, and sample-makers—the new kind of workers who work hard to create not just garments, but fashion.

Acknowledgements

My many thanks to Eugenia Paulicelli and Hazel Clark for their comments and suggestions on and editing of this chapter.

Notes

1. All names of individuals in this chapter are changed.
2. In Le Sentier of Paris the work is done by West Indian, Southeast Asian, and Chinese workers, and in Milan, by Chinese sewers. In London fashion depends on the South Asian community, and in New York City on Latin Americans and Asians. See Green (1997).

References

Appelbaum, R. and Gereffi, G. (2004) "Power and Profits in the Apparel Commodity Chain," in E. Bonacich (ed.), *Global Production: The Apparel Industry in the Pacific Rim*, Philadelphia: Temple University Press.

Bagli, C. V. (1998) "Holding on in the Garment Center," *New York Times*, March 2: B1.

Berger, J. (2004) "The Shrinking and Fading Garment Center; As Manufacturing Shifts in Fashion Industry, Gritty Lofts Become Upscale Apartments," *New York Times*, August 23: B1.

Berman, M. (2006) *On the Town: One Hundred Years of Spectacle in Times Square*, New York: Random House.

Bonacich, E. (ed.) (2004) *Global Production: The Apparel Industry in the Pacific Rim*, Philadelphia: Temple University Press.

Carnoy, M., Castells, M., Cohen, S., and Cardosa, F. H. (eds.) (1993) *The New World Economy in the Information Age*, University Park, PA: Penn State University Press.

Casanova, P. (2005) *The World Republic of Letters (Convergences: Inventories of the Present)*, M. B. DeBevoise (trans.), Cambridge, MA: Harvard University Press.

Castells, M. (1989) *The Informational City*, Oxford: Basil Blackwell.

Chauncey, G. (1995) *Gay New York: Gender, Urban Culture, and the Making of the Gay Male World, 1890–1940*, New York: Basic Books.

Chen, D. W. (1997) "Manufacturing and Design Links are Encouraged," *New York Times*, February 4: B6.

Chesluk., B. (2007) *Money Jungle: Imagining the New York Times Square*, New Brunswick: Rutgers University Press.

Chin, M. M. (2005) *Sewing Women: Immigrants and the New York City Garment Industry*, New York: Columbia University Press.

Collins, G. (1995) "The Media Business: Advertising in the 'I Love New York' Campaign, a New Kind of Broadway Revival," *New York Times*, September 20: D5.

Foley, B. (1998) "Lang Sets Early Date For His New York Show," *Women's Wear Daily*, July 7: 2.

Gereffi, G., Spencer, D., and Bair, J. (eds.) (2002) *Free Trade and Uneven Development: The North American Apparel Industry after NAFTA*, Philadelphia: Temple University Press.

Green, N. (1997) *Ready-to-Wear and Ready-to-Work: A Century of Industry and Immigrants in Paris and New York*, Durham: Duke University Press.

Holusha., J. (1996) "New Times Square Tower Lures a Key Tenant," *New York Times*, October 25: B6.

Kleinfield, N. R. (1993) "Buttonholes to Go," *New York Times*, January 16: V1.

Lambert, B. (1995) "Can the Garment District Refashion Itself?" *New York Times*, August 6: CY4.

Light, I. and Bhachu, P. (eds.) (1993) *Immigration and Entrepreneurship: Culture, Capital, and Ethnic Networks*, New Brunswick: Transaction.

Lowe, L. (1996) *Immigrant Acts: On Asian American Cultural Politics*, Durham and London: Duke University Press.

Luther, M. (1993) "High Status of Couture No Longer All Sewn Up," *Christian Science Monitor*, February 11: 10–11.

Morris, B. (1993) "When America Stole the Runway from Paris Couture," *New York Times*, September 10: C1.

Muschamp, H. (1996) "Smaller is Better: Conde Nast Meets Times Square," *New York Times*, May 18: 21–22.

Park, K. (1997) *The Korean American Dream: Immigrants and Small Business in New York*, Ithaca, NY: Cornell University Press.

Pogrebin, R. (1998) "Vogue's Untimely Issue Heralds the New Tower," *New York Times*, July 24: B5.

Ross, A. (2004) *Low Pay, High Profile: The Global Push for Fair Labor*, New York: The New Press.

Sansoni, S. (2000) "Rags to Digits," *Forbes*, April 17: 412.

Scheffer, M. (1998) "Trading Places: Fashion, Retailers, and the Changing Geography of Clothing Production," *International Journal of Operations and Production Management*, 18(12): 1189–1204.

Smith, P. (1997) "Tommy Hilfiger in the Age of Mass Customization," in A. Ross (ed.), *No Sweat: Fashion, Free Trade, and the Rights of Garment Workers,* New York and London: Verso.

Soyer, D. (ed.) (2005) *A Coat of Many Colors: Immigration, Globalization and Reform in New York's Garment Industry*, New York: Fordham University Press.

Trachtenberg, J. A. (1986) "'My Daughter, She Will Speak Better:' Korean Immigrants Put in Long Hours in Garment Lofts to Raise Standard of Living," *Forbes*, October 6: 68.

Tsing, A. L. (2005) *Friction: An Ethnography of Global Connection*, Princeton, NJ: Princeton University Press.

Waldinger, R.D. (1986) *Through the Eye of the Needle: Immigrants and Enterprise in New York's Garment Trades*, New York: New York University Press.

Wilson, E. (1998) "The Fashion District Gets New Look: More than Pins and Needles," *Women's Wear Daily* , April 28: 1.

Women's Wear Daily (1990) "SA to City Hall: Give Us Respect, and a Lot More (Apparel Designers on New York's Seventh Ave.)" July 17: 1.

—— (1994) "Industry Tells NY's New Mayor What It Wants," January 11: 1.

—— (1995) "Rudy's Fashion Agenda: Fashion Center at FIT, Start of Tax-Free Zones," January 24: 1.

Zukin, S. (1995) *The Cultures of Cities*, Cambridge, MA: Blackwell.

Index

Note: page numbers in *italics* refer to illustrations. Page numbers followed by *n* refer to information in a note.

Abbas, Ackbar 179, 189
aesthetics: and artisan production 17; "clothing competence" in Zambia 114, 118–119; grammar of style and jeans 129, 132–134, 141; suit aesthetics in Zambia 119–121, 122, 125
Agreement on Textiles and Clothing (ATC) 195–196
Albanians in Greece 146–147, 147; origins of fustanella 147, 148
Althusser, Louis 95, 99
Amado, Jorge 168–169
America: American fashion photography in postwar France 41–51; and "China style" 183–189; Cold War consumption strategy in Soviet Russia 76–77; jeans production 135, 136, 138–141, 142; *see also* New York
amiche, Le (film) 56, 59–61, 60, 61, 62
Anand, Chetan 33
Andaz (film) 28–32, 29, 31, 38
Andrianou, Molly 161
Anglo-Indians: attitudes towards 34–35
Antonioni, Michelangelo 53–70
ao dai (Vietnamese national costume) 92

apamwamba women's dress in Zambia 118, 121–124, 124, 125
Appadurai, Arjun 151, 178
Arnold, Rebecca 42–43, 46–47
artisan production of cloth 14, 16–18
autonomy and artisanal cloth production 14, 18
Avedon, Richard 41, 42, 44, 47–49, 48, 51
avventura, L' (film) 54, 55–56, 55, 62, 63–64, 65–66, 68, 69, 69

Barbier, Armele 191*n*
bark garments 20–21
Barthes, Roland 42, 43, 45–46, 49, 54, 69–70
Bartlett, Djurdja 74, 84, 155, 157
Bassman, Lillian 46
Bataille, Georges 21–22
batiking 18
Baudelaire, Charles 160
Baudrillard, Jean 154, 168
Benjamin, Walter 46, 47, 50–51, 160, 162
Bergman, Ingrid 62–63
Berselli, Adriana 54, 55, 56, 64, 70*n*
Bhabha, Homi 105
Biki (Italian designer) 64
Blanc de Chine 178, 179–180, 182–183, 189, 190, 191; Bleu de Chine range 183, 185; New York store 183–184, 187–189, 188
Blass, Bill 200–201
Blitz News Magazine (Indian magazine) 28, 32

Blow-Up (film) 56, 66
body shape: and Japanese designers
    188–189; and taste in Soviet Russia
    81–82, *83*; and women's dress in
    Zambia 123–124, *125*; *see also*
    female body
Bonita, Maria 170
Bonnell, Victoria 78
Bosè, Lucia 57, *58*
Bourdieu, Pierre 165, 172
branding 2; branded clothing and self-
    enhancement 14, 24–25; Brazilian
    fashion brands 166–167; and
    "Chinese style" 179–180, 186; jeans
    production 132, *133*, 134–139, 142;
    and modern production methods
    130, *131*; of New York by Giuliani
    202
Brazilian fashion
    164–176; cultural identity and
    fashion 168–172; fashion industry
    165–168, 174–175; global context
    174–175; Herchcovitch case study
    172–174; "Latin style" 164–165;
    and street culture 165, 167–168,
    168–170
Breward, C. 1–2
Brodovitch, Alexey 42–43, 46
Bryant Park and New York Fashion
    Week 205–206
Buchli, Victor 90*n*
bui (grunge style in Vietnam) 92, 97,
    106
Butt, Vinita 36
Buziol, Claudio 135
Byron, Lord 148

California: jeans production 135, 136,
    138, 142
capitalist hierarchies and consumption
    13–14, 22–25
cars and postwar Paris 48–49
Casanova, P. 194–195
cedar bark garments 20–21
Chá, Rosa 164, 166, *168*, 175
Chan, Alan 191*n*
Chan, Jackie 188
charitable donations of clothing 113

cheongsam (*qipao*): Chinese designs
    180–181, *181*, 183, 187, 190;
    Galliano collection 178
Chilkat "blankets" 14, 17, 23
China: consumption of luxury goods
    191*n*
"China style" and Hong Kong
    designers 177–191
chitenge clothing in Zambia 122,
    123–124, *124*
Chulamanda, George 119
cinema costume: and fashion in Soviet
    Russia 79; in films of Antonioni
    53–70; and national fashion in
    Indian cinema 28–39
class differences and clothing: in
    Antonioni's films 54; *apamwamba*
    women's dress in Zambia 118,
    121–124, *125*; and *Doi moi*
    policies in Vietnam 95, 106–107;
    equality as aim in Soviet Russia 74;
    funding unpaid fashion internships
    205; in Indian cinema 35–37; and
    secondhand clothing market in
    Zambia 118
cloth and clothing and self-
    enhancement 13–25
"clothing competence" in Zambia 114,
    118–119
clustering and jeans production
    138–139, 142
Cohn, Bernard S. 16
Cold War consumption strategy in
    Soviet Russia 76–77
colonization and Hong Kong 179,
    189–190
color of clothing: regulation in Soviet
    Russia 82–84
Communist Youth League in Vietnam
    95, 99, 100, 101–102; Spring
    Fashion Contest 92–94, *93*, *94*,
    95–96, 101, 102, 103–105, 106, 107
Compania Maritima 166
connotation: and fashion photography
    45–46; material objects in Soviet
    Russia 90*n*
consumption: and capitalist hierarchies
    13–14, 22–25; consumerism in

US 22–25; and *Doi moi* policies
in Vietnam 96–97, 101, 106–107;
and fashion magazines in Greece
158–160; and gift theory 14, 15,
21–22; luxury goods in China 191*n*;
middle classes and fashion in Soviet
Russia 76–80, 89; and production
of clothing 128–143; Western-style
clothing in Zambia 112
contracting out production 25, 131,
139; offshore production and
New York garment industry 194,
195–196, 197, 203
Coopa-Roca (Brazilian fashion
cooperative) 167–168
Council of Fashion Designers of
America (CFDA) 206
courtly societies and consumption of
cloth 13–25
Craik, Jennifer 188
credit system and consumerism in US
23
Cronaca di un amore (film) 57–59, *58*
Cu Mai Cong 97
cultural capital 128; "cultural
discount" as remuneration 205–206
"cultural economy of distance" 178
cultural identity: and Brazilian fashion
168–172; in post-colonial Hong
Kong 179, 189–190
customization of jeans 129, 136–137

Da Matta, Roberto 168–170
Dang Canh Khanh 100
Dashkova, Tat'iana 84
Daslu store in Brazil 167
Daspu (clothing collective in Brazil)
167–168
DaVida (prostitutes' collective in Brazil)
167
de la Renta, Oscar 207
Debord, Guy 49–50, 158
debt and consumerism in US 23
"decent dress" for women in Zambia
118, 121–123, 125
Dener (Brazilian designer) 165
denim production 128–129, 138–139,
141

denotation: and fashion photography
45–46; and material objects in Soviet
Russia 90*n*
deserto rosso, Il (film) 55–56, 64,
66–68, *67*
designer jeans 137, 138
Devi, Jayananda Nandini 30
Dicken, Peter 25
Diesel jeans *134*, 135, 137, 138
differentiation production techniques
131, 168; jeans brands 132, 133,
134–137, *134*, 138, 139; localization
138–141
distressed jeans 135–136
Doi moi (Renovation) policies
in Vietnam 92, 95–96; and
consumption 96–97, 101, 106–107;
role of youth 99–102
Douglas, Mary 17
Dumont, Louis 18
Dunham, Vera S. 89*n*
Dutt, Guru 35, 37
dyeing: ritual and spirituality 16–17

eclisse, L' (film) 62, 64, 66, 68
Eco, Umberto 156
Elias, Norbert 89*n*
elites and cloth in courtly societies
18–19, 20–22, 23
enhancement and cloth and clothing 13,
14–16
"ensemble" and color in Soviet Russia
83–84
ethnic identity and Greek dress
145–155
ethnography: consumption and gift
theory 14, 15, 21–22; courtly and
capitalist hierarchies 14–25; intern's
experience of New York fashion
industry 194–208
Evans, C. 1–2
everyday: clothes in Soviet Russia
84–86
Evisu jeans 135, 136, 138
exoticism: of Chinese goods
178–179; self-exoticization of
Chinese designers 179–183,
190

Fabric of Cultures project 1
fabric technologies: and jeans 132–133,
    136, 137, 139, 142; natural materials
    in Brazil 164–165
fashion as art 156–157
Fashion Center Business
    Improvement District (FCBID), New
    York 202
fashion contest in Vietnam 92–94, *93,
    94*, 95–96, 101, 102, 103–105, 106,
    107
fashion magazines and modernization
    in Greece 155–162
fashion photography: Antonioni as
    influence 56; postwar American
    photography 41–51
"fashionization" 156, 157
female body: and "decent dress" in
    Zambia 122–123, 125; and Soviet
    Russia 73, 81–82, *83*; *see also* body
    shape
film *see* cinema costume
Filmfare (Indian magazine) 28
Finkelstein, Joanne 150
fit and jeans production 132, 136
flâneur 46, 160
flexible accumulation production model
    129
Fontana sisters (designers) 59–60
Fordist/modernist production methods
    128–129; jeans production 135,
    141
Fox, James J. 15
Fraga, Ronaldo 170, *171*
France: American fashion photography
    and postwar Paris 41–51; jeans
    production and market 135, 137,
    139, 142; *see also* Paris
Frankel, S. 178
Free (Greek magazine) 152–153, *152,
    153*
Freyre, Gilberto 164
Fukuyama, Francis 158
fustanella as Greek national dress
    147–154, *149, 151*, 155, 161;
    historical origins 147–150; modern
    interpretations 151–154
fustanellitsa 150, *151*

G-Star jeans *134*, 135, 136, 137, 138
Galliano, John 178, 180
garment industry in New York
    194–208; decline of traditional
    industry 195–196, 207; labor
    demands of design industry 203–204;
    production for fashion industry
    196–203; transformation of district
    into design area 200–203, 207
Gattinoni, Ferdinanda 60, 70*n*
gender: and artisan cloth production
    17–18; body and fashion discourse in
    Soviet Russia 73–90; gender relations
    and costume in Indian cinema 28–32;
    and secondhand clothing in Zambia
    112–126; and Soviet discourse 77–78
General Agreement on Tariffs and
    Trade (GATT) 195–196
generation gap and youth studies 97, 98
gift theory 14, 15; excessive giving
    21–22, 23
Girbaud, François and Marithé 135,
    138
Giuliani, Rudolph 202
global trade: exports from China 177;
    global jeans production 138–141,
    142; trade acts and New York
    garment industry decline 195–196,
    203
global value chain model 128
globalization: and consumption
    in Zambia 112; and fashion 2,
    113–114; global brand identities
    131; jeans as garment archetype
    128–129, 132; and local 3, 112, 125,
    137–141; and postwar Paris 42; and
    production methods 131, 139–141;
    see also global trade
goat hair 21
Golikova, N. 81
Gradskova, Yulia 78
grammar of style and jeans 129,
    132–134, 141
Greece: ethnic identity and national
    dress 145–155, 161–162; influence of
    fashion magazines 155–162
Gronow, Jukka 89*n*
Grundberg, Andy 46–47

grunge (*bui*) fashion in Vietnam 92, 97, 106
Gurchenko, Liudmila 79
Gynaika (Greek magazine) 158

Harper's Bazaar (American magazine) 41, 42–43, 45
Harrison, Martin 46, 50
Harvey, David 128, 129–130, 131, 139, 142, 159–160
Hatten, Fause 175
Herchcovitch, Alexandre 164, 170, 172–174, *173*, 175
Herman, Stan 201–202, 206
hierarchies and consumption of cloth and clothing 13–25
Ho Chi Minh Communist Youth League 95, 99, 100, 101–102
Hollander, Anne 38*n*, 154, 156
"homogenizing heterogeneity" 3
Hong Kong: and "China style" 179–183, 190; colonization and cultural identity 179, 189–190
House of Fashion (Dom modelei) in Soviet Russia 75
Hudson Bay Company 19, 20, 21

Ianês, Mauricio: Brazilian Color Chart 170
identity: clothing and identity in Antonioni's films 53–70; interpellation of youth in Vietnam 95, 98, 99–102; young people and fashion in Vietnam 105–106, 107; *see also* cultural identity; national identities and fashion; self and clothing
ideology: and clothing in Soviet Russia 84, 86–89; interpellation of youth in Vietnam 95, 98, 99–102
Illustrated Weekly of India (magazine) 28, 33, 36
immigrant labor in New York fashion industry 197–199, 201
Indian cinema costume and national fashion 28–39
inequality: under capitalism 13, 14, 22; *see also* class differences

Inka society and cloth 19
international trade *see* global trade
interns and New York fashion industry 194–208; duties of interns 205–206
interpellation of youth in Vietnam 95, 98, 99–102
Italy: Italian style in films of Antonioni 53–70; jeans production 135, 136, 138–139, 142

Japan: Japanese designers and the body 188–189; jeans production 135, 136, 138–139, 142
jeans: Brazilian brands 166; as garment archetype 128–129, 132; globalization and production 137–141, 142; luxury brands 137; technical grammar 132–137, *134*, 141; retail presentation of *140*; and young men's dress in Zambia 120, 125
Joshi, O. P. 30
Journal du textile 137

Kant, Immanuel 157
Karan, Donna 181–182
Kasbekar, A. 34
Khan, Mehboob 32
Kireeva, L. 84, 88
Korean labor and New York garment industry 198, 199
Kwakiutl people in American Northwest 19–20

labor: demands of New York design industry 203–205, 208; low labor-cost production methods 131, 142; low-cost labor for New York garment industry 195–196, 197–199, 201; for textile production 24–25; unpaid intern labor for New York Fashion Week 205–206
landscape and power 41–42, 50
Lang, Helmut 207
language and advertising in Greek fashion magazines 160–161
"Latin style" and Brazilian fashion 164–165
Lauren, Ralph 181

Le Masne de Chermont, Raphael 186
Lear, Edward 145–146
Lele people 17–18
Levi's jeans 132, 134–135, *134*, 136,
    137–138, 140–141, 142
life cycle: of clothes and fashion in
    Soviet Russia 74; and global fashion
    industry 203
Lima, André *169*, 170
local and global 3, 112, 125; and jeans
    production 137–141
Louie, A. 190
Luce, Claire Booth 60
Lusaka, Zambia 112–126
luxury goods: consumption in China
    191*n*; luxury-brand jeans 137,
    138

McCarthy, Terry 100
machine production 24
McRobbie, Angela 102
Magrini, Gritt 66
Mallis, Fern 206
Manning, Robert 23
manufacturing 2; Brazilian clothing
    industry 165–166; ethnography
    and artisan production of cloth 14,
    16–18; expansion in China 177;
    garment industry in New York
    194–203; manufacturers' retail
    outlets 130; production methods and
    consumption of clothing 128–143;
    see also jeans; production; textile
    industry
Marie Claire (fashion magazine) 152,
    161, *161*
Marr, David 98
Martin, Richard 206–207
materiality and morality in Vietnam 95,
    106, 107
Mauss, Marcel 14, 15, 21
Maynard, M. 150, 151
media: and "decent dress" on television
    in Zambia 121–122; and fashion
    information in Soviet Russia 78–80;
    influence of fashion magazines in
    Greece 155–162; and moral panic
    about youth in Vietnam 96–97;

and state ideology in Vietnam 102;
    women's magazines in Soviet Russia
    78, 80–88
memory and clothing 70
men: dress and young men in Zambia
    116, 119–121, *121*, 122, 125
middle classes and consumption:
    apamwamba women's dress in
    Zambia 118, 121–124, 125; in Soviet
    Russia 76–80, 89; in Vietnam 101,
    106–107
Miele, Carlos 166–167, 175
mien lap jackets 182
miniskirts: and "decent dress" in
    Zambia 122; in Soviet Russia 86–88,
    87
Mitchell, W. T. 41–42, 50
Miyake, Issey 189
modernist production *see* Fordist/
    modernist production methods
morality: and clothing in Soviet Russia
    86–88; "decent dress" for women
    in Zambia 118, 121–123, 125; and
    materiality in Vietnam 95, 106, 107;
    moral panic about youth in Vietnam
    94–95, 96–98; young people and
    clothing in Vietnam 102–107
Morisset, Pierre 135, 138
Morumbi Fashion in Brazil 165
Moyer, Eileen 126*n*
Murra, John 19

national identities and fashion 2;
    American fashion photography
    and postwar Paris 41–51; Indian
    cinema costume and national fashion
    28–39; and national dress in Greece
    145–155, 161–162
Native Americans: potlatching on
    Northwest Coast 19–22, 23
natural materials in Brazil 164–165
Netherlands: jeans production 138
New York: as brand 202; Chinese
    designers in 183–189; fashion and
    postwar Europe 46–47, 50; *see also*
    garment industry in New York
New York Fashion Week 194,
    195, 207–208; garment district

production for 196–203; unpaid
intern labor 205–206
Ngoma, Samuel 112
Nguyen Bich Thuan 102
Nguyen Minh Hoa 97
Nguyen Phuong An 100
Nguyen Thi Oanh 97, 106
Nguyen-Vo, Thu-Huong 101
Nilan, Pam 106–107
Nivi-style saris 30–31, 34, 38
Nopcsa, Baron 148
North American Free Trade Agreement
(NAFTA) 195–196
notte, La (film) 64–66, 68
Nudie Jeans 136, 138
Nuttall, Sarah 124

obesity and fashion in Soviet Russia
81–82, 83
offshore labor and New York garment
industry 195–196, 197, 203
Ohmann, Richard 159
Ooi, Joanne 186
Orientalism 3; self-exoticization of
Chinese designers 179–183, 190; in
Western fashion 177, 178–179, 186
Oswell, David 98
Other 3, 157; see also Orientalism
Otto, king of the Greeks 149–150
outsiders in Italian style in films 62–63
outsourcing see contracting out
production

Papa, Matilda 152
Papantoniou, Ioanna 147, 148, 149,
150, 154
Paris: American designers in 206–207;
and American fashion photography
after WWII 41–51
Parker, Suzy 43, 44, 45, 47–49, 48
Passenger, The (film) 63, 64
personalization of jeans 136–137
Petropoulos, Elias 149, 150
Phiri, Mary 122
photography see fashion photography
Phytoervas Fashion in Brazil 165
pocket features of jeans 133, 134, 134
Polhemus, Ted 170

post-Fordist/postmodern production
methods 128, 141, 142
potlatching and Chilkat "blankets" 14,
19–22, 23
Pratt, Mary Louise 42
production: artisan production of cloth
14, 16–18; and capitalist hierarchies
13–14; production methods and
consumption of clothing 128–143;
see also contracting out production;
jeans; manufacturing
profitability: jeans 137; ratios 130–131
Pyaasa (film) 28, 35–37, 37, 38

qipao see cheongsam

Rabotnitsa (Russian magazine) 75–76,
75, 78, 79, 80, 81, 82, 83, 84–86,
85; on fashion and behavior 86, 87,
88
racial identity and costume in Indian
cinema 32–35
Rajadhyaksha, A. 32
Rajan, Rajeswari 34
Ramani, Sheila 39n
Reeve, Lydia 183
regional clusters in jeans production
138–139, 142
Reid, Susan E. 76–77, 78
retailing: Chinese designers in New
York 183–189; manufacturers as
retailers 130
Rhodes, Zandra 174
ritual and cloth 15–16, 16–17;
potlatches and Chilkat "blankets"
20–22, 23
Roerich, Devika Rani 38
Rohdie, S. 56
Rosa Chá (Brazilian fashion company)
164, 166, 168, 175
Rosen, Stanley 98
Ross, Andrew 205
Ross, Kristin 48–49
Rossellini, Roberto 62–63
Rosso, Renzo 135
rotation of current assets ratio
130–131
Russia see Soviet Russia and fashion

Russian Revolution and fashion 73
Rydstrøm, Helle 99

Said, Edward 157
St. Clair, William 146
Salish people 20
sample-makers: low-cost labor for New
    York fashion industry 196–199, 201
São Paulo Fashion Week 165, 166,
    170–172, 175
saris: in Indian cinema costume 30–31,
    31, 34–35; Nivi-style saris 30–31,
    34, 38
Sarmi, Count Ferdinando 58–59
Scheffer, Y. M. 131
Schneider, Jane 112
Schor, Juliet 23
secondhand clothing in Zambia
    112–126; and international trade
    113, 116; local markets 112, 113,
    115–118, *117*
self and clothing 114; and identity
    in Antonioni's films 53–70; self-
    enhancement and cloth 13, 14–25; in
    Soviet Russia 86–88
Semenova, E. 79
Sennett, Richard 106
7 For All Mankind jeans *134*, 136, 138
Shanghai Tang 178, 179–182, 183,
    190, 191; Imperial Tailor in Hong
    Kong 180; New York store 183–184,
    185–187
signora senza camelie, La (film) 57,
    61–62
Siliya, Dora 122
Smith, Paul 181
Snow, Carmel 42–43, 59
social mobility and Indian cinema
    32–33
social relations: hierarchies and
    consumption 13–25; *see also* class
    differences and clothing; middle
    classes and consumption
socialism: *Doi moi* (Renovation)
    policies in Vietnam 92, 95–96,
    99–102; socialist clothing in Vietnam
    103–107; *see also* Soviet Russia
Sofroniou, Tassos 152–153, *152, 153*

Sommer, Marcelo 167
Soviet Russia and fashion 73–90; Soviet
    regulation of taste 73–74, 80–89;
    state view on 73–74, 74–76, 80–88;
    Western influences 76–80, 86–89
spectacle 49–50, 158
spirituality of cloth and clothing 14–16,
    16–17
squandering 21–22, 23
state: and fashion in Soviet Russia
    73–74, 74–76, 80–88; interpellation
    of youth in Vietnam 95, 98, 99–102
Stockler, Mary 171
street culture and fashion in Brazil 165,
    167–168, 168–170
subcontracting production 131, 139,
    197
suit aesthetics in Zambia 116, 119–121,
    121, 122, 125
Suliotes (Albanian rebels) 148
Susser, Ida 112
synthetic fibers 24

Tam, Vivienne 179, 180, 190
Tang, David 180, 181–182, 185, 186
taste: Soviet regulation 77, 78, 80–89
Tattersall, Robin *44*, 47–48, *48*
Taxi Driver (Indian film) 28, 33–35, 38
Taylorist production mode 128, 129
technical grammar of jeans 129,
    132–137, 141
Ter-Ovakimian, I. A. 86
textile industry 2; in Brazil 166;
    contracting out production 25;
    denim production 128–129,
    138–139, 141; labor requirements
    24–25; *see also* fabric technologies;
    manufacturing
Thomas, Mandy 102
Tikhomirova, Anna 90*n*
Tlingit people in American Northwest
    20–21
Tommy Hilfiger jeans 138, 141
Torres, Lolita 79, *80*
trade *see* global trade
trade acts and New York garment
    industry decline 195–196, 203
trousers for women in Soviet Russia 88

Tsarouxis, Yannis 149
Tsing, A. L. 194
Tuoi Tre (Youth) (Vietnamese newspaper) 97, 101, 103
Turner, Terrence 106
turnover time in fashion industry 129–130, 131, 141, 142

Uberoi, P. 35
United States *see* America

Vainshtein, Olga 81, 82
Valéry, Paul 43
Veblen, Thorstein 153, 155–156, 159, 160, 161–162
Veloso, Kamala 31
Versollato, Ocimar 165
Viaggio in Italia (film) 62–63
Vietnam: appropriate fashion for youth 92–108; *Doi moi* (Renovation) policies 92, 95–96, 99–102; materiality and morality 95, 106, 107; moral panic about youth 94–95, 96–98
Vitti, Monica 69, 70n
Vlachs in Greece 146, 147
Vogue in Greece 155–156, 157, 158–159, *159*, 160
volatility of fashion markets 129–130

Wal-Mart: branded clothing and self-enhancement 14, 24–25
washing jeans 133–134, 142; geographical spread of process 138–139; and product differentiation 135–136, 137; and productivity 134–135
Weiner, Annette B. 15
Welters, Linda 147–148
Western influences: appropriate fashion for youth in Vietnam 92–108;

and secondhand clothing markets in Zambia 112, 113, 114–115, 115–118; in Soviet Russia 76–80, 86–89; *Vogue* in Greece 155–156
Willemen, P. 32
Winnifrith, Tom 146, 162n
women: body shape and taste in Soviet Russia 81–82, *83*; "decent dress" in Zambia 118, 121–123, 125; Indian cinema costume and national fashion 28–39; *see also* female body
women's magazines in Soviet Russia 78, 80–88
Woolf, Virginia 145, 146, 160
work clothes in Soviet Russia 84–85, *85*
"world cultural space" 194–195
World of Suzie Wong, The (film) 183, 191n
World Trade Organization (WTO) 196

Yeoh, Michelle 188
Yeung, Kin 182
young people: appropriate fashions in Vietnam 92–108; gender and secondhand clothing in Zambia 112–126; state interpellation of youth in Vietnam 95, 98, 99–102
Youth League *see* Communist Youth League in Vietnam
youth studies 97–98
Yue Minjun 182

Zabriskie Point (film) 66
Zambia and secondhand clothing 112–126; "clothing competence" 114, 118–119; construction of "the latest" in fashion 114, 115; "decent dress" for women 118, 121–123, 125; local markets 112, 113, 115–118, *117*
Zukin, Sharon 22–23, 24

eBooks – at www.eBookstore.tandf.co.uk

A library at your fingertips!

eBooks are electronic versions of printed books. You can store them on your PC/laptop or browse them online.

They have advantages for anyone needing rapid access to a wide variety of published, copyright information.

eBooks can help your research by enabling you to bookmark chapters, annotate text and use instant searches to find specific words or phrases. Several eBook files would fit on even a small laptop or PDA.

NEW: Save money by eSubscribing: cheap, online access to any eBook for as long as you need it.

Annual subscription packages

We now offer special low-cost bulk subscriptions to packages of eBooks in certain subject areas. These are available to libraries or to individuals.

For more information please contact webmaster.ebooks@tandf.co.uk

We're continually developing the eBook concept, so keep up to date by visiting the website.

www.eBookstore.tandf.co.uk